The Economic Performance of the European Union

The Economic Performance of the European Union

Issues, Trends and Policies

Edited by

Antonin Rusek
Susquehanna University, USA

Lubor Lacina
Mendel University, Czech Republic

Jarko Fidrmuc
Ludwig-Maximilians-Universität Munich, Germany

palgrave
macmillan

First published 2009 by
PALGRAVE MACMILLAN

Palgrave Macmillan in the UK is an imprint of Macmillan Publishers Limited, registered in England, company number 785998, of Houndmills, Basingstoke, Hampshire, RG21 6XS.

Palgrave Macmillan in the US is a division of St Martin's Press LLC, 175 Fifth Avenue, New York, NY 10010.

Palgrave Macmillan is the global academic imprint of the above companies and has companies and representatives throughout the world.

Palgrave® and Macmillan® are registered trademarks in the United States, the United Kingdom, Europe and other countries.

ISBN-13: 978–0–230–22227–4 hardback
ISBN-10: 0–230–22227–7 hardback

This book is printed on paper suitable for recycling and made from fully managed and sustained forest sources. Logging, pulping and manufacturing processes are expected to conform to the environmental regulations of the country of origin.

A catalogue record for this book is available from the British Library.

Library of Congress Cataloging-in-Publication Data

The economic performance of the European Union : issues, trends and policies / edited Antonin Rusek, Lubor Lacina, Jarko Fidrmuc.
p. cm.
Includes bibliographical references and index.
ISBN 978–0–230–22227–4
1. European Union countries—Economic conditions. 2. European Union countries–Economic policy. 3. Monetary policy—European Union countries. 4. European Union. I. Rusek, Antonin. II. Lacina, Lubor, 1969– III. Fidrmuc, Jarko.
HC240.E2755 2008
330.94—dc22

2008030100

10 9 8 7 6 5 4 3 2 1
18 17 16 15 14 13 12 11 10 09

Printed and bound in Great Britain by
CPI Antony Rowe, Chippenham and Eastbourne

Contents

Part II EU Expansion: New Members in the EU Environment

List of Figures

List of Tables

Acknowledgements

We would like to thank Taiba Batool, publishing editor at Palgrave Macmillan, and Eric Dubber, assistant editor at Palgrave Macmillan, for their support and patience in dealing with editorial arrangements encompassing three continents. And our special thanks go to Dr Barbara Slater, the copy editor at Palgrave Macmillan. Without her patient work, this volume would not exist. Finally, we would like to appreciate the willingness of the journal *Review of International Political Economy* to let us include the work (Chapter 5) whose first version was initially published by them.

List of Contributors

Karl Aiginger, Austrian Institute of Economic Research, Vienna University of Economics and Business Administration, University of Linz, Austria

Ivana Bátorová, Comenius University, Bratislava, Slovakia

Istvan Benczes, Corvinus University, Budapest, Hungary

Jarko Fidrmuc, Department of Economics, Ludwig-Maximilians-Universität Munich, Germany

Jan Filáček, Czech National Bank, Prague, Czech Republic

Roman Horváth, Czech National Bank and Institute of Economic Studies, Charles University, Prague, Czech Republic

David Howarth, School of Social and Political Studies, University of Edinburgh, UK

Svatopluk Kapounek, Department of Finance, Mendel University, Brno, Czech Republic

Evžen Kočenda, CERGE-EI, Charles University and the Academy of Sciences, Prague, Czech Republic; The William Davidson Institute, Michigan, USA; CEPR, London, UK

Iika Korhonen, Bank of Finland, Helsinki, Finland

Ali M. Kutan, Southern Illinois University Edwardsville, Illinois, USA; The Center for European Integration Studies (ZEI), Bonn, Germany; The Emerging Markets Group, London, UK; The William Davidson Institute, Michigan, USA

Lubor Lacina, Department of Finance, Mendel University, Brno, Czech Republic

Jitka Poměnková, Department of Statistics and Operational Analysis, Mendel University, Brno, Czech Republic

Petr Rozmahel, Department of Economics, Mendel University, Brno, Czech Republic

Antonin Rusek, Department of Economics, Susquehanna University, Selinsgrove, USA

Margit Schratzenstaller, Austrian Institute of Economic Research (WIFO), Vienna, Austria

Michal Skořepa, Czech National Bank and Institute of Economic Studies, Charles University, Prague, Czech Republic

Milan Sojka, Department of Economics, Mendel University, Brno, Czech Republic and Charles University, Prague, Czech Republic

Taner M. Yigit, Bilkent University, Ankara, Turkey

Introduction

This volume explores the economic performance of the European Union, the underlying trends and economic policies. The emphasis is placed on the post-1999, 'euro' period. The experiences and the functioning of both the European Union (EU) as a whole and the European Economic and Monetary Union (EMU) are explored in the context of the twofold challenges of EU expansion (post-2004) and the increasingly globalized world economy.

In 2008, European countries celebrated the fiftieth anniversary of the creation of the European Common Market. This initial grouping of six countries has grown into a large economic and political organization with 27 member countries, and today it encompasses most of what is conventionally considered the European continent.

The nature of this European integration process also evolved over time. Conceived initially as a customs union and an attempt to create a common market for trade in goods, today's European Union is a complex integrated political and economic system. Many argue that, especially in the last 15 years, the European Union has increasingly acquired the attributes of a transnational state – that is, it has evolved from a group of states wishing to cooperate on a treaty basis into a form of confederation. While this view remains controversial it cannot be denied that whereas the public rationale for the process of European integration was predominantly economic, the driving forces behind it were predominantly political. Nothing reflects this reality better than the European dynamic in the last 17 years.

The collapse of the Soviet empire and the unification of Germany in 1992 established a new political and economic reality both in Europe and in the world at large, which provoked a twofold political response from European leaders. On the one hand they aimed at a deepening of European political and economic integration. The result of this effort was the so-called Maastricht Treaty. Here the concept of Economic and Monetary Union was formally established and its basic characteristics defined. These included the goal of the common currency (later – and today – known as the euro) and a commitment to deepen further the processes of economic liberalization and the removal of the barriers preventing the (newly renamed) European Union from becoming a single market. EMU is considered by many to be one of the EU's finest achievements. In the words of Wim Duisenberg (the first President of the European Central Bank): 'The Eurozone is much more than just a currency. It is a symbol of European integration in every sense of the world' (quoted from Tilford, 2006).

On the other hand, the European leaders committed themselves to the expansion of the new EU to the East. This process resulted in the admission of 10 new member states to the EU in May 2004 (Estonia, Lithuania, Latvia, Poland, the Czech Republic, Hungary, Slovakia, Slovenia, Malta, Cyprus) and two other new members (Bulgaria and Romania) joined in January 2007.

But while there were sound political reasons for this response, economically both steps were somewhat controversial. With regard to the creation of the common currency, many economists pointed out that even the core EU members were not able to satisfy the criteria for so-called optimum currency areas (OCA). This was bound to create problems and tensions once the common currency was introduced. Similarly, with the expansion of the EU to the East, which meant that membership was extended to countries whose standards of living and economic levels compared only to the poorest among the original 15 EU members (Greece and Portugal), problems were bound to arise from the inevitable conflict between the political will to broaden and deepen economic integration and economic reality. And this was only aggravated by the impact of the continuing economic globalization and the changing competitive position of the EU in the world.

These problems and tensions today shape a new reality for the EU which in turn requires new and innovative solutions that should be preceded by a thorough analysis.

Contributors to this volume analyse various aspects of this new reality, providing a balanced and multifaceted look at EU dynamics in the last decade. The issues covered include the discussion of the Eurozone dynamics and cohesion, the problems of taxation and fiscal policies in general and the various issues pertaining to the 'new' member states.

The underlying idea that connects all the contributions is the analysis of the problems that have affected the European Union in the past decade and the challenges and dilemmas that the EU will face in the coming years.

The book is divided into three parts. Part I provides an analysis of systemic performance and currency issues from the EU-wide perspective.

In Chapter 1 Karl Aiginger analyses the challenges to the European economic and social model inherent in the continuing process of globalization. He points out that making economies fit for the dynamics of globalization is high on the reform agenda of all current EU members. However, there are competing needs to reduce persistently high unemployment and to cope with the new challenge of climate change. The European Social Model, with its high costs, large governments and regulated markets, is for some critics the culprit responsible for the slow growth in 'old Europe', that is, in the member countries of the pre-enlargement European Union (EU-15).

Aiginger's contribution reports the basic characteristics of the 'European' model, and the differences between various sub-models applied in different European countries. He shows that while economic performance across Europe and the US was very similar up to the 1990s, with Europe catching up in productivity, since the early 1990s, the gap between US and European performance has once again widened in relation to output growth, productivity and employment.

However, the performance of the Scandinavian countries has been much better than that of the big continental economies. The author claims that important changes in policy were initiated in the Scandinavian countries (five pillars of success are defined). Additionally these countries outperform the continental countries in many indicators on the adaptability of their economies.

The question remains whether it was the existing set of institutions in these countries or the changes made in political priorities since the early or mid-1990s that made the Scandinavian countries better able to cope with globalization than Germany, Italy and France. The evidence highlights the importance of policy changes.

In Chapter 2 Svatopluk Kapounek and Lubor Lacina investigate the relationship between economic growth in the Eurozone (the subgroup of EU countries which adopted the euro as their common currency) and the European Central Bank's inflation target. Their analysis emphasizes that 'The primary objective of the European central bank (ECB) and its monetary policy, as defined in Article 105 of the Treaty Establishing the European Community, is to maintain price stability. "Without prejudice to the objective of price stability", the Eurosystem will also "support the general economic policies in the Community with a view to contributing to the achievement of the objectives of the Community". These include a "high level of employment" and "sustainable and non-inflationary growth".'

The reasoning behind this monetary policy target definition is as follows: 'price stability contributes to high levels of economic growth and employment – mainly as a result of improvements in the transparency of the price mechanism, the more efficient allocation of resources, a reduction in inflation risk premia and interest rates (which reduce real interest rates and increase incentives to invest), reductions of distortions caused by inflation or deflation and last but not least as a result of the creation of conditions essential for the formation of stable rational expectations. Therefore it is not possible to determine price stability as a final target of macroeconomic policy; it is more plausible to regard price stability as an operating target or a macroeconomic tool necessary for achieving high levels of economic growth and employment. [The authors] identify this assumption with the monetary policy of the ECB.'

The aim of the analysis is to answer the question 'whether the ECB's monetary policy target (inflation below but close to 2 per cent) is optimal for the EMU member states or not. The authors consider the possibility that the ECB's monetary policy could have been one of the factors that contributed to the recent slowdown in economic growth in the Eurozone.'

In Chapter 3, Antonin Rusek analyses the dynamics of the real exchange rates of the euro for the Eurozone as a whole and for the four largest Eurozone countries (Germany, France, Italy and Spain) individually.

His analysis is based on the notion that real exchange rate misalignments are perceived to be the cause of the loss of competitiveness, growth slowdowns and currency crises in the case of overvaluation, and to underlie overheating and inflation in cases of undervaluation, and, indeed, sectoral misallocations of resources and global economic imbalances. In a currency union covering sovereign countries with imperfectly integrated markets and limited fiscal transfers, the divergent dynamics of real effective exchange rates in the individual countries – both actual and equilibrium – will exacerbate both economic and political tensions (in addition to the above-mentioned problems) and may lead to the collapse of not only the monetary union per se, but the underlying integration processes as well.

The empirical part of the chapter employs the estimation of the BEER (behavioural equilibrium exchange rate – the concept pioneered by Clark and MacDonald) for both the Eurozone (that is, for the euro) as a whole and its large member countries – Germany, Italy, Spain and France – individually for the 1999–2006 period. Those estimates are then used both to estimate the degree of the euro's misalignment and the magnitude, persistence and the direction of divergence tendencies within the Eurozone itself.

The exchange rate policy strategy in a large currency area is discussed in Chapter 4 by Svatopluk Kapounek and Jitka Poměnková. They assume that the central banks use two operating targets for monetary policy in open economies: the short-term interest rate and the nominal exchange rate. With the additional assumption of short-term price rigidities, these two operating targets can be expressed as the real short-term interest rate and the real exchange rate. The combination of these two variables affects both aggregate demand and economic growth.

While the effects of exchange rate changes are significant in smaller economies, the central banks of large currency areas are able to prevent an unwanted real appreciation of their currency through the combination of interest rates and flexibility in exchange rates. The central banks of small countries, however, do not have free and autonomous monetary policy and capital mobility is an important limiting factor. Monetary policy of central banks in small countries is often determined by the monetary policy of central banks in the large currency areas. The monetary authorities in the large currency areas are able to stabilize or target their currency without losing control over domestic interest rates and consequently without negative impacts on aggregate demand and economic growth. Chapter 4 focuses on the differences between central banks' exchange rate policy strategies in small open economies and in large currency areas. With the help of a monetary condition index, the authors identify causalities between short-term real interest rate changes, real exchange rate changes and economic growth.

In Chapter 5 David Howarth analyses the December 2002 reform of decision-making in the European Central Bank's (ECB) Governing Council in terms of national economy size reflected in the bargaining power of the ECB Governing Council members and member state macroeconomic interest. The National Central Bank (NCB) governors of the largest member states were concerned about the impact on ECB monetary policymaking of equal representation being extended to future member states. By eliminating equal voting rights, the reform distorts the meaning of equality, representativeness and *ad personam* participation as guiding principles of ECB decision-making, moving from equal member state representation towards an emphasis placed upon Eurozone economy representation. At the same time, two possible concerns watered down efforts to modify 'representativeness' and prevent enlargement contributing to inefficiency in Governing Council decision-making. First, the current smaller member state NCB governors opposed a significant reduction of their 'voice' in ECB monetary policymaking. Second, legitimacy concerns ensured persistent support for the maintenance of a large and 'decentralized' Governing Council.

The second part of the book analyses the issues pertaining to the 'new' member states – that is, the countries which joined the EU in 2004.

In Chapter 6 Evžen Kočenda, Ali M. Kutan and Taner M. Yigit address the issues raised by fiscal convergence in monetary union. Specifically, they ask whether the new EU member states had a better fiscal discipline than the Eurozone members. They examine the progress of the ten 'new' European Union (EU) members with respect to satisfying the official Maastricht criteria, and against the performance of EU-15. The study includes alternative measures of fiscal convergence and employs vastly flexible tests of convergence, allowing for structural breaks. Their results suggest poor progress on convergence in general, and, more importantly, they find that the new members are as undisciplined as EU-15, if not more so. These results suggest that monetary unions may not provide fiscal discipline. The authors also provide some suggestions through which the new member states could improve their fiscal discipline in order to meet the Maastricht criteria.

In Chapter 7 Petr Rozmahel analyses business cycle similarity and the EMU enlargement using the concordance index for Central and Eastern European countries. He evaluates the similarities between the business cycles of the 'new' member economies and the Eurozone countries. And he finds that the long-term similarity of business cycles in countries planning to form a common monetary union decreases the importance of national monetary policy. This statement is in line with general conclusions of the 'new' theory of optimum currency areas. The chapter sheds some light on the process of business cycle similarity measuring and points out that contemporary studies usually simplify this problem by measuring a simple correlation of cyclical developments in GDP. The main aim of Rozmahel's approach is to characterize and apply the concordance index to the Central and Eastern European Countries (CEECs) acceding to the Eurozone. The concordance index embodies an alternative and rarely used approach to the measurement of business cycle similarity. This method needs to identify technically the actual business cycles in analysed economies – the turning points and phases of the cycles.

The chapter also includes a comparison with the traditional correlation methods. A potential impact of the endogenous OCA hypothesis on the contemporary approach to the assessment of candidate countries' preparedness to adopt the euro is discussed in the conclusion to the chapter.

In Chapter 8 Jan Filáček, Roman Horváth and Michal Skořepa address the conduct of monetary policy before the adoption of the euro and related challenges for the new EU member states. Their contribution argues that the main issues for monetary policy in the new EU member states before their adoption of the euro are typically rooted in the challenge of fulfilling both the Maastricht inflation and exchange rate criteria in the context of an equilibrium real exchange rate appreciation. The authors first distinguish between the wording, the written interpretation and the 'revealed' interpretation of the inflation and exchange rate criteria. They then discuss the options for monetary policy in the period of the fulfilment of these criteria in terms of its transparency, its continuity with the previous monetary policy regime, the choice of central parity for the ERM II, the setting of the fluctuation bandwidth, the probability of the fulfilment of both criteria and the impact on economic stability.

In Chapter 9 István Benczes considers fiscal consolidation and the adoption of the euro in the old and new member states of the EU. He points out that the experience of the old EU member states with fiscal consolidations that were implemented in the past 25 years makes it possible to make comprehensive assessments on the role and effectiveness of fiscal policy and also on the real and alleged macroeconomic consequences of adjustments. Accordingly, he raises two main points. First, according to the standard (Keynesian) textbook approach, a fiscal adjustment is able to reduce indebtedness but it also triggers a deterioration in economic activity. Yet, the great abundance of empirical evidence in the last almost 25 years does not give definitive support to this general conviction. Rather, EU countries often experienced a further increase in their debt ratios in times of consolidation, and, more surprisingly, fiscal retrenchment was not necessarily followed by a drop in economic output. Second, the new member states of the EU are obliged to adopt the single currency as soon as they are capable of meeting the Maastricht convergence criteria. The challenge for countries in Central and Eastern Europe is therefore to introduce the euro without compromising their growth potential. The chapter argues accordingly that there is in fact no trade-off between the catching up and the fiscal discipline – just the opposite, it is the relatively low level of redistribution and the lack of (permanent) deficit-financing that can prove to be conducive to growth both in new and old member states.

Part III provides some insights into the miscellaneous issues of EU policies, performance and its relations to the rest of today's globalized world.

In Chapter 10 Margit Schratzenstaller looks at company taxation in the EU, current developments in this area and their implications for the harmonization debate. She shows that tax competition between member states tends to result in an erosion as well as a convergence of company taxation in the EU. Besides statutory tax rates, several other characteristics of national company tax systems are gradually aligning: for example the integration of corporate and shareholder taxation. Another common trend is the systematic reduction of the tax burden on profits and capital income vis-à-vis labour income. Practically all EU company tax systems are characterized by the non-neutrality of taxation with regard to the legal form of firms (incorporated firms are taxed more favourably than non-incorporated firms) and to capital structure (debt-financing enjoys tax advantages compared to equity financing). At the same time company taxes are significantly lower in the new member states. Moreover, there is no convergence as yet between company taxes in the new and the old member states. Finally, there is increasing empirical evidence that the erosion of company taxation in the EU member countries is not only affected by decreasing tax rates, but also by the shifting of profits from high-tax to low-tax countries.

Despite the increasing erosion of company taxes in the EU member states, the current discussion and policy initiatives at EU level concentrate on the elimination of 'unfair tax competition', that is, of tax breaks offered exclusively to foreign investors and thus considered as discriminatory. 'Fair tax competition' is no matter of concern to the European Commission, as it is expected to be efficiency-enhancing.

After presenting the most important developments within company tax systems in the member states, Margit Schratzenstaller critically examines the current harmonization initiatives at the EU level against this background. Finally, she puts forward an alternative suggestion to harmonize company taxation in the EU.

A post-Keynesian view of ECB policy and its impact on the economic development of new member states is provided by Milan Sojka in Chapter 11. In the first part of the chapter, the basic principles of the contemporary Post-Keynesian theory of the relative endogeneity of money are briefly outlined. The second part concentrates on the Post-Keynesian criticism of the institutional arrangement of the ECB and its monetary policy. The closing part looks at issues concerning the potential effects of ECB policy in the given institutional framework on the economic development of the Czech economy and the economies of other Central and Eastern European states after joining the Eurozone. Possible adverse effects on the process of real convergence are discussed and alternative policies devised to eliminate this danger are presented.

The last chapter, written by Jarko Fidrmuc, Iikka Korhonen and Ivana Bátorová analyses the relationships between the EU and the rest of the world in the globalized environment. It looks at business cycles in China and in selected OECD countries between 1992 and 2006. It is shown that, although negative correlation dominates for nearly all countries, large differences can be seen for various frequencies of cyclical development. On the one hand, nearly all OECD countries show positive correlations of very short-run developments that might correspond to intensive supplier linkages. On the other hand, business cycle frequencies (cycles with periods between 1.5 and 8 years) are typically negative. Nevertheless, countries facing a comparably longer history of intensive trading links tend also to show slightly higher correlations of business cycles with China.

ANTONIN RUSEK, LUBOR LACINA, JARKO FIDRMUC
SELINSGROVE, BRNO, MUNICH

References

Clark, Peter B. and R. MacDonald (1998). 'Exchange Rates and Economic Fundamentals: a Methodological Comparison of BEERs and FEERs', IMF Working Paper WP/98?67, Washington DC, May.
Tilford, Simon (2006). 'Will the Eurozone Crack?' Centre for European Reform, London, September.

Part I

EU Perspectives: Systemic Performance and Currency Issues

1
The Swedish Economic Model: Lessons to be Learned

Karl Aiginger

1.1 Introduction

The European Union has not equalled the US with respect to the growth of output, productivity or employment since the early or mid-1990s. Unemployment is now higher than in the US, and employment rates are lower – both in contrast to past trends (Aiginger, 2004). Many international analyses, such as that of the OECD, the IMF and the European Commission, blame – explicitly or implicitly – high welfare costs and low market flexibility for this disappointing performance. The European socio-economic model with its emphasis on social expenditures and high taxes is seen as a barrier to competitiveness in a globalizing world. However, contradicting this assertion is the fact that the three European countries which performed best in the past fifteen years with regard to growth, employment rates and fiscal prudence, Sweden, Finland and Denmark, belong to the Scandinavian type of the European model. This is the most comprehensive type, with the highest emphasis on social cohesion, redistribution and ecological awareness. Among these, Sweden may be seen as the prototype, with its long history of welfare, and its high taxes. Sweden experienced a long and steady decline of its lead in per capita income versus the European average, accompanied with recurrent devaluations, and a deep crisis in 1992/93. Since then Sweden has ventured courageous reforms which have made it one of the best performing countries in Europe, essentially maintaining its high standards of welfare and social cohesion, while making the labour market more flexible and budgets sustainable.

The chapter is structured as follows. In the next section we define the European model. This is not only a 'social model', but also shapes incentives, efficiency and competitiveness, and has an impact on education, innovation and health. We therefore prefer to speak of a model of European society or a socio-economic model (Aiginger and Guger, 2005, 2006). We further distinguish between different types of European models with Sweden as a member – maybe even the prototype – of the Scandinavian model type and analyse performance differences across models in the long run and since the 1990s. Section 1.3 outlines elements of change in the economic policy of the Scandinavian countries, concentrating again on Sweden. A three-tier policy strategy for the most successful countries is outlined (following Aiginger, 2004). Section 1.4 looks at some recent problems re-emerging in Sweden, and at the measures proposed by the OECD or planned by the new government. Section 1.5 discusses whether there are lessons to be learned from policy changes in Sweden for the new member countries of the EU. In an appendix we describe common elements of the strategies of Scandinavian countries which could indicate the substance of a 'Reformed European Model'.

1.2 The European socio-economic model

We follow Aiginger and Guger (2005) and define the European socio-economic model in terms of responsibility, regulation and redistribution:

- *Responsibility*. The broad responsibility of society for the welfare of individuals, sheltering them against poverty, and providing support in case of illness, disability, unemployment and old age; society encourages, and actively promotes and often provides, education, health care, and the support of families (the latter through transfers as well as the provision of care and housing facilities).
- *Regulation*. Labour relations are institutionalized; they are based on social dialogue, labour laws and collective agreements. The business environment is regulated and is shaped by social partners (on the branch and firm level). Administrative and economic regulation for product markets exists. Business start-ups depend on permits and partly on the qualifications of owners or managers.
- *Redistribution*. Transfers, financial support and social services are open to all groups; differences in incomes are limited by redistributive financial transfers, taxation, taxes on property and on bequests.

If we differentiate between types of the European model, the Scandinavian model is the most comprehensive, with a high degree of emphasis on redistribution and social benefits financed by taxes. The Scandinavian model relies on institutions working closely together with the government; trade unions are strongly involved in the administration of unemployment insurance and training; and the model is characterized by an active labour market policy and high employment rates. The continental model emphasizes employment as the basis of social transfers. Transfers are financed through the contributions of employers and employees. Social partners play an important role in industrial relations, and wage bargaining is centralized. Redistribution and the inclusion of outsiders are not high on the agenda. The Anglo-Saxon model emphasizes the responsibility of individuals for themselves, its labour market is not regulated and its competition policy is ambitious. Social transfers are smaller than in the other models, more targeted and 'means tested'. Labour relations are decentralized, and bargaining takes place primarily at the firm level. The Scandinavian, the continental and the Anglo-Saxon model are the three main models; we add a Mediterranean model and a group of countries still looking for a model – the group of new member countries. In the Mediterranean countries, social transfers are small; families still play a significant role in the provision of security and shelter. Trade unions and employer representatives are important to the generally centralized bargaining process for wages and work conditions. Employment rates, particularly those of women, are low.

The Scandinavian model applies at least in Sweden, Finland and Denmark. Some studies include Norway, but many do not, since it is rich in oil and is not a member of the EU. Whether the Netherlands are part of the Scandinavian model or nor is in debate. But unquestionably Sweden is the prototype. It has the longest history in welfare, and enjoyed a lead against the European average in GDP per capita of more than 30 per cent for a long time after World War II.

Looking at the growth dynamics in the various types of models, the long-run dynamics are all very similar (Table 1.1). Taking 1960/1990, for example, the long-term growth rates range between 2.6 per cent and 3.6 per cent for three main European models (Anglo-Saxon, Scandinavian and continental), as well as for the Anglo-Saxon overseas group (3.6 per cent). It is higher only in the Mediterranean model, and there is little variation within models (with the lowest growth rates for the United Kingdom and New Zealand; see Table 1.1). Performance in the 1990s (1990/2005) however diverged.[1] The Scandinavian group enjoyed a growth rate of 2.5 per cent for these 15 years – despite a severe crisis in many countries in the early 1990s – while the growth rates of the countries associated with the continental model plummeted to 1.7 per cent as a result of low growth in Germany and Italy. France, Austria and Belgium surpassed the group average, but no single country reached the level of dynamics attained by the Scandinavian group.[2]

Table 1.1 Performance in growth and employment: long run versus 1990/2007

	GDP growth p.a. in %		Unemployment rate		Employment rate		GDP per capita at PPP 2005 1,000 €
	1960/1990	1990/2007	1990	2007	1990	2007	
Scandinavian model	3.4	2.5	4.7	4.1	73.5	76.8	33.6
Denmark	3.0	2.2	7.2	3.0	76.8	79.6	31.1
Finland	3.9	2.4	3.2	6.7	74.1	70.9	29.2
Netherlands	3.4	2.6	5.8	3.1	65.0	77.3	32.7
Sweden	2.9	2.3	1.7	6.1	83.0	74.8	29.8
Norway	3.8	3.2	5.2	2.6	75.0	80.2	46.2
Continental model	3.5	1.7	7.3	7.5	63.4	67.2	27.7
Germany	3.2	1.7	6.2	8.1	69.5	73.1	28.2
France	3.8	1.9	8.5	8.6	59.7	61.9	27.6
Italy	4.0	1.4	8.9	5.9	57.4	63.8	25.4
Belgium	3.4	2.1	6.6	7.5	58.3	63.1	30.5
Austria	3.5	2.3	3.1	4.2	69.2	70.0	32.0
Anglo-Saxon model Europe	2.6	2.7	7.3	5.3	70.7	72.0	29.9
Ireland	4.2	6.4	13.4	4.5	54.6	70.5	35.5
United Kingdom	2.5	2.5	6.9	5.3	71.8	72.1	29.5
Mediterrean model	4.6	2.9	10.9	8.1	55.8	66.5	24.2
Greece	4.5	3.2	6.4	8.4	54.7	56.7	24.3
Portugal	4.8	2.1	4.8	8.0	71.1	72.5	18.2
Spain	4.6	3.1	13.0	8.1	53.2	67.3	25.3

Anglo-Saxon model overseas	3.6	3.0	5.7	4.7	71.9	73.4	36.3
US	3.5	2.9	5.5	4.6	72.2	73.3	37.1
Canada	4.0	2.8	8.1	6.1	71.2	75.1	30.4
Australia	3.8	3.5	6.9	4.6	69.2	74.5	30.7
New Zealand	2.4	2.9	7.8	3.9	53.7	60.6	22.6
EU-15	3.4	2.1	8.0	7.2	64.2	68.2	27.7
Japan	6.1	1.4	2.1	3.9	74.7	76.7	27.8
Catching-up model	–	3.2	–	7.9	–	60.2	16.1
Czech Republic	–	1.9	–	5.9	–	68.0	20.2
Estonia	–	–	–	4.9	–	71.8	17.7
Cyprus	–	4.1	–	4.3	–	69.9	22.9
Latvia	–	1.4	–	5.8	–	69.6	15.0
Lithuania	–	1.3	–	4.2	–	65.8	15.2
Hungary	–	3.1	–	7.3	–	56.2	16.1
Malta	–	–	–	6.8	–	54.7	18.7
Poland	–	3.9	–	9.4	–	56.4	13.6
Slovenia	–	2.9	–	4.9	–	66.9	22.6
Slovakia	–	5.1	–	11.2	–	60.3	16.4
EU-15/US	0.96	0.71	1.45	1.57	0.89	0.93	0.75

Source: Eurostat (AMECO); as to sub-aggregates weighted average over countries; EU-15 reported.

1.3 Reform strategies in Sweden, 1993–2002

Following crises in the late 1980s (Denmark) and the early 1990s (Sweden and Finland), the Scandinavian countries in general and Sweden in particular pursued a three-pronged strategy with the following aims (Aiginger, 2004a):

- to reduce or contain private and public costs, specifically to balance wage dynamics and productivity as well as public expenditure and taxes;
- to reform institutions, and to make labour and product markets more competitive, but not by means of a simple deregulation strategy, but by targeted reforms such as training, education, and increasing geographical mobility and incentives to work;
- to boost long-run growth and productivity by supporting and encouraging innovation, education and the diffusion of new technologies.

We now describe these policy changes specifically in relation to Sweden which had gradually lost its position as one of the leading European countries in per capita GDP by underperforming in growth over the greater part of the post-World War II period (Figure 1.1). In the early

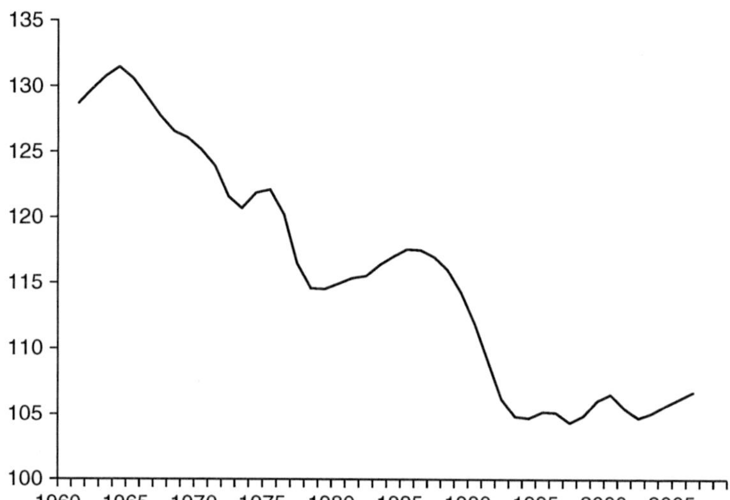

Figure 1.1 Sweden: falling down and forging ahead again
Note: GDP per capita; EU-15 = 100; moving average over three years.
Source: Eurostat (AMECO).

1990s, exports, GDP and employment decreased, leading the OECD to open its 1994 report with the comment that 'the current recession is comparable in depth to that of the 1930s' (OECD, 1994). The serious crisis – second only to that in Finland – had several causes: the Russian crisis affected Sweden more strongly than it affected continental countries, and Sweden suffered a particular crisis in its financial sectors (following deregulation without allowance for bad loans and a tax system which favoured borrowing). Competitiveness suffered from high and rising costs without parallel increases in productivity and Swedish industry remained specialized in capital-intensive basic goods subject to strong price competition (steel, paper) and without product differentiation or specialization in high-tech segments. See Lindbeck et al. (1994) for the responsibility of the welfare state from cradle to grave as the cause of Swedish problems.

1.3.1 Restoring balance

The short-run policy response was to bring costs into balance. The first element of this strategy was yet another devaluation of the Swedish krona, namely of 18 per cent versus the euro at the beginning of the 1990s. The second element in this direction was a discretionary fiscal stability package which amounted to 7.5 per cent of GDP and was negotiated between the government and the opposition Socialist Party. This consisted in part of rises in tax and in part of cuts in government expenditure. The budget cuts did include moderate cuts in benefits and transfers, but did not change the system in principle: higher incomes had to take a higher burden in the combined impact of tax increases and transfer deductions; thus both the opposition and the trade unions could accept the package. The government committed itself to long-term expenditure limits, with different targets for 27 expenditure categories (Brandner, 2003). The fiscal stability package, the long-term commitment to expenditure limits, the declining costs of the bailing-out of banks and a strong cyclical element inherent in Swedish budgets led to a switch from a deficit of nearly 10 per cent in 1993 into a persistent surplus over the past ten years (see Figure 1.2). The policy goal of government is now to have a surplus of 2 per cent for a full business cycle.

Wage moderation was tried – unsuccessfully at first – as a centralized bargaining outcome (Rehmberg moderation) which looked moderate as it was negotiated in 1991, but proved excessive in the second year. The next two-year contract for 1993–95 also proved ex post to be moderate,

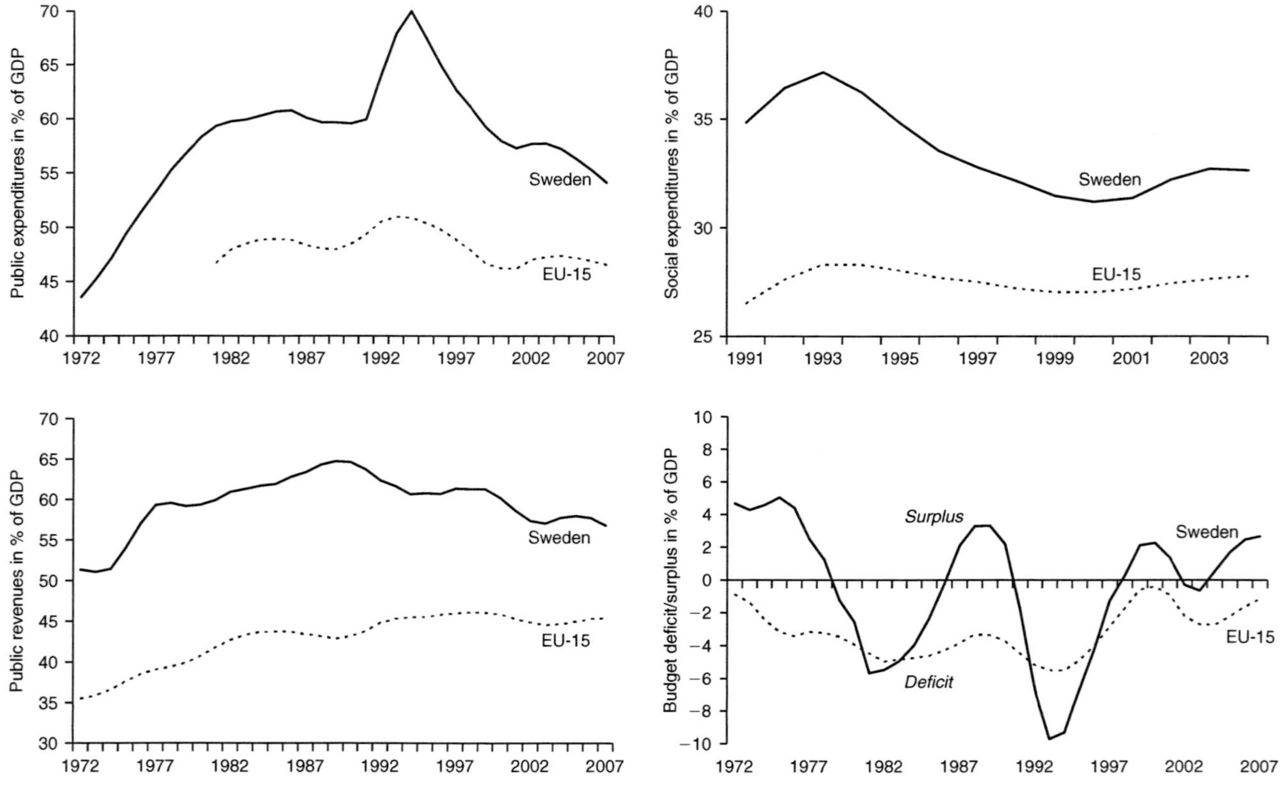

Figure 1.2 Fiscal restraint and fiscal prudence
Source: Eurostat (AMECO).

leading to the first decline in unit labour costs in post-World War II history (OECD, 1994, p. 39).

1.3.2 Changing incentives

Elements of welfare to work reforms were introduced. An active labour market policy and low capital taxes had long been constituent elements of the Swedish system (Marterbauer, 2001). Institutional reforms remodelled the competition and monetary authority with the goal that tough 'after-care' should ensure that this time the devaluation would prove successful in the long term. Labour market regulation, which had been slightly stricter than the European average in 1990, is now below the European average. The main changes related to temporary contracts, where tight regulation in 1990 was changed to one of the least regulated frameworks: the overall index for labour market regulation dropped from 3.4 in 1990 to 2.4 in 1998, the fourth lowest in Europe. The tax wedge (the difference between gross and net wages) is now lower in Sweden than in Germany (despite the generally high taxes) (Figure 1.3). Regulation of product markets had been less stringent in 1990, but further deregulation increased the difference compared to other European countries. With the exception of the United Kingdom, Sweden now has the most deregulated product markets in Europe.

Regarding incentives, the responsibility for the first two weeks of sickness was transferred to employers (whose contribution to social security was reduced in turn). Compensation for the first day of sick leave was cancelled, sickness compensation which had been as high as 100 per cent, was reduced to between 65 per cent and 90 per cent depending on the length of insurance and supplementary insurance (OECD, 1994, p. 95). Replacement ratios for unemployment were reduced from 90 per cent to 80 per cent, the first five days remain uncompensated and work insurance assistance was reduced. In the public sector, transfers from central government to local governments were reduced if the local authorities increased taxes. Government agencies introduced competition, enforced contracting out, including social services and vouchers for private schools, and general practitioners were allowed to compete with public services in the health sector (OECD, 1994, p. 91). Municipalities took full responsibility for schools and care for the elderly, receiving lump-sum transfers from central government without monies being directed to specific services, thus increasing cost-consciousness as well as the ability to meet demand.

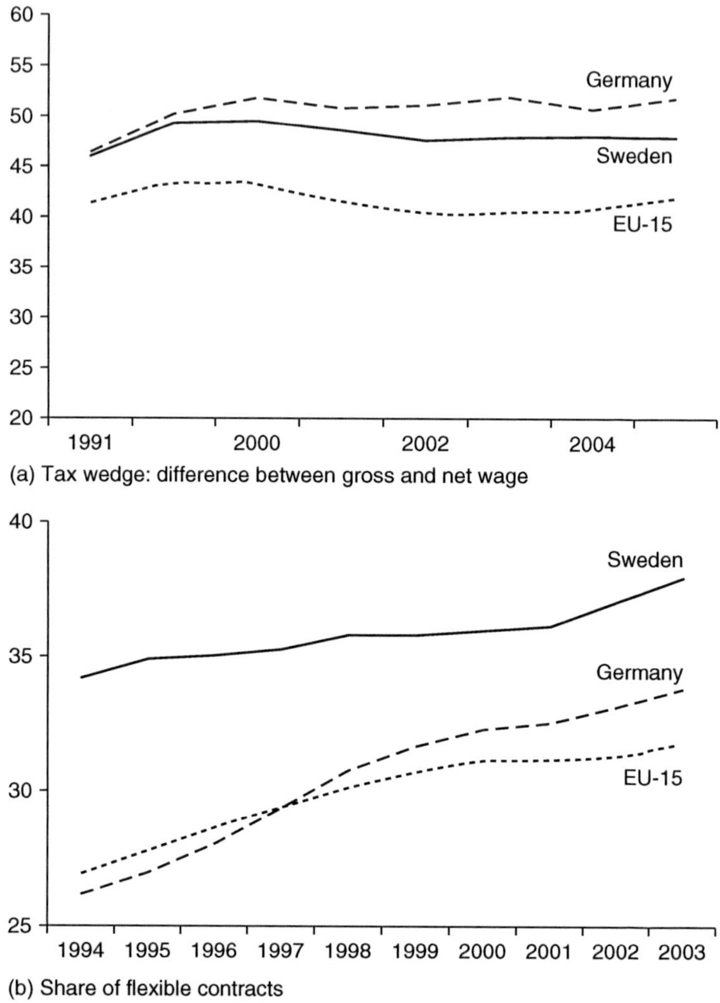

Figure 1.3 Flexibility of labour

(a) *Note*: Tax wedge is defined as 'Income tax plus employee and employer contributions (as % of labour costs); labour costs = gross wage earnings less personal income tax plus employee social security contributions.'

Source: IFO Database for Institutional Comparisons in Europe (DICE).

(b) *Note*: Part-time plus fixed-term contracts as a percentage of all contracts.

Source: Eurostat, EU Labour Force Survey and National Accounts.

1.3.3 Leader in research and ICT

Policies to enhance long-term growth included the development of pervasive and comprehensive programmes in order to promote information technology: the distribution of PCs for private use was made attractive by tax deductions, education expenses were enforced, alliances for electronic commerce were created and the use of ICT in government became compulsory. Sweden is today the European leader in information technology, having surpassed the US according to many indicators. It achieved this position and its lead in research by way of a consistent long-run government-assisted policy maintained during a severe crisis in the first half of the 1990s. High-tech schools and universities were established throughout the country; expenditures on education in Sweden have been the highest in Europe since 2001 and are increasing. The research/GDP ratio rose from 2.2 per cent in 1981 to 3.8 per cent in 1999. Research expenditures relative to GDP are higher than in the US and are among the highest in Europe. Sweden is ranked first in the set of 16 growth drivers. It had a good position already at the start, but enforced it to a larger degree than all other countries except Finland. It is among the top three countries in 15 indicators and leads in seven (Aiginger 2004b; see also Table 1.2).

Economic growth rebounded, and between 1996 and 2007 GDP growth was one of the highest in Europe. Particularly impressive has been Sweden's growth of output and productivity, with the strongest results in manufacturing, particularly in the telecom industries. Sweden is still a leading welfare state, and a high tax country. It has some features that might not be expected a priori from a country with strong government: corporate taxes are generally low, the labour market is flexible insofar as wages react to unemployment; pre-tax income differences are large (the smaller differences in final incomes originate from taxes and transfers). Sweden invests in active labour market policies, with carrot and stick strategies of obligations and training. The ratio of social expenditures to GDP declined – mainly as a result of reduced expenditure on passive measures since unemployment decreased – but are still 5 per cent above the EU average after a 10 percentage point difference in the early 1990s. The overall tax rate is above the EU average by 14 points, corporate taxes were decreased from 30 per cent to 28 per cent, and are 2.5 points below the EU average. The most impressive part of the strategy is the high and increasing investment in research, in education and in telecom expenditures (see Figure 1.4). The echo of the past devaluation is reflected in the below-European average real GDP per head.

Table 1.2 Investment into the future: Sweden surpasses the US (% GDP)

	1992	2006	1992–2006
Scandinavian model	13.3	15.6	2.3
Denmark	13.95	16.93	3.0
Finland	13.34	15.90	2.6
Netherlands	12.10	13.24	1.1
Sweden	14.70	18.16	3.5
Continental model	10.8	12.5	1.7
Germany	11.40	12.86	1.5
France	11.72	13.36	1.6
Italy	8.59	10.45	1.9
Belgium	11.58	13.71	2.1
Austria	11.16	13.71	2.5
Anglo-Saxon model Europe	11.9	13.3	1.5
Ireland	10.77	9.83	−0.9
United Kingdom	11.93	13.58	1.7
Mediterrean model	7.5	10.1	2.6
Greece	5.46	8.70	3.2
Portugal	9.02	12.20	3.2
Spain	7.61	10.02	2.4
Anglo-Saxon model Overseas	11.07	13.20	2.1
USA	11.07	13.20	2.1
EU-15	10.5	12.8	2.2
Japan	10.58	14.50	3.9
EU-15/USA	0.95	0.81	−0.14

Note: As to sub-aggregates weighted average over countries; EU-15 weighted.
Source: OECD (MSTI); Eurostat.

1.4 The recurrence of some problems

Swedish growth is proving remarkably high and stable. Between 2000 and 2007 average annual economic growth amounted to 2.8 per cent. GDP per capita, which had been only 4 per cent higher than the EU-15 average in 1998 was again 8 per cent ahead in 2007. This is still far from the 30 per cent lead that Sweden had in 1960, but is nonetheless an impressive turnaround. Unemployment is at 6.1 per cent, slightly lower than the EU average (EU-15, 7.2 per cent) but far higher than the best-performing countries (Denmark, Netherlands,

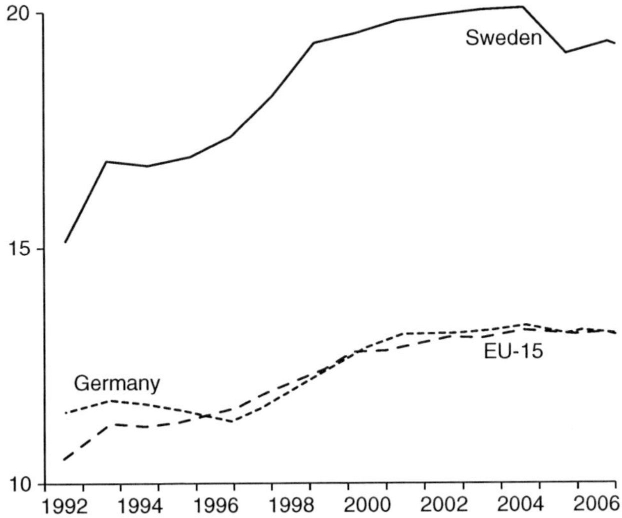

Figure 1.4 Investment into the future: expenditures in R&D, education and ICT as a percentage of GDP
Source: Eurostat, Structural Indicators.

United Kingdom, Austria); youth unemployment, however, is one of the highest in Western Europe (Swedish Government, 2006, p. 52).

Thus it would be fair to say that some of the incentive problems in the comprehensive social system have not been solved and that more recently some have recurred. The OECD (2005) reports that:

- the employment rate – particularly among males – had not yet recovered to its 1990 peak, as a result of longer periods of education, late entry and low rates of immigration.
- Sickness and disability absences are much higher than in most OECD countries, mainly because sickness benefits are generous and easy to get.
- Unemployed people would get back faster to work if the unemployment insurance and Activity Guarantee Programmes were overhauled (and the 'last in first out' rule in dismissals was softened).

Now we have to recall that the OECD was always critical of Swedish economic policy, since it neither followed the free market approach, as propagated in the OECD Job Study, nor the usual recommendations of the Paris Consensus (parodied as 'deregulate and wait' in Aiginger, 2006). But even admirers of the Swedish attempt to reconcile welfare with efficiency and full employment have to admit that keeping an economy with high social and ecological responsibility competitive needs a careful design of incentives at the margin, stringent incentives to work and offers to re-qualify. In other words a continuing reform is needed to encourage activity rates, lifelong learning and retraining. The goal to react quickly to changes in demand is of particular importance in a comprehensive social system.

Signs of strain are also showing in the budget balance. Though much better than in most other European countries, the structural surplus of the budget is below its target of 2 per cent of GDP in the 'best' years of the business cycle. The OECD calculates that Sweden has been about half a percentage point below its target for several years. Public sector reforms – though again admirable because of Sweden's top-down budget process and multi-year expenditure ceiling – do not rely on outside competition and benchmarks. Public financing still implies public production (OECD, 2005, p. 32).

As far as sickness and disability schemes are concerned, the old problem seems to recur. 'On a normal day nearly one fifth of potential work force is on sick leave or receiving a disability benefit' (OECD, 2005). The initially high sickness rate had declined as a result of, inter alia, shifting the financial load to firms and cancelling the payment for the first day off. But it returned to an all time high in 2006 (edging back in the business upswing). Government has set the target of halving the number of sick-listed people by 2008. Increasing the burden for firms (either by ensuring that they pay a share of the expenses, or by experience rating) will be one instrument; making extensions of sickness certificates more difficult (for instance not allowing this to be done by telephone) and encouraging a culture of mutual obligations are other possible solutions. Incapacity to work should not be focused on the ability to work in a particular job, but to work in general.

The unemployment insurance replacement ratio, which amounted to 80 per cent and is one of the highest in Europe, is to be lowered after 200 days, and after 300 days it will switch into a job or qualification guarantee. The precondition for unemployment insurance is raised from 70 to 80 hours of work per month and the period for meeting this minimum is extended to one year. Social contributions will be increased, with part-time workers paying the same amount as full-time workers. These changes follow the policy mix in Denmark (with more obligation and more offers to help). A carrot and stick strategy had been applied very softly in Sweden up until now. This had prevented the reduction of unemployment to the Danish level.

1.5 Are there lessons to be learned for the new member countries?

Are there lessons to be drawn from this analysis for the development of the European socio-economic model? The first conclusion is that the European model is no barrier to competitiveness, so long as it is reformed in the direction of fostering change and growth and improving incentives and qualifications. This is clearly demonstrated by the Scandinavian countries, which now combine – after several crises, devaluations, unsuccessful fiscal consolidations – rapid growth, full employment and fiscal prudence with a comprehensive welfare system and a high priority for ecological concerns and fairness.

The second conclusion is that the successful countries had to undergo substantial changes to be able to adapt their particular versions of the European socio-economic model to the challenges of globalization. The reform strategy rested on five pillars: managed and balanced flexibility, making wages significantly higher than unemployment support or welfare subsidies and at the same time making welfare conditional on participation in government-sponsored training or retraining schemes, fiscal consolidation plus quality of government, fostering investment into the future and following a consistent long-run strategy, embedded in trust and strong institutions.

Third, as far as institutions were concerned, the Scandinavian countries always had more inclusive institutions, and less insider-outsider problems. They managed to maintain and to exploit this property: the coverage of collective agreements is increasing and trade union membership is stable, both in contrast to continental economies. The inclusiveness of institutions and the trust in society enabled these countries to deregulate contracts and to make use of part-time work and fixed-term contracts without increasing poverty and exclusion.

Our fourth conclusion is that quadripartite decision-making seems to be more open for radical change than bipartite policymaking, since at least two partners (government and experts) will represent general interests. And the strong position of firm representatives and of trade unions enables the countries to cope with the burden of change and with the reintegration of losers.

The fifth conclusion is that the burden of change is acceptable if it is derived from a positive vision and if the burden is distributed in a fair way. Complex reforms – such as increasing flexibility and security at the same time – are feasible in trusting societies. Strong and inclusive institutions will mitigate the pressure from specific interests, thus preventing Olson's petrification hypothesis (Olson, 1986). In the ideal case they will help to foster externalities (for example, innovation, education, lifelong learning) thus making the economies more competitive.

Drawing conclusions from countries which have experienced a market-oriented welfare state for decades is of limited comparative value for countries which only fifteen years ago were run as planned economies in which government and institutions played very specific roles. It is even more difficult if we acknowledge the differences between the socio-economic models within 'old' Europe. Furthermore, we need to take into account the early success of the Scandinavian model, its demise in the 1980s and the early 1990s and now the resurrection after the crisis.

Nonetheless, there are some pointers towards what policy measures might be important for the further development of the 'catching-up model':

- institutions should be inclusive, avoiding a dichotomy between outsiders and insiders;
- specific positions in existing firms, industries and individual jobs should not be guaranteed; mobility, upgrading skills, finding new jobs should, however, be encouraged;
- part-time jobs, learning on the job, transition jobs between education and permanent jobs and sabbaticals should be encouraged. Part-time, entry and exit should be a choice and the jobs should be connected with social benefits (pro rata);
- microeconomic changes and willingness to adapt to new challenges need a high and stable macroeconomic growth rate;
- the role of economic policy does not decrease in periods of integration and globalization, only the instruments change. Enforcing activities with high external effects, such as innovation, education, lifelong learning and technological excellence becomes a priority;
- the burden of change is not equally distributed by market forces; those less trained, with lower skills and newcomers have to be assisted and re-qualified if they lose jobs.

A comprehensive welfare state is no barrier to change, but it needs permanent reforms to adapt the system and to encourage people to accept new challenges. The reformed European model is based on a trusting society, high mobility, a challenging environment and excellence in innovation and education. The new member countries need not follow a specific type of the model. Maybe the Baltic countries will follow the Scandinavian type, while Slovakia, Hungary, Poland and the Czech Republic might follow the continental type. But all can learn from the past problems and the new strength of the Swedish model.

Appendix 1.1 Towards a new European model

As regards institutional structures and policies, the strategies of the most successful European countries (Denmark, Finland and Sweden) show some elements which may encourage us to speak about a 'reformed European social model'. Some of the features of a new European model and its difference to the traditional model are summarized in Table A1.1.

The new reformed model, as represented by successful policy reforms, differs from the old welfare state in the following ways:

- The social system remains inclusive and tight, but benefits are increasingly made contingent on certain obligations; replacement rates are lower than they used to be in order to provide stronger incentives to work but still remain high by international standards.
- Taxes are relatively high, but in line with expenditure, aiming at positive balances in the medium term, to cover future pensions and to repay current debt; business taxes are relatively low as compared to personal taxes, and the tax wedge for low incomes is kept low.
- Wages are high, but the position of the individual is not guaranteed, as business conditions vary. The assistance and training opportunities offered to people who lose their jobs are personalized, less bureaucratic and less centralized. The public services are complemented by private agencies.
- Welfare-to-work elements have been introduced, generally on a decentralized – sometimes even private – basis; the background philosophy being one of giving help without incriminating the unemployed for being inactive.
- Part-time work and the adaptation of work to lifecycles are encouraged – not prevented. Social benefits are extended pro rata to part-time work, which is valued as a right of the individual and as an instrument of personal choice, rather than an inevitability preventing gender equality.

Table A1.1 The old welfare model versus a new European model of a reformed welfare state

Old model of European welfare	The reformed European model
Welfare pillar	
Security in existing jobs	Promoting mobility, assistance in finding a new job
High replacement ratios	Incentives to accept new jobs (return to labour force)
Structural change in existing firms (often large firms)	Job creation in new firms, service, self-employment
Comprehensive health coverage, pensions, education	Coverage dependent on personal obligations
Regulation of labour & product markets	Flexibility as a strategy for firms and as a right for employees
Focus on stable, full-time jobs	Part-time work as individual choice (softened by some rules)
Early retirement	Encouraging employment for elderly workforce
Policy pillar	
Focus on (price) stability	Focus on growth and new technologies
Asymmetric fiscal policy (deficits)	Fiscal prudence (but flexible in crisis)
Incentives for physical investment	Research, education, and new technologies are the basis
Subsidies for ailing firms (public ownership)	Industrial areas, university nexus
Industrial policy for large firms	Start-ups, venture capital, services
Local champions, permissive competition policy	Enforce current strengths (cluster and regional policy) and competition

- Technology policy and the adoption of new technologies, rather than the subsidization of old industries, are a precondition for the survival of the welfare state, and lead to more challenging and more interesting work.

The new European model differs from the United States model in at least the following ways:

- Even where welfare costs are streamlined and incentives improved, the welfare system offers comprehensive insurance against economic and social risks and a broad coverage of health risks.

- Environmental and social goals, as well as the equity of income distribution and the prevention of poverty remain high on the political agenda.
- Government and public institutions play a proactive role in promoting innovation, efficiency, structural change, higher qualifications and lifelong learning. Public institutions also provide the largest share of education and health care, which is open to all residents, and is of high quality and available at affordable rates.
- Social partners (institutions representing employers and employees) negotiate wage formation, develop labour laws and co-determine economic policy in general.
- Government is large and taxes are high, even if there are mechanisms to limit increases in spending and goals for achieving a sound fiscal policy ('fiscal rules') in periods of high demand. Firms are partly sheltered from high tax rates; there are high taxes on consumption and specifically on energy.

Notes

1. The countries in the Mediterranean model group and those in the Anglo-Saxon countries in Europe came closest to the US, with GDP growth rates of 2.9 per cent and 3.0 per cent, mainly since the initial starting point was at a relatively low level of GDP per capita. This holds for Spain, Portugal, Greece and Ireland; the high growth of the United Kingdom can either be interpreted by the dynamics of a 'liberal model' or by geography (trade with the US, Scandinavia) or as a reflection of slow growth in the past decades.
2. This evidence on economic performance is based on four indicators. It is supported and expanded in Aiginger (2004a), who uses a set of 12 indicators on the dynamics of output, productivity and employment, as well as on the level and changes of unemployment and fiscal balances to derive a more comprehensive 'performance evaluation' of countries since 1995.

References

Aiginger, K. (2004a). 'The Three Tier Strategy Followed by Successful European Countries in the 1990s', *International Review of Applied Economics*, 18(4): 399–422.

Aiginger, K. (2004b). 'Copying the US or Developing the New European Model: Policy Strategies of Successful European Countries in the Nineties', paper presented to the UN-ECE spring seminar, Competitiveness and Economic Growth in ECE Region, Geneva, February.

Aiginger, K. (2006). 'Competitiveness: from a Dangerous Obsession to a Welfare Creating Ability with Positive Externalities', Special Issue on Competitiveness, *Journal of Industry, Competition and Trade*, 6(2): 161–77.

Aiginger, K. and A. Guger (2005). 'The European Social Model: from an Alleged Barrier to a Competitive Advantage', *Journal of Progressive Politics*, 4(3): 40–7.
Aiginger, K. and A. Guger (2006). 'The European Socio-Economic Model', in A. Giddens, P. Diamond and R. Liddle (eds), *Global Europe, Social Europe*, Cambridge: Polity, pp. 124–50.
Brandner, P. (2003). 'Budgetpolitik der Niederlande, Finnlands und Schwedens – Lehren für nachhaltige Konsolidierungen?', Projektbericht, Institute for Advanced Studies, Vienna.
Lindbeck, A., P. Molander, T. Persson, O. Peterson, A. Sandmo, B. Swedenborg and N. Thysgesen (1994). *Turning Sweden Around*, Cambridge, MA: The MIT Press.
Marterbauer, M. (2001). 'Rehn-Meidner and Austrokeynesianism: Two Post-Keynesian Roads to High Employment', in H. Milner, E. Wadensjö and Rehn Gösta (eds), *The Swedish Model and Labour Market Policies*, Aldershot: Ashgate.
OECD (2005). 'Country Report: Sweden', Paris: OECD.
OECD (1994). 'Country Report: Sweden', Paris: OECD.
Olson, M. (1986). 'A Theory of the Incentives Facing Political Organizations: Neo-Corporatism and the Hegemonic State', *International Political Science Review*, 7(2): 165–89.
Swedish Government (2006). 'The Swedish Reform Programme for Growth and Jobs 2006–2008', Stockholm.

2

The European Central Bank Inflation Target and Economic Growth in the Eurozone

Svatopluk Kapounek and Lubor Lacina

2.1 Introduction

The primary objective of the European Central Bank (ECB) and its monetary policy, as defined in Article 105 of the Treaty Establishing the European Community, is to maintain price stability. 'Without prejudice to the objective of price stability', the Eurosystem will also 'support the general economic policies in the Community with a view to contributing to the achievement of the objectives of the Community'. These include a 'high level of employment' and 'sustainable and non-inflationary growth'. 'The ECB's Governing Council has defined price stability as a year-on-year increase in the Harmonised Index of Consumer Prices (HICP) for the euro area of below 2%. Price stability is to be maintained over the medium term. The Governing Council has also clarified that, in the pursuit of price stability, it aims to maintain inflation rates below, but close to, 2% over the medium term' (ECB, 2007a).

The reasoning behind this monetary policy target definition is as follows: price stability contributes to high levels of economic growth and employment – mainly as a result of improvements in the transparency of the price mechanism, the more efficient allocation of resources, reductions in inflation risk premia and interest rates (which reduce real interest rates and increase incentives to invest), reductions of distortions caused by inflation or deflation and last but not least as a result of the creation of conditions essential for the formation of stable rational expectations. Therefore it is not possible to determine price stability as a final target of macroeconomic policy; it is more plausible to regard price stability as an operating target or a macroeconomic tool necessary for achieving high levels of economic growth and employment. In this chapter we identify this assumption with the monetary policy of the ECB.

The aim of the following analysis is to answer the question whether the ECB's monetary policy target (inflation below but close to 2 per cent) is optimal for the EMU member states or not. The authors consider the possibility that the ECB's monetary policy could have been one of the factors that contributed to the recent slowdown in economic growth in the Eurozone.

2.2 Theoretical background: monetary policy versus economic growth

Price stability, an increase in economic growth, full employment and the quality of life are often mentioned among the final goals of central banks. But there is no theoretical or empirical consensus as to whether central banks are actually able to exert influence over economic growth.

According to classical economic theory (and its supply side-oriented models) real output is in the long run determined by the production capacity of the economy, which cannot be directly influenced by the central bank's monetary policy. But monetary policy can be used to influence the accumulation of capital, that is, the value of investments, and consequently the level of technological advance. On the other hand Keynesian economic theory asserts that real output could be influenced by monetary policy to the extent to which the monetary policy is capable of influencing aggregate demand.

From the previous paragraph it can be assumed that in demand-side economics monetary policy is seen as an effective tool to influence economic growth. Supply-side economics, however, maintains that monetary expansion exerts influence over real output only in the short run. In the long run any increase in real output will be offset by price increases.

Nonetheless, in supply-side economic theory monetary policy is an effective tool for influencing real output if it is able to maintain price stability effectively. Price stability increases the transparency of the price mechanism and so helps to improve the allocation of resources. Moreover price stability further reduces inflation risks and inflation premia in interest rates. Lower real interest rates have a positive impact on investment, which leads in turn to innovations and technological advances that determine the long-run real output of the economy. Furthermore, price stability reduces distortions caused by inflation or deflation and creates conditions essential for the formation of stable rational expectations. Many economists (for example, Angeloni et al., 2002) therefore assume that price stability is the essential tool in the maintenance of economic growth. The impact of the central bank's monetary policy on real output is therefore indirect, but significant.

The main assumptions of the ECB's monetary policy are based on monetarist doctrines. Even the ECB publicly states that:

> the natural role of monetary policy in the economy is to maintain price stability. Monetary policy can affect real activity only in the shorter term. But ultimately it can only influence the price level in the economy ... The Treaty provisions also imply that, in the actual implementation of monetary policy decisions aimed at maintaining price stability, the Eurosystem should also take into account the broader economic goals of the Community. In particular, given that monetary policy can affect real activity in the shorter term, the ECB typically should avoid generating excessive fluctuations in output and employment if this is in line with the pursuit of its primary objective.
>
> (ECB, 2007b)

On the assumption that there is a dichotomy between the real and monetary sectors, real activity is perceived as being determined only by real factors, such as the availability of capital, marginal labour and capital productivities, natural resources, technology developments and so on. On the other hand nominal wages and prices are determined solely by monetary factors. Therefore an increase in the money supply leads only to increases in nominal wages and prices, as the neutrality of money is assumed.

It is also assumed that through the ECB's transmission mechanism, funds in the banking system and interbank interest rates can be determined. These changes in the interbank interest rates affect the lending and deposit rates of commercial banks. Expectations of economic agents of future official interest rate developments affect medium and long-term interbank interest rates. The ECB also supposes that 'monetary policy can also guide economic agents' expectations of future inflation and thus influence price developments. A central bank with a high degree of credibility firmly anchors expectations of price stability. In this case, economic agents do not have to increase their prices for fear of higher inflation or reduce them for fear of deflation.' The changes in interest rates and economic agents' expectations may also lead to adjustments in asset prices and the exchange rate of the euro (ECB, 2007a, 2007b).

Given the aim of this chapter the following assumption is very important:

> Changes in interest rates affect saving and investment decisions of households and firms. For example, everything else being equal, higher interest rates make it less attractive to take out loans for financing consumption or investment. In addition, consumption and investment are also affected by movements in asset prices via wealth effects and effects on the value of collateral. For example, as equity prices rise, share-owning households become wealthier and may choose to increase their consumption. Conversely, when equity prices fall, households may reduce consumption. Asset prices can also have impact on aggregate demand via the value of collateral that allows borrowers to get more loans and/or to reduce the risk premia demanded by lenders/banks.
>
> (ECB, 2007c)

Besides the impact on savings and investments, interest rate rises increase the risk of borrowers being unable to repay their loans. Monetary restrictions therefore lead to reductions in the amounts that banks lend to households and firms. This assumption is very important (see below). It is possible to assume that monetary restrictions are more effective in reducing the amounts of loans than monetary expansions are in increasing them. In the case of a monetary expansion, households and small companies cannot change their investments and consumptions because of limited flexibility due to liquidity restraints (Revenda, 2004, pp. 219–40).[1] In the discussion below we assume that monetary restrictions have more effect on the supply of credit and hence on aggregate demand than is the case with monetary expansion vis-á-vis credit expansion.

The ECB summarizes the effect of monetary policy on domestic demand as follows: 'Changes in consumption and investment will change the level of domestic demand for goods and services relative to domestic supply. When demand exceeds supply, upward price pressure is likely to occur. In addition, changes in aggregate demand may translate into tighter or looser conditions in labour and intermediate product markets. This in turn can affect price and wage-setting in the respective market' (ECB, 2007c).

Although the ECB's assumptions and its monetary policy objectives have a monetarist character, the transmission mechanism includes many Keynesian elements. On the one hand, the ECB's monetary policy assumes that the money supply in the mid- and long term affects aggregate demand and prices. On the other hand, the relationship between interest rates and saving and investment decisions is typical of a Keynesian transmission mechanism. Keynesians assume that lower interest rates stimulate investment demand and autonomous consumption along with aggregate demand and output.

On the basis of Keynesian theory and the assumption that monetary expansion need not lead to an increase in investment and consumption on the grounds of access to credit of households and small companies, the authors assume that the sensitivity of investments and aggregate demand is different in the case of monetary expansion and restriction. Consequently monetary restriction, represented by an increase in interest rates, has a more significant impact on investment and aggregate demand than monetary expansion.[2]

In the analysis below, we accept the Keynesian assumption that investment and aggregate demand impact on real output and abstract from the neutrality of money in the long run.

2.3 Methodology

Empirical analyses focused on the impact of monetary policies on economic growth and inflation frequently provide insignificant results. This could be explained by the fact that in the low-inflation environment, where year-on-year change in inflation (measured as HICP) is lower than 5 per cent, there does not appear to be any causality between inflation and the velocity of money in the economy (De Grauwe, 2004, pp. 211–14).

Another – paradoxical – explanation could be the success of central banks in reducing inflation, because inflation biases are reduced even before they can appear. For this reason there are no historical time series displaying the effects of applications of monetary or/and fiscal policies available for empirical analysis.

Other possible reasons for the insignificant results offered by quantitative empirical analysis are the transmission mechanism and time lags between inflation and other shocks in the economy, the central bank's reactions, financial market adjustments and final effects in the real economy. Monetary policy lags are estimated to be 8–12 months in the Eurozone. Furthermore, the monetary transmission lags are different in each member state of the Eurozone.

However, the main reasons why we reject the application of quantitative statistical methodology to the analysis of the ECB's single monetary policy and its impact on the inflation rate and economic growth in the Eurozone are the insufficient number of observations (only 36 quarters) and permanently low inflation rates in the years 1998–2006. In these low-inflation countries it is not possible to analyse monetary restrictions and expansions, because the ECB's official refinancing rates fluctuate between 2 and 4.75 per cent. Determining the role of monetary restriction in such an environment would prove contentious.

In the following analysis, monetary expansion (restriction) is defined as a positive (negative) gap between the aggregate inflation rate in the Eurozone and the same rate in individual member states. The authors assume that inflation rate differences between the member states, combined with the ECB's single monetary policy, targeted on the primary objective – price stability – have an impact on the long-term trend of economic growth.

This long-term trend can be estimated with statistical filters (Woodford, 2001). Canova (1999) occupies himself with the identification of the trends and cyclical parts in the actual economic data by using the Kalman filter, Hodrick-Prescott filter and the band-pass filter. Of those, the Hodrick-Prescott filter is the most commonly used.

This filter is defined as:

$$Min\left\{\sum_{t=1}^{T}(Y_t - Y_t^*)^2 + \lambda\sum_{t=2}^{T-1}\left[(Y_{t+1}^* - Y_t^*) - (Y_t^* - Y_{t-1}^*)\right]\right\} \tag{2.1}$$

where λ is the parameter determining degree of the trend smoothing. For the purposes of this analysis the value of $\lambda = 1600$ is used, which is commonly considered to be appropriate for quarterly observations and assessments of long-term trends in GDP growth (see Figures 2.1 and 2.2 below).

Tables 2.4 and 2.5 (below) in the following analytical part include simple cross-correlation indexes without any time lags.

2.4 Empirical analysis: impact of monetary restriction and expansion on the aggregate economy growth in the Eurozone

In accordance with the primary target, the ECB tries to maintain aggregate inflation at under 2 per cent (Table 2.1). In years when aggregate inflation remains below this level ECB monetary policy can be assumed to be successful although inflation in the individual Eurozone member states fluctuates.

Table 2.1 Annual average rate of change, all-items HICP (Harmonized Index of Consumer Prices)

	Eurozone*	Belgium	Czech Republic	Germany	Ireland	Greece	Spain	France	Italy
1997	1.6	1.5	8.0	1.5	1.3	5.4	1.9	1.3	1.9
1998	1.1	0.9	9.7	0.6	2.1	4.5	1.8	0.7	2.0
1999	1.1	1.1	1.8	0.6	2.5	2.1	2.2	0.6	1.7
2000	2.1	2.7	3.9	1.4	5.3	2.9	3.5	1.8	2.6
2001	2.3	2.4	4.5	1.9	4.0	3.7	2.8	1.8	2.3
2002	2.2	1.6	1.4	1.4	4.7	3.9	3.6	1.9	2.6
2003	2.1	1.5	−0.1	1.0	4.0	3.4	3.1	2.2	2.8
2004	2.1	1.9	2.6	1.8	2.3	3.0	3.1	2.3	2.3
2005	2.2	2.5	1.6	1.9	2.2	3.5	3.4	1.9	2.2
2006	2.2	2.3	2.1	1.8	2.7	3.3	3.6	1.9	2.2
Average	1.9	1.8	3.6	1.4	3.1	3.6	2.9	1.6	2.3

	Luxembourg	Hungary	Netherlands	Austria	Poland	Portugal	Slovenia	Slovakia	Finland
1997	1.4	18.5	1.9	1.2	15.0	1.9	8.3	6.0	1.2
1998	1.0	14.2	1.8	0.8	11.8	2.2	7.9	6.7	1.3
1999	1.0	10.0	2.0	0.5	7.2	2.2	6.1	10.4	1.3
2000	3.8	10.0	2.3	2.0	10.1	2.8	8.9	12.2	2.9
2001	2.4	9.1	5.1	2.3	5.3	4.4	8.6	7.2	2.7
2002	2.1	5.2	3.9	1.7	1.9	3.7	7.5	3.5	2.0
2003	2.5	4.7	2.2	1.3	0.7	3.3	5.7	8.4	1.3
2004	3.2	6.8	1.4	2.0	3.6	2.5	3.7	7.5	0.1
2005	3.8	3.5	1.5	2.1	2.2	2.1	2.5	2.8	0.8
2006	3.0	4.0	1.7	1.7	1.3	3.0	2.5	4.3	1.3
Average	2.4	8.6	2.4	1.6	5.9	2.8	6.2	6.9	1.5

Note: *Eurozone – euro area (EU-11, 2000; EU-12, 2006, EU-13).
Source: Eurostat (5 March 2007).

In this chapter we define monetary restriction (expansion) as a change in the money supply or in interest rates which causes a reduction (increase) in inflation. This assumption allows us to say that in countries with inflation below the aggregate inflation rate in the Eurozone, the ECB's monetary policy appears inappropriately restrictive. On the other hand, in those countries where inflation exceeds the aggregate level of the Eurozone, the ECB policy results in inappropriate expansion. Monetary restriction is obvious in Belgium, Germany, France, Austria and Finland (Table 2.1). At the same time, Germany, Belgium, France and Austria are among those states with lower rates of economic growth in the Eurozone (Table 2.2).

The relationship between the inflation gap[3] and real economic indicators is more significant in the case of domestic demand[4] (Table 2.3). Italy is the only state with lower domestic demand than the Eurozone's aggregate without assumption of inappropriate monetary restriction.

Ireland, Greece, Spain, Italy, Luxembourg, the Netherlands and Portugal are those states with inflation higher than the aggregate level in the Eurozone. With the assumption that in these countries the ECB's monetary policy is inappropriately expansive, higher economic growth is to be expected. With the exception of Italy and Portugal all these countries do have higher economic growth. The relationship between the inflation gap and domestic demand is also significant (Table 2.3).

For a comparison of the impact of monetary restriction and expansion on aggregate economic growth in the Eurozone it is important to recognize the shares of different member states in the aggregate. Belgium, Germany, France, Austria and Finland comprise 64.1 per cent of Eurozone GDP. The share of Ireland, Greece, Spain, Italy, Luxembourg, The Netherlands and Portugal is 35.9 per cent.[5] Obviously, lower economic growth in countries with lower inflation cannot be balanced with higher economic growth in countries where inflation exceeds aggregate inflation and the monetary policy of the ECB acts expansively.

The long-term trend of the Eurozone's GDP growth represented by time series smoothed by HP filter indicates a permanent decrease (Figure 2.1). The Eurozone significantly falls behind the long-term trend of US GDP growth (Figure 2.2).

In the current analysis we concentrate on the roles of monetary policy and an inflation target. Variables such as capital endowments, marginal labour and capital productivities, natural resources, technological changes and so on indeed impact both real activity and GDP growth, but they are considered to be exogenous here.

Table 2.2 GDP at constant prices, percentage change on previous period

	Eurozone*	Belgium	Czech Republic	Germany	Ireland	Greece	Spain	France	Italy
1997	2.5	3.5	−0.7	1.8	11.7	3.6	3.9	2.2	1.9
1998	2.8	1.7	−0.8	2.0	8.5	3.4	4.5	3.5	1.4
1999	3.0	3.4	1.3	2.0	10.7	3.4	4.7	3.2	1.9
2000	3.8	3.7	3.6	3.2	9.4	4.5	5.0	4.0	3.6
2001	1.9	0.8	2.5	1.2	5.8	5.1	3.6	1.9	1.8
2002	0.9	1.5	1.9	0.0	6.0	3.8	2.7	1.0	0.3
2003	0.8	1.0	3.6	−0.2	4.3	4.8	3.0	1.1	0.0
2004	2.0	3.0	4.2	1.2	4.3	4.7	3.2	2.3	1.2
2005	1.4	1.1	6.1	0.9	5.5	3.7	3.5	1.2	0.1
2006	2.6	3.1	6.0	2.7	5.3	3.8	3.9	2.2	1.9
Average	2.2	2.3	2.8	1.5	7.2	4.1	3.8	2.3	1.4

	Luxembourg	Hungary	Netherlands	Austria	Poland	Portugal	Slovenia	Slovakia	Finland
1997	5.9	4.6	4.3	1.8	7.1	4.2	4.8	5.7	6.1
1998	6.5	4.9	3.9	3.6	5.0	4.8	3.9	3.7	5.2
1999	8.4	4.2	4.7	3.3	4.5	3.9	5.4	0.3	3.9
2000	8.4	5.2	3.9	3.4	4.2	3.9	4.1	0.7	5.0
2001	2.5	4.1	1.9	0.8	1.1	2.0	2.7	3.2	2.6
2002	3.8	4.3	0.1	0.9	1.4	0.8	3.5	4.1	1.6
2003	1.3	4.1	0.3	1.1	3.8	−1.1	2.7	4.2	1.8
2004	3.6	4.9	2.0	2.4	5.3	1.2	4.4	5.4	3.7
2005	4.0	4.2	1.5	2.0	3.5	0.4	4.0	6.0	2.9
2006	5.5	3.9	2.9	3.1	5.2	1.2	4.8	8.3	5.5
Average	5.0	4.4	2.6	2.2	4.1	2.1	4.0	4.2	3.8

Note: *Eurozone – euro area (EU-11, 2000; EU-12, 2006, EU-13).
Source: Eurostat (5 March 2007).

Table 2.3 Domestic demand at constant prices, percentage change on previous period

	Eurozone*	Belgium	Czech Republic	Germany	Ireland	Greece	Spain	France	Italy
1997	2.0	2.8	−1.1	1.0	10.2	3.5	3.4	0.9	3.0
1998	3.6	2.2	−1.4	2.4	9.8	4.6	6.2	4.1	3.3
1999	3.6	2.9	1.2	2.8	7.4	3.8	6.4	3.7	3.2
2000	3.3	3.9	3.8	2.2	9.0	5.6	5.3	4.5	2.8
2001	1.2	0.3	3.7	−0.5	4.0	3.1	3.8	1.8	1.6
2002	0.4	0.8	3.9	−2.0	4.1	4.8	3.2	1.1	1.3
2003	1.5	1.0	4.4	0.7	3.4	5.4	3.8	1.8	0.9
2004	1.8	3.1	3.2	0.0	4.8	4.7	4.8	3.1	1.1
2005	1.6	1.6	1.6	0.5	7.9	2.3	5.0	2.1	0.3
2006	2.3	2.3	4.0	1.6	6.3	3.9	4.6	2.4	1.6
Average	2.1	2.1	2.3	0.9	6.7	4.2	4.7	2.6	1.9

	Luxembourg	Hungary	Netherlands	Austria	Poland	Portugal	Slovenia	Slovakia	Finland
1997	6.4	4.9	4.4	0.6	9.4	5.5	4.9	6.2	5.0
1998	6.4	8.2	5.1	2.4	6.4	6.9	5.1	4.7	4.6
1999	8.0	5.1	4.9	3.0	5.3	5.8	8.8	−5.9	0.9
2000	4.3	7.2	2.7	3.1	2.9	3.3	1.3	0.4	3.7
2001	4.5	2.2	2.3	−0.2	−1.6	1.7	0.8	8.0	2.2
2002	2.5	6.5	−0.4	−1.0	0.7	0.0	2.3	4.1	1.4
2003	4.0	6.5	0.5	2.5	2.3	−2.2	4.9	−1.3	4.0
2004	2.6	4.2	0.5	1.6	5.6	2.3	5.2	6.2	3.0
2005	5.2	0.6	0.9	1.2	1.8	0.8	1.9	8.6	4.5
2006	2.5	−0.6	2.8	1.9	5.2	0.1	3.9	6.2	2.8
Average	4.6	4.5	2.4	1.5	3.8	2.4	3.9	3.7	3.2

Note: *Eurozone – euro area (EU-11, 2000; EU-12, 2006, EU-13).
Source: Eurostat (5 March 2007).

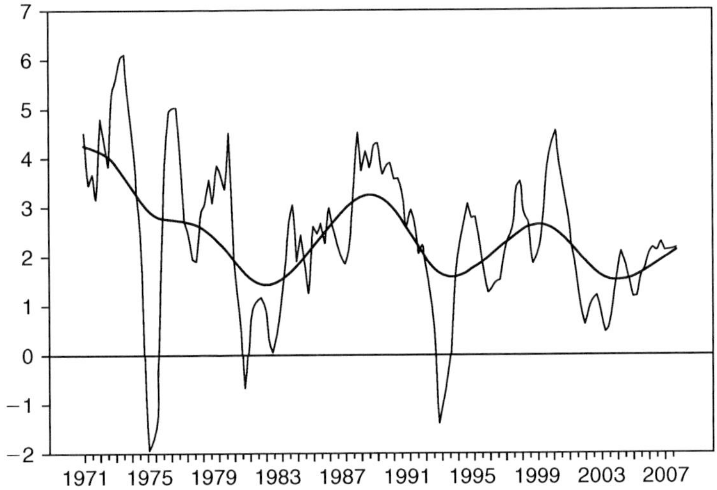

Figure 2.1 GDP growth in the Eurozone (quarterly data, percentage change on the same period previous year, constant prices)
Source: Eurostat (10 November 2006), HP filter ($\lambda = 1600$).

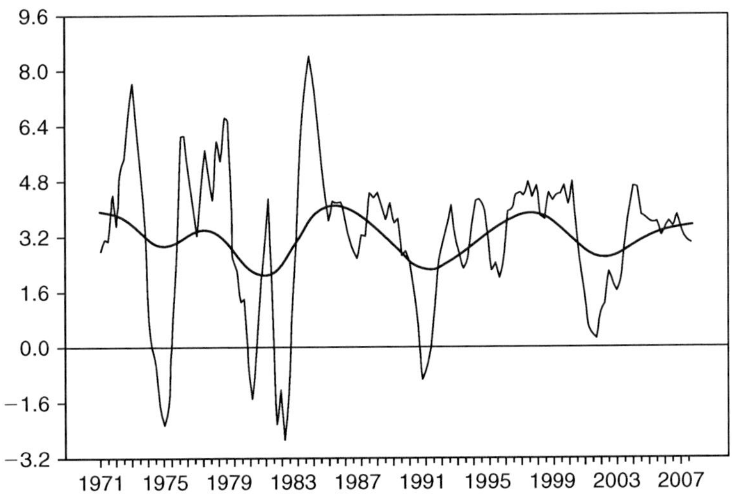

Figure 2.2 GDP growth in the US (quarterly data, percentage change on the same period previous year, constant prices)
Source: Eurostat (10 November 2006), HP filter ($\lambda = 1600$).

Table 2.1 shows the different inflation rate levels in the EMU member states. We assume that these differences are very important for a single monetary policy target of the ECB. The smaller differences between the inflation rates imply a greater success of monetary policy instruments and the reduction of a differential impact of the single monetary policy. The correlation between the inflation rates in the Eurozone is presented in Table 2.4. The average correlation index of inflation rates between the Eurozone member states and aggregate inflation is 0.558 (for EU-13).

The same correlation index for the US is 0.798[6] (Table 2.5). However, a better comparison of these correlation indexes could be attained by comparing the aggregate against a selection of five Eurozone member states. The index of correlation between monthly inflation in Eurozone (EU-13) and Germany, France, Belgium, Luxembourg and the Netherlands is 0.724. Therefore we assume that the correlation among the inflation in US regions is higher than among Eurozone member states.

It follows that the ECB's primary target of inflation below 2 per cent is unrealistic for all the Eurozone member states. Thus, the ECB's monetary policy appears to be permanently unsuccessful in Ireland, Greece, Spain, Italy, Luxembourg and Portugal.

In contrast to the ECB's single monetary policy strategy, the Federal Reserve System (FED) defines its monetary policy strategy on two major objectives: price stability and a sustainable rate of growth of output. The FED's monetary policy is based on the analysis of a large body of economic and financial data and its model consists of a wide spectrum of objectives. Thus, its Central Bank Council can consider (at least to a degree) different objectives together with price stability. The priorities are then able to change according to conditions in the real economy.

2.5 Conclusions

The maintenance of price stability is the primary objective of the Eurosystem and the single goal of the ECB's monetary policy. Underlying this single monetary policy objective is monetarist economic theory. However, the transmission mechanism logic as applied also contains many Keynesian assumptions. We accept the assumptions that monetary policy affects banks and money-market interest rates and that the interest rates have a significant role in savings, investment decisions, consumption and in the formation of economic agents' expectations. We also assume that interest rates and the supply of credit leads to changes in aggregate demand and real output. These assumptions are consistent with the ECB operational approach. Table 2.6 shows the responses of real

Table 2.4 Cross-correlation, monthly HICP, annual rate of change, EU-13, 1997–2006

	Euro area	Belgium	Germany	Ireland	Greece	Spain	France	Italy	Luxem-bourg	Nether-lands	Austria	Portugal	Slovenia	Finland
Euro area		0.7326	0.8219	0.4955	0.0351	0.8151	0.9111	0.6935	0.7653	0.3894	0.8585	0.5581	−0.1059	0.2833
		119	119	119	119	119	119	119	119	119	119	119	119	119
		0.000	0.000	0.000	0.705	0.000	0.000	0.000	0.000	0.000	0.000	0.000	0.252	0.002
Belgium	0.7326		0.6997	0.3624	−0.0522	0.6217	0.6108	0.3523	0.7114	0.2238	0.7398	0.3148	−0.0889	0.3679
	119		119	119	119	119	119	119	119	119	119	119	119	119
	0.000		0.000	0.000	0.573	0.000	0.000	0.000	0.000	0.014	0.000	0.001	0.336	0.000
Germany	0.8219	0.6997		0.0741	0.1524	0.551	0.7036	0.2643	0.6553	0.198	0.7716	0.2529	−0.2015	0.087
	119	119		119	119	119	119	119	119	119	119	119	119	119
	0.000	0.000		0.423	0.098	0.000	0.000	0.004	0.000	0.031	0.000	0.006	0.028	0.347
Ireland	0.4955	0.3624	0.0741		−0.2358	0.5777	0.3974	0.6655	0.3619	0.5581	0.4086	0.6404	0.3682	0.6912
	119	119	119		119	119	119	119	119	119	119	119	119	119
	0.000	0.000	0.423		0.010	0.000	0.000	0.000	0.000	0.000	0.000	0.000	0.000	0.000
Greece	0.0351	−0.0522	0.1524	−0.2358		−0.261	−0.023	−0.012	−0.247	0.0841	−0.005	0.017	0.3135	−0.0154
	119	119	119	119		119	119	119	119	119	119	119	119	119
	0.705	0.573	0.098	0.010		0.004	0.804	0.900	0.007	0.363	0.955	0.854	0.001	0.868
Spain	0.8151	0.6217	0.551	0.5777	−0.261		0.7466	0.6587	0.7953	0.1668	0.6649	0.4983	−0.2772	0.2136
	119	119	119	119	119		119	119	119	119	119	119	119	119
	0.000	0.000	0.000	0.000	0.004		0.000	0.000	0.000	0.070	0.000	0.000	0.002	0.020
France	0.9111	0.6108	0.7036	0.3974	−0.023	0.7466		0.6978	0.7403	0.1615	0.7653	0.39	−0.2462	0.0538
	119	119	119	119	119	119		119	119	119	119	119	119	119
	0.000	0.000	0.000	0.000	0.804	0.000		0.000	0.000	0.079	0.000	0.000	0.007	0.561

(Continued)

Table 2.4 (*Continued*)

	Euro area	Belgium	Germany	Ireland	Greece	Spain	France	Italy	Luxem-bourg	Nether-lands	Austria	Portugal	Slovenia	Finland
Italy	0.6935	0.3523	0.2643	0.6655	−0.0116	0.6587	0.6978		0.5045	0.2513	0.5074	0.4919	0.0856	0.2776
	119	119	119	119	119	119	119		119	119	119	119	119	119
	0.000	0.000	0.004	0.000	0.900	0.000	0.000		0.000	0.006	0.000	0.000	0.354	0.002
Luxembourg	0.7653	0.7114	0.6553	0.3619	−0.247	0.7953	0.7403	0.5045		−0.031	0.7376	0.2509	−0.287	0.1443
	119	119	119	119	119	119	119	119		119	119	119	119	119
	0.000	0.000	0.000	0.000	0.007	0.000	0.000	0.000		0.739	0.000	0.006	0.002	0.117
Netherlands	0.3894	0.2238	0.198	0.5581	0.0841	0.1668	0.1615	0.2513	−0.0309		0.3525	0.7313	0.5457	0.6895
	119	119	119	119	119	119	119	119	119		119	119	119	119
	0.000	0.014	0.031	0.000	0.363	0.070	0.079	0.006	0.739		0.000	0.000	0.000	0.000
Austria	0.8585	0.7398	0.7716	0.4086	−0.0052	0.6649	0.7653	0.5074	0.7376	0.3525		0.418	−0.0671	0.2722
	119	119	119	119	119	119	119	119	119	119		119	119	119
	0.000	0.000	0.000	0.000	0.955	0.000	0.000	0.000	0.000	0.000		0.000	0.468	0.003
Portugal	0.5581	0.3148	0.2529	0.6404	0.017	0.4983	0.39	0.4919	0.2509	0.7313	0.418		0.1882	0.4381
	119	119	119	119	119	119	119	119	119	119	119		119	119
	0.000	0.001	0.006	0.000	0.854	0.000	0.000	0.000	0.006	0.000	0.000		0.040	0.000
Slovenia	−0.1059	−0.0889	−0.2015	0.3682	0.3135	−0.2772	−0.2462	0.0856	−0.287	0.5457	−0.067	0.1882		0.6983
	119	119	119	119	119	119	119	119	119	119	119	119		119
	0.252	0.336	0.028	0.000	0.001	0.002	0.007	0.354	0.002	0.000	0.468	0.040		0.000
Finland	0.2833	0.3679	0.087	0.6912	−0.0154	0.2136	0.0538	0.2776	0.1443	0.6895	0.2722	0.4381	0.6983	
	119	119	119	119	119	119	119	119	119	119	119	119	119	
	0.002	0.000	0.347	0.000	0.868	0.020	0.561	0.002	0.117	0.000	0.003	0.000	0.000	

Source: Authors' calculations.

Table 2.5 Cross-correlation, monthly consumer prices index, annual rate of change, US cities, 1990–2006

	US city average	New York-Northern New Jersey-Long Island	Philadelphia-Wilmington-Atlantic City	Chicago-Gary-Kenosha	Los Angeles-Riverside-Orange County	San Francisco-Oakland-San Jose
US city average		0.9034 148 0.000	0.884 148 0.000	0.8706 148 0.000	0.8038 148 0.000	0.5274 148 0.000
New York-	0.9034 148 0.000		0.857 148 0.000	0.7216 148 0.000	0.8597 148 0.000	0.4136 148 0.000
Philadelphia-	0.884 148 0.000	0.857 148 0.000		0.7178 148 0.000	0.79 148 0.000	0.3657 148 0.000
Chicago-	0.8706 148 0.000	0.7216 148 0.000	0.7178 148 0.000		0.6394 148 0.000	0.4857 148 0.000
Los Angeles-	0.8038 148 0.000	0.8597 148 0.000	0.79 148 0.000	0.6394 148 0.000		0.5362 148 0.000
San Francisco-	0.5274 148 0.000	0.4136 148 0.000	0.3657 148 0.000	0.4857 148 0.000	0.5362 148 0.000	

Source: Author's calculations.

Table 2.6 Estimates of responses of real GDP and consumer prices to 1 percentage point increase in the policy-controlled interest rates in the Eurozone

	Real GDP				**Consumer prices**			
	Year 1	**Year 2**	**Year 3**	**Year 4**	**Year 1**	**Year 2**	**Year 3**	**Year 4**
Model 1	−0.34	−0.71	−0.71	−0.63	−0.15	−0.30	−0.38	−0.49
Model 2	−0.22	−0.38	−0.31	−0.14	−0.09	−0.21	−0.31	−0.40
Model 3	−0.34	−0.47	−0.37	−0.28	−0.06	−0.10	−0.19	−0.31

Notes: Model 1 is the Area-Wide Model for the Euro Area (Fagan et al., 2001); Model 2 is the CNB Macroeconomic Model (Benes and Vavra, 2004); Model 3 is the NiGEM Model of the UK National Institute for Economic and Social Research.
Source: 'Recent Findings on Monetary Policy Transmission', ECB's Monthly Bulletin, October 2002.

GDP and consumer prices to a two-year increase of 100 basis points in the policy-controlled interest rates of the euro area. Figures are expressed in per cent from baseline. Simulations are performed using the ECB's area-wide model (AWM), the NCB's macroeconomic models (NCB) and the multi-country model of the NIESR (NiGEM).

The output and price responses to monetary policy were analysed using vector-autoregression (VAR) models. From Table 2.6 it is obvious that output reactions are more sensitive to the increases of a policy-controlled interest rate than are consumer prices. The ECB summarizes these results as follows:

> First, impact of monetary policy is neutral in the long run, i.e. a permanent change in the money supply (associated here with a temporary change, in the opposite direction, in the central bank instrument, the policy-controlled interest rate) has no significant long-run effect on real GDP, but does lead to a permanent change in the price level. This evidence is consistent with that given in the large body of theoretical and empirical literature on money neutrality. Second, monetary policy changes do have a temporary impact on output. This short-run non-neutrality is attributable to nominal and real rigidities in the goods and labour markets, which prevent prices from quickly adjusting after a change in monetary policy. This highlights the importance of the structural characteristics of the wage and price setting mechanisms in terms of enhancing the effectiveness of monetary policy on prices and reducing its costs in terms of output fluctuations.
>
> (ECB, 2002, pp. 45)

The ECB also recognizes the problem of differences in monetary policy effects on output. The reason is not only different transmission mechanisms in each member state but also the different effects of monetary policy on euro area output in booms and in downturns. In downturns, policy-controlled interest rates have more significant negative effects on output.

The different effects of monetary policy on output in the individual countries of the euro area were analysed by Mojon and Peersman (2003, pp. 56–74), who confirmed the assumption, that 'contractionary monetary policy shock leads to a temporary fall in GDP that peaks between three and six quarters after the shock and a gradual decrease in the price level'. The consumption response is smaller than that in investments and exports. If the response of investments to the monetary policy contraction exceeds that of consumption, then the Keynesian assumptions could be accepted and the conclusion reached that monetary policy restriction causes economic growth to decline in the long run. The neutrality of money in the long run cannot be generally accepted.

Significant monetary policy effects on economic growth are also confirmed by van Els et al. (2003) and Peersman and Smets (2003). All of the above-mentioned empirical studies are based on the long-run time series before the ECB was established. The estimation of the impact of the ECB's monetary policy on economic growth and the inflation rate is not exact because the European integration process affects financial markets and transmission mechanisms differently in each of the Eurozone member states. And, of course, the ECB's single monetary policy is different from the autonomous monetary policies of the Eurozone member states before the year 1998.

We also assume that monetary expansion has a lower impact on economic growth than monetary restriction. This assumption is based on the Keynesian theory of the liquidity trap. Also very important is the fact that monetary restriction is more effective in reducing the amount of loans than monetary expansion is in expanding the amount of loans. In the case of a monetary expansion, households and small companies cannot change their investments and consumptions because of limited flexibility stemming from liquidity constraints.

The different sensitivities of member states to monetary restriction and expansion and the growth of output present a problem for the Eurozone. There are different levels of inflation in different member states, while the ECB targets aggregate inflation for the Eurozone as a whole. We assume that the inflation gap (defined as the difference between aggregate inflation in the Eurozone and each of the EMU member states) is a problem for the central bank and its primary objective of price stability. It is not possible to apply a different monetary policy for each state and in many states in the Eurozone the ECB appears to act with an inappropriate monetary restriction or expansion. At the same time, the monetary restriction effect is not fully compensated by the monetary expansion effect on economic growth. Therefore we conclude that the ECB's single monetary policy is one of the factors underlying the decline in the long-term trend of economic growth in the Eurozone.

The question that remains is that of the role of monetary policy. Barron et al. (2006, pp. 144–5) discussed the effectiveness of monetary policy. They 'presume that the goal of the monetary authority focuses solely on output. In particular, suppose that the monetary authority desires to set the money supply in order to minimize the fluctuation in the log of output around some desired level.' The price level stabilization reduces nominal disturbances that tend to contribute to the aggregate demand volatility and the real short-term output fluctuations.

How can the ECB reduce nominal disturbances in the monetary union with the inflation rate differences? Why does the ECB target aggregate inflation rate, insofar as this inflation target is not implemented in the individual EMU member states? The German model of central banking reduces the flexibility of the ECB in the real conditions of the Eurozone. The adoption of a wider spectrum of objectives appears to be an interesting alternative option. This might not only enhance the credibility of the central bank but could also promote debate about the ECB's impact on economic growth in the Eurozone.

Notes

1. The significance of this assumption is determined by the funding possibilities of households and companies. Higher degree of financial dependence on the banking system increases this assumption.
2. Neutral monetary policy is defined as a change in the money supply or interest rate which has no impact on inflation. Monetary restriction (or expansion) is a change in the money supply or interest rate associated with the reduction (or increase) of inflation in the economy.
3. The inflation gap is defined as the difference between aggregate inflation in the Eurozone and each of the EMU member states.
4. Domestic demand covers gross capital formation and final consumption expenditure of households, governments and companies.
5. The GDP data are calculated in millions of euros at constant 2006 prices.
6. The authors accept a minimum of 100 observations for time series correlation analysis. New York, Northern New Jersey, Long Island; Philadelphia,

Wilmington, Atlantic City; Chicago, Gary, Kenosha; Los Angeles, Riverside, Orange County and San Francisco, Oakland, San Jose provided disposable data. The cross-correlation was counted with the US city average consumer prices index.

References

Angeloni, I. et al. (2002). 'Monetary Transmission in the Euro Area: Where Do We Stand?', European Central Bank, Working Paper No. 114, January.

Barron, J.M. et al. (2006). *Understanding Macroeconomic Theory*, New York: Routledge.

Benes, J. and D. Vavra (2004). 'SDGE Models to Support Monetary Policy', CNB/CERGE-EI Macro Workshop, Prague, May.

Canova, F. (1999). 'Does Detrending Matter for the Determination of the Reference Cycle and the Selection of Turning Points? ' *Economic Journal*, 109(452): 126–50.

De Grauwe, P. (2004). *Economics of Monetary Union*, Sixth Edition, Oxford: Oxford University Press.

ECB (2002). 'Recent Findings on Monetary Policy Transmission', ECB's Monthly Bulletin, October.

ECB (2007a). 'Benefits of Price Stability', 5 January, http://www.ecb.int/mopo/intro/html/benefits.en.html.

ECB (2007b). 'Objective of Monetary Policy', 5 January, http://www.ecb.int/mopo/intro/html/objective.en.html.

ECB (2007c). 'Transmission Mechanism of Monetary Policy', 10 February, http://www.ecb.int/mopo/intro/html/transmission.en.html.

Fagan, G., J. Henry and R. Mestre (2001). 'An Area-Wide Model (AWM) for the Euro Area', ECB Working Paper no. 42, Frankfurt, January.

Mojon, B. and G. Peersman (2003). 'A VAR Description of the Effects of Monetary Policy in the Individual Countries of the Euro Area', in I. Angeloni, A.K. Kashyap and B. Mojon (eds), *Monetary Policy Transmission in the Euro Area. A Study by the Eurosystem Monetary Transmission Network*, Cambridge: Cambridge University Press.

Peersman G. and F. Smets (2003). 'The Monetary Transmission Mechanism in the Euro Area: Evidence from VAR Analysis', in I. Angeloni, A.K. Kashyap and B. Mojon (eds), *Monetary Policy Transmission in the Euro Area. A Study by the Eurosystem Monetary Transmission Network*, Cambridge: Cambridge University Press.

Revenda, Z. (2004). *Centrální bankovnictví*, Prague: Management Press.

UK National Institute of Economic and Social Research, http://nimodel.niesr.ac.uk/.

Van Els, P., A. Locarno, J. Morgan and J.P. Villetelle (2003). 'The Effects of Monetary Policy in the Euro Area: Evidence from Structural Macroeconomic Models', in I. Angeloni, A.K. Kashyap and B. Mojon (eds), *Monetary Policy Transmission in the Euro Area. A Study by the Eurosystem Monetary Transmission Network*, Cambridge: Cambridge University Press.

Woodford, M. (2001). 'The Taylor Rule and Optimal Monetary Policy', *American Economic Review: Papers and Proceedings*, 91: 232–7.

3
Real Effective Exchange Rate for the Euro: Equilibrium and Misalignment

Antonin Rusek

3.1 Introduction

The real exchange rate is among the most important categories in both macroeconomic and international economics analyses. The dynamics of the real exchange rate influence (and are in turn influenced by) the dynamics of both real and financial sectors of all economies. Empirically, real exchange rate misalignments are perceived to be the causes of the loss of competitiveness, growth slowdowns and currency crises in cases of an overvaluation, overheating and inflation in cases of an undervaluation, sectoral misallocations of resources and global economic imbalances.

In the case of a currency union that includes sovereign countries, the dynamics of the real exchange rate take on an additional importance. When a currency union encompasses sovereign countries with imperfectly integrated markets and limited fiscal transfers, the divergent dynamics of real effective exchange rates in the individual countries – both actual and as an equilibrium – will exacerbate both economic and political tensions and may lead to the collapse of not only the monetary union per se but of the underlying integration processes as well.

The reason for this is that members of a currency union lose power over both monetary policy to influence the domestic economic dynamic and the nominal exchange rate as a tool to counter unfavourable developments vis-à-vis the rest of the global economy.

That, in turn, places an increased burden on the remaining economic policy tools, namely microeconomic policies (which encompass both the regulations in general and labour market policies) and the fiscal policy in all its aspects. But the use of both microeconomic and fiscal policies to deal with unfavourable economic developments more often than not leads to economic hardship, which results in government unpopularity and rising political and social tension.

Under such circumstances individual governments attempt to influence the common monetary (and hence the exchange rate) policy in their favour. But because individual countries face different economic circumstances (and, in fact, may have governments with different economic preferences), attempts to influence the central monetary authority are likely to lead to rising tensions and disagreements between countries. This might eventually endanger the existence of the monetary union itself.

Whether a currency union is in the process of increasing economic cohesion or increasing divergence is an empirical question. After all, in an entity like the EMU (European Economic and Monetary Union, commonly called the Eurozone) a degree of difference between member states is natural. It is the consequence of different historical, economic and political traditions, as they express themselves in differing legal systems, regulations, labour markets, social welfare and economic policy institutions. Removing those differences is a very long-run process – where the 'long run' goes far beyond its Keynesian meaning.

In the medium term 'cohesion' is supposedly facilitated by the removal of obstacles to the movement of goods and services and capital among the Eurozone (and EU) member nations, by the harmonization of goods, services, capital and labour market regulations among these states and by a harmonization of public taxes and public services (that is, the fiscal policy area). And whereas significant progress was made in these areas in the 1990s, the process slowed down radically after the introduction of the euro in 1999 (Tilford, 2006).

This raises the question of whether the introduction of the common currency resulted in an increased cohesion among the Eurozone countries? Or did it lead to increasing divergence (as the discussion above has hinted is certainly possible)?

The dynamics of the real exchange rates may indicate possible answers. Even if the nominal exchange rate is the same for all Eurozone participants, the real exchange rates may differ. This is the result of different levels of inflation in the individual countries and different trade patterns that generate different weights in the calculations of the 'effective' real exchange rates.

However, one would assume that as cohesion in the Eurozone increases (that is, it gradually becomes single economic area) the real effective exchange rates should converge as well – or at least they should not diverge. And this process should be observable not only for the actual real effective exchange rates, but, perhaps more importantly, for their 'equilibrium' values as well. Therefore, the questions this chapter seeks to answer are:

1. Do the 'equilibrium' real exchange rates for the Eurozone as a whole and its largest member states (Germany, Italy, Spain, France) converge or diverge?
2. In this context, are the 'equilibrium' real exchange rates for the individual countries in the Eurozone 'overvalued' or 'undervalued'? (This addresses the medium to long-term impact of the common monetary policy on the individual member states.)
3. And third, are the actual real exchange rates for the individual countries in the Eurozone overvalued or undervalued with respect to both Eurozone and individual country's equilibria?

The analysis below seeks to answer these questions. The discussion is divided into six parts. The next part provides a basic overview of the 'equilibrium' real exchange rate concepts and literature. Section 3.3 provides the basic discussion of MacDonald's BEER (behavioural equilibrium exchange rate) concept, which is then used in the further analysis. Section 3.4 reports econometric results which are then discussed in Section 3.5. Section 3.6 concludes.

3.2 'Equilibrium' real effective exchange rate: modelling concepts and literature

A misaligned real exchange rate is commonly thought of as one of the main reasons for economic disequilibria. However, it is obvious that the notion of 'misalignment' of the real exchange rate requires the idea of the 'equilibrium' real exchange rate. But the latter is not a simple concept: the real exchange rate affects not only a single market (or a single economic sector) but the multitude of markets and sectors – both real and financial. Moreover, even if the 'equilibrium' real effective exchange rate can be defined theoretically, the complexity of this concept generates difficulties in operationalizing the notion of the equilibrium real effective exchange rate for the purposes of empirical estimation and study.

The current economic and econometric approaches generally follow one of three basic analytical models that have been developed in the economic literature. Chronologically first is the FEER (fundamental equilibrium exchange rate) approach, developed by John Williamson (1994) and Simon Wren-Lewis et al. (1998). Subsequently, variants of this approach were applied by others for a variety of real effective exchange rates involving many different countries. (Examples of work in the FEER tradition are Baffes et al., 1997; Bayoumi et al., 2005; Feyzioglu, 1997; Wren, 2003. This approach is analysed and compared to others by Siregar and Rajan, 2006.)

This model is derived from the (rather standard) economic assumption that the equilibrium real effective exchange rate is the one which is compatible with both the internal and external equilibria.

In the empirical work, the small multi-equation macroeconomic model is specified and estimated using observed values of the relevant economic variables. Equilibrium real effective exchange rate is then calculated using presumed long-term (equilibrium) values of the economic variables. (That is why some call this approach an equilibrium calculation rather than an estimation.) The degree of the misalignment is then calculated by comparing the actual real effective exchange rate with its calculated equilibrium values.

This approach is critiqued in two areas. First, the use of and the implied need to estimate the multi-equation macroeconomic model introduces possible inconsistencies – and hence biases – into the values of estimated coefficients. This comes from the fact that the number of variables in even relatively small models is often large relative to the number of available observations. That makes the direct and consistent estimation of the multi-equation model unfeasible. Hence, the single equation estimations must be used, tying them together by methods such as seemingly unrelated regressions and trying to restore the coefficient consistency with subsequent calibrations. This technique, even if necessary under the circumstances (the lack of sufficiently long reliable data), casts a shadow over the 'estimated' coefficients and hence over the reliability of the calculated equilibrium real effective exchange rate itself.

Second, the specifications of both internal and external equilibria are often controversial. This is less so as far as the internal equilibrium is concerned, where concepts such as output at its potential level or the NAIRU level of unemployment are generally accepted as the internal equilibrium indicators. But even here things are sometime controversial, given demographic and preference dynamics, changing the retirement age, changing work participation rates and so on.

More contentious is the specification of an external equilibrium. It is generally recognized that the assumption of a zero external balance in the medium term is broadly unrealistic, given both the domestic savings–investment nexus and the medium-term fiscal nexus. In these circumstances assumptions regarding the medium-term 'external equilibrium' contain a strong normative element, which then affects the calculations of the equilibrium real effective exchange rates.

The NATREX (natural real exchange rate) class of models, first elucidated by Jerome Stein (1994), reflects an attempt to address some of the perceived shortcomings of the FEER approach. Here the assumption of the internal equilibrium is preserved, usually approximated by the NAIRU concept. However, the external position is modelled as a dynamic interaction between the long-term values of domestic savings and investments, which then determine the current account and hence the long-term capital flows. Both the long-term dynamics of domestic savings and investments are determined by economic fundamentals (relative productivity, relative wealth, rate of return differentials and so on). Short-term and cyclical influences are excluded from the determination of the equilibrium real effective exchange rate. Due to its construction the NATREX model is stock flow consistent.

The real effective exchange rate determined by the NATREX class of models is sometimes described as 'dynamic', in contrast to the equilibrium rate determined by FEER models. The reason is that in NATREX models the equilibrium rate changes, reflecting the long-term dynamics of domestic savings and investments. It follows that in a very long run (a stationary state equilibrium) all agents will be satisfied with their asset positions. That implies that both gross and net capital flows will cease, hence domestic savings must equal domestic investments. Current account – that is, the external position – is balanced. In this sense the strictly theoretical long-term FEER equilibrium real effective exchange rate is the limit value for the NATREX equilibrium real effective exchange rate.

Given its complexity and the simultaneous equations structure, the estimations of the NATREX models run into the same kinds of difficulties as FEER approaches. To avoid some of the problems, most of the empirical research utilizing the NATREX approach uses reduced form estimations. That of course raises the question of both the stability of estimated coefficients (given the long-run dynamics of factors determining the saving–investment nexus, the Lucas type critique is certainly possible) and the values of fundamentals free of short-term and cyclical variations. For more detailed discussions of NATREX type models and their estimations see Gandolfo and Felettigh (1998), Siregar and Rajan (2006) and Stein (1994, 1999).

Both FEER and NATREX approaches define the equilibrium real effective exchange rate as the one corresponding to some definition of the general macroeconomic equilibrium. In contrast, in the BEER (behavioral equilibrium exchange rate) approach the equilibrium rate is the one consistent with the prevailing level of economic fundamentals.

First specified by Clark and MacDonald (1998), the BEER approach is essentially derived from the simple assumption of an uncovered interest parity (a more detailed discussion of the BEER approach is provided in the next section). The result is a single equation suitable for estimating purposes. This makes the BEER approach especially useful in situations for which there are only relatively short time series available, as is in the case of the subject of this chapter. Works utilizing the BEER approach include Clark and MacDonald (1998, 2000), Dias and MacDonald (2007), MacDonald (1997, 1999, 2000), Maeso-Fernandez et al. (2001) and Osbat et al. (2003). BEER, FEER and NATREX models are compared in Siregar and Rajan (2006).

Hence, the equilibrium real effective exchange rates of the euro as a whole and the euro for the largest Eurozone countries (Germany, Italy, Spain, France) will be estimated via the application of the BEER methodology. The BEER type of the model is derived in Section 3.3. This model will be estimated in Section 3.4 and results will be discussed in Section 3.5.

3.3 The BEER type of the equilibrium real effective exchange rate model

Let us specify the uncovered interest parity in real terms as:

$$Es_{t+1} - s_t = r - r^* \tag{3.1}$$

Where s_t is the real exchange rate (which here is defined as a foreign currency per unit of the domestic currency times domestic to foreign price ratios – that is, an increase in s_t is an appreciation and vice versa). Es_{t+1} is the expected future value of the real exchange rate. $Es_{t+1} - s_t$ is then the expected rate of change of the real exchange rate s (assuming that (3.1) is in logs). $r - r^*$ is the domestic to foreign interest rate differential, where r is the domestic real interest rate (defined generally as a nominal interest rate minus the expected rate of inflation) and the r^* is the 'world' real interest rate.

We can rewrite (3.1) as

$$s_t = Es_{t+1} - (r - r^*) \tag{3.2}$$

that is, the real exchange rate is the function of its own expected value and the real interest rate differential.

The BEER approach assumes that the expected real exchange rate is the function of economic fundamentals only. That is:

$$Es_{t+1} = f(Z_t) \tag{3.3}$$

where Z_t is the vector of economic fundamentals characterizing an economy at the period t.

From the empirical standpoint, the actual real exchange rate s can be influenced not only by its expected value (that is, the economic fundamentals) and the interest rate differential, but also by a variety of other short-term variables – some of them cyclical, some reflecting short-term shocks. Let us denote the vector of such variables as A_t, which influences the real exchange rate via some function $g(A_t)$.

By substituting (3.3) into (3.2) and adding $g(A_t)$, we get

$$s_t = f(Z_t) - (r - r^*) + g(A_t) = F(Z_t, r - r^*, A_t) \tag{3.4}$$

where $F(\ldots)$ is a general functional form.

Expression (3.4) is the general BEER formulation of the real exchange rate. From here the equilibrium real exchange rate can be defined as the function of the economic fundamentals only, where the fundamentals' values Z_t^E are cleared of the random short-term influences and measurement errors. That is, $Z_t^E = Z_t + \varepsilon_t$, where ε_t represents random and measurement errors and $E(\varepsilon_t) = 0$.

The equilibrium real exchange rate then can be expressed as:

$$s_t^E = F^E(Z_t^E) \tag{3.5}$$

where s_t^E denotes the equilibrium real exchange rate.

Assuming that the variables in expression (3.4) are cointegrated (that is, the coefficients reflect the long-run equilibrium relationships) then the relevant coefficients in (3.4) and (3.5) may be assumed to be the same. Hence the estimate of (3.4) can be used to calculate the equilibrium and, implicitly, the misalignment of the real exchange rate from expression (3.5).

To estimate (3.4), we need to specify the set of variables for vectors Z_t and A_t. In the economic literature, the often used set of variables to represent the economic fundamentals (that is, the vector Z_t) are the terms of trade (*TOT*), the relative price of traded to non-traded goods (*TNT*) and the net foreign assets (*NFA*). (For the relevant literature, see, for example,

Clark and MacDonald, 1998; MacDonald, 2000; Maeso-Fernandez et al., 2001; Siregar and Rajan, 2006.)

It goes beyond the scope of this analysis (which is primarily empirical) to discuss in detail this choice of variables. The interested reader is referred to the authors mentioned above for more detailed and thoroughly argued explanations.

However, one should mention that this set of variables is based on the stock-flow consistent model of an open economy specified by Frenkel and Mussa (1986) (Clark and MacDonald, 1998; MacDonald, 2000). In general, they represent the fundamental characteristics of an economy, such as relative productivity and growth, international competitiveness and its changes, agents' preferences, the domestic investments–savings nexus, general fiscal stance and so on (again, see the literature listed above for clear and consistent arguments).

The vector A_t contains only one variable, namely the ratio of the share of the domestic public debt in GDP (*DGDP*) to the same share for the rest of the world (*DGDP**) – that is, $A_t = D_t = (DGDP/DGDP^*)$. This variable was originally specified by Clark and MacDonald (2000) (and subsequently used by others) as a measure of the risk premium. However, one may argue that in the context of a currency union where national governments are deprived of the tools of monetary and nominal exchange rate policies, fiscal policies are primarily used as countercyclical tools and to counter outside shocks. And this will certainly be reflected in short-term variations of the debt to GDP ratios.

Substituting the expressions for Z_t and A_t into (3.4), we get:

$$s_t = F(TOT_t, TNT_t, NFA_t, r - r^*, D_t) \tag{3.6}$$

By the same logic, (3.5) can be replaced by:

$$s_t^E = F^E(TOT_t^E, TNT_t^E, NFA_t^E, D_t^E) \tag{3.7}$$

where TOT_t^E, TNT_t^E, NFA_t^E are values representing the economic fundamentals minus their short-term shock effects and measurement errors. D_t^E is some 'equilibrium' value of D_t.

In the following analysis (3.6) will be used to estimate the real effective exchange rate, whereas (3.7) (utilizing coefficients obtained by estimating (3.6)) will be used to calculate the 'equilibrium' real effective exchange rate.

3.4 Estimation

For the purposes of the econometric estimation, equation (3.6) is expressed in linear semi-logarithmic form as:

$$\begin{aligned}\text{Log}\, s_t &= \alpha_0 + \alpha_1 * \log TOT_t + \alpha_2 * \log TNT_t + \alpha_3 * NFA_t + \alpha_4 * (r - r^*) \\ &\quad + \alpha_5 * \log D_t + \varepsilon_t \qquad (3.8)\end{aligned}$$

where Log s_t is the log of the real effective exchange rate, log TOT_t is the log of terms of trade (defined here as prices of exports over prices of imports), log TNT_t is the log of the ratio of the producer to consumer price indexes (used here as the proxy for the tradables to non-tradables price ratio), NFA_t is the ratio of net foreign assets to GDP (both in euro terms), $(r - r^*)$ is the real interest rate differential, log D_t is the log of the ratio of the share of the domestic public debt in GDP to the same share for the world and ε_t is the error term.

To understand the possible signs of the estimated coefficients, some discussion of how data used in (3.8) are constructed is necessary. The real effective exchange rate s is reported by the ECB as the foreign currency per unit of domestic currency times domestic over foreign consumer price indexes. Weighted average is then calculated for 41 trading partners. In this approach an increase in s indicates a real appreciation and vice versa.

Terms of trade (TOT) are the ratio of the export to import price indexes, reported by Eurostat in euros. Generally, we would assume the TOT coefficient α_1 to be positive. An increase of export relative to import prices improves the trade balance, *ceteris paribus*. Supply of the foreign currency increases relative to demand, leading to a nominal appreciation in the domestic currency (euros in our case). And if, as is often observed, the variability of nominal exchange rates dominates the variability of price indexes, the nominal exchange rate appreciation will lead to the real exchange rate appreciation.

It is, however, possible that an increase in both export and import prices is caused by a foreign inflation in excess of the domestic one. If this inflation differential exceeds the nominal appreciation, both export and import price indexes in the domestic currency will increase. The relative magnitudes of those increases will be determined by relative inflations and the structure of trade – that is, measured TOT can increase. However, for a given consumer prices dynamic, the foreign consumer inflation can exceed the domestic nominal appreciation to the extent that *s* depreciates. Consequently, the sign of α_1 has to be determined from the data.

The proxy for the productivity dynamics, the tradables to non-tradables price ratio (TNT), is itself proxied by the ratio of the domestic producer to consumer price indexes. This practice, albeit common in the economic literature, has important consequences.

Theoretically, the use of the TNT variable to measure the impact of productivity on the real exchange rate is derived from the so-called Balassa-Samuelson relationship. It is premised on the assumption that it is the international trade and competition – that is tradables – that carry the productivity advances. Rising productivity facilitates rising wages in the tradables sector. The labour market competition then forces rising wages in the non-tradables sector as well. But here the productivity lags, hence rising wages will lead to rising prices. The TNT variable would decline but domestic inflation accelerates – hence *s*, *ceteris paribus*, increases. This would result in a negative sign for the α_2 coefficient.

But again, given the real structure of the world economy and the actual construction of the TNT variable, an alternative mechanism can be constructed. Let us assume the New Keynesian description of the globalized world economy, where consumer prices are kept in check by a strongly anti-inflationary stance by central banks, slack often exists in the degree of resource utilization and oligopolistic producers exercise a discernible degree of market power on the world scale. In such an economy the producer price dynamics may not be entirely passed through to consumer prices Econometrically speaking, the TNT variable as constructed will be non-stationary, indicating at best a limited impact of the Balassa-Samuelson mechanism.

Any ability of domestic producers (as measured by the producer price index) to exercise some market power in the globalized world market can then be interpreted as an indication of an improved competitiveness, generated by productivity and innovation growth, perhaps aided by a shift in the preference structure which determines the composition of a global demand. Implicitly it indicates the possible improvement in a trade balance. This means an increase of the flow supply of foreign currencies relative to the domestic flow demand for the same. Both nominal and real exchange rates have a tendency to appreciate. Hence α_2 can be positive and its actual sign will depend on the data.

NFA (net foreign assets) is the variable which reflects the complex processes of domestic private and public savings and investments, domestic and foreign preferences for portfolio compositions (home bias?), tax systems and so on. In general we would assume the relevant coefficient

α_3 to be negative. An improvement in NFA – a relative increase in the acquisition of foreign assets – implies an increase in the flow demand for foreign currencies relative to supply, implying the tendency for both nominal and real depreciations.

But again, one has to keep in mind that econometric estimates (especially the ones using the cointegration approach) indicate a correlation, not causality. When we take into account the speed and flexibility of financial markets and the fact that we utilize quarterly observations, we may envisage an alternative scenario. That is, a real appreciation of a domestic currency makes foreign assets relatively cheaper, resulting in the higher NFA. And this will be only enhanced if markets (or some segments thereof) expect a future real depreciation – which, *ceteris paribus*, improves domestic currency returns on foreign assets. Hence the α_3 could be positive. Again, the actual sign depends on the data.

The standard expression for the real uncovered interest parity implies α_4 to be positive.

D_t is the ratio of the share of the domestic public debt in GDP to the same share for the rest of the world. It was introduced by Clark and MacDonald (1998) as a measure of a relative risk in holding domestic assets. As a such, the relevant coefficient (α_5) should be negative. An increased risk associated with domestic assets should lead to reduced holdings, *ceteris paribus*, and hence to both nominal and real depreciations.

In the real economy, however, D_t measures not only the risk, but it also reflects the short-term and cyclical reactions of governments to changing underlying economic conditions. That is especially true within a currency union, where changes in national governments' borrowing and spending are the only policy tools available in the short term. Moreover, if markets believe that debt difficulties in a currency union member state will be mitigated by other member states and/or the common monetary authority, the reaction to an increased risk due to a rising public debt can be muted. But markets may perceive an increased public debt as an increased inflation potential (even in the monetary union). In such an admittedly unusual but not impossible case a rise in D_t may result in real exchange rate appreciation (that is, the positive α_5) via a rising domestic inflation.

To conclude the discussion of the coefficient signs we must keep in mind that even the BEER type of equation is an implicit reduced form of the underlying (even if generally unspecified) economic model. To make less conditional statements about coefficients in expression (3.8) would require structural models tailored to particular economies in particular

Table 3.1 Estimates of REER for the Eurozone and its four largest countries

	Eurozone	Germany	Italy	Spain	France
Log *TOT*		4.715	6.259	0.079	−1.457
(t-stat)		(16.255)	(12.811)	(0.500)	(6.447)
Log *TNT*	6.470	3.969	10.038	0.330	−2.987
(t-stat)	(6.282)	(6.270)	(13.145)	(1.723)	(22.684)
NFA	−0.813	−0.179	−0.855	−0.031	0.454
(t-stat)	(7.146)	(11.445)	(16.982)	(4.481)	(28.391)
$(r - r^*)$	0.094	0.022		0.007	0.057
(t-stat)	(9.122)	(3.019)		(2.880)	(29.400)
Log D	−2.567	−1.725	1.503	−0.306	−1.740
(t-stat)	(8.798)	(12.874)	(8.765)	(10.965)	(23.688)
Constant	4.104	4.499	2.464	4.496	4.530
(t-stat)	(42.218)	(105.603)	(14.558)	(140.416)	(316.051)
Rbar^2	0.731	0.558	0.677	0.586	0.621

Notes: All coefficients are from the estimate of equation (3.8) by the Johansen cointegration technique, using CATS2 program in RATS. All variables that the exclusion test indicated should be included are reported, even if the t-test indicates that they may not be statistically significant. In contrast, if the exclusion test indicated that a variable is not a part of the cointegrated vector, such a variable was excluded – hence no value is reported.

circumstances. But this not only goes far beyond the intended scope of this analysis, but it may be well impossible given the still relative paucity of the available data.

All data needed for the estimates of (3.8) were found to be I(1). (See the results in Appendix 3.2.) Hence the cointegration approach pioneered by Johansen (1988) was applied, using the CATS2 program in RATS software. Results for both the Eurozone and its four largest member countries (Germany, Italy, Spain and France) are reported in Table 3.1.

To calculate the 'equilibrium' values, the expression (3.7) can be written as

$$Log\ s_t^E = \alpha_0 + \alpha_1 * \log TOT_t^E + \alpha_2 * \log TNT_t^E + \alpha_3 * NFA_t^E + \alpha_5 * D_t^E \quad (3.9)$$

where α_0, α_1, α_2, α_3, α_5 are the estimated coefficients, TOT_t^E, TNT_t^E and NFA_t^E are medium-term values (excluding random effects and measurement errors) of the observed TOT_t, TNT_t and NFA_t obtained by applying the Hodrick-Prescott filter and D_t^E is the average value of D_t over the estimation range. Real interest rates are equalized in the equilibrium.

(3.8) was estimated and (3.9) was calculated over the euro period, using the quarterly data from 1999:1 to 2006:4. Pre 1999:1 data (available from sources in euro terms where needed) were used for lags in the Johansen technique.

The actual real effective exchange rates for the Eurozone and its four largest members (Germany, Italy, Spain, France) and their 'equilibrium' values are displayed in Figures 3.1a and 3.1b.

Utilizing results from (3.9), the degrees of misalignment were calculated using the formula Misalignment $= (s_t/s_t^E) - 1.0$. Those results are reported and discussed below.

3.5 Results: what do they tell us?

Real equilibrium exchange rates (REERs) for the Eurozone as a whole and its four largest members (Germany, Italy, Spain, France) are reported in Figure 3.1a. The corresponding equilibrium values are shown in Figure 3.1b. In order to evaluate whether both the actual REERs and their equilibrium values converged or diverged during the 'euro period', the root mean squared deviation (RMSD) of the 'national' REERs from the Eurozone was calculated and its time series properties analysed. Results are in Table 3.2. Graphs of these root mean squared deviations are in Figures 3.2a and 3.2b.

The analysis started with tests for stationarity, using both ADF and Perron tests. As indicated in Table 3.2, even for a shorter period – 2001:4 to 2006:4 (this was dictated by the fact that both Akaike and Schwartz test indicated the 10 lags as optimal for both unit root tests) – the results are

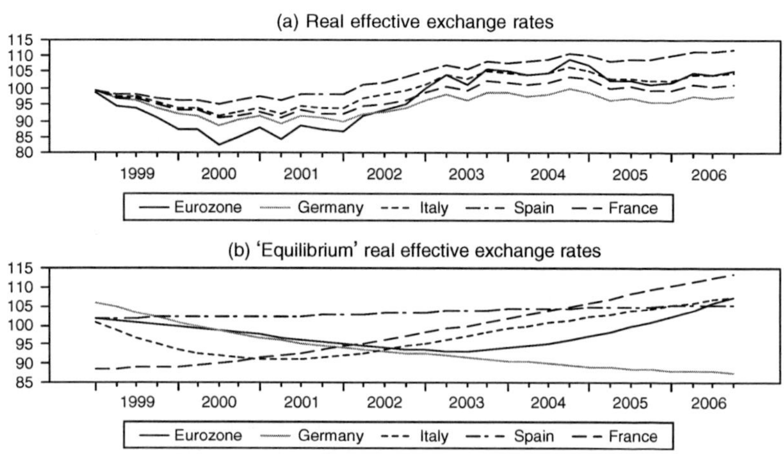

Figure 3.1 Real effective exchange rates, 1991:1–2006:4

negative. As far as RMSD for actual REERs is concerned, ADF and Perron tests indicate different results. The stationarity hypothesis is therefore rejected, albeit weakly. For RSMD for 'equilibrium' REERs, stationarity is clearly rejected.

Stationarity being rejected, the next step was to evaluate whether both the actual and the equilibrium REERs converge or diverge over time. Simple OLS regression of both REERs on the constant and the time trend (see results in Table 3.2) indicates that even for a shorter period, 2001:4

Table 3.2 Root mean squared deviations and their properties

	ADF test	**Perron test**
RMSD actual	−2.5755	−3.48219
(5% critical values for tests)	(−3.004)	(−2.956)
RMSD equilibrium	11.96497	0.40411
(5% critical values for tests)	(−3.004)	(−2.956)

OLS Estimates: RMSDs against constant and trend
Actual REERs
RMSD = 9.437*Constant −0.077* Trend
(5.07) (2.35)
$Rbar^2 = 0.165$
'Equilibrium' REERs
RMSD = −7.005*Constant + 0.242* Trend
(8.10) (15.92)
$Rbar^2 = 0.916$

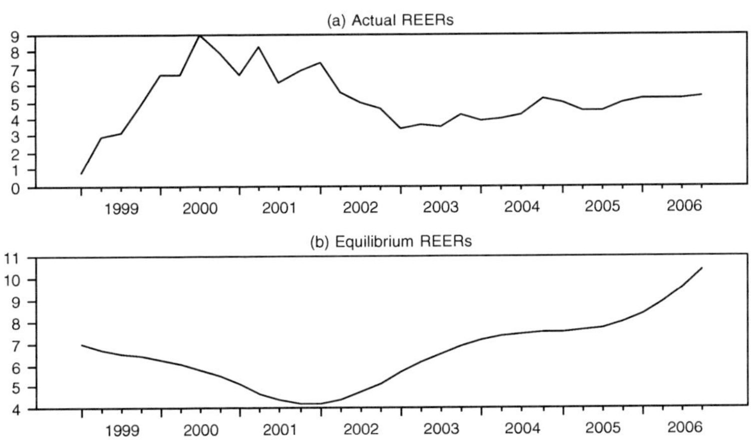

Figure 3.2 Root mean squared deviations of REERs, 1991:1–2006:4

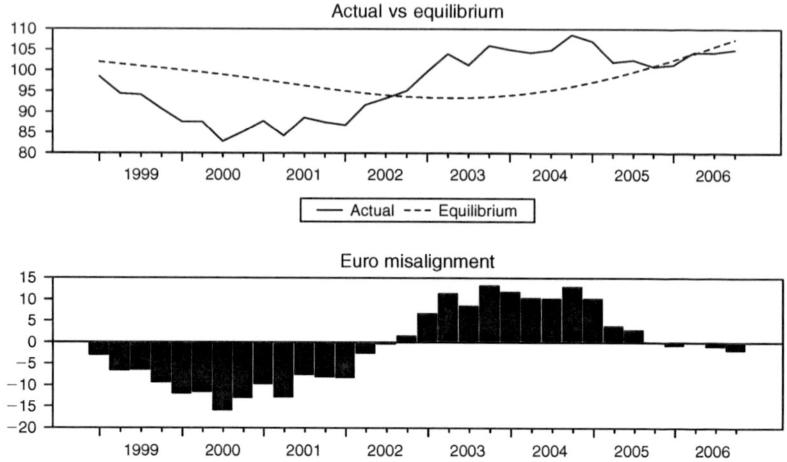

Figure 3.3 Real effective exchange rate for the Eurozone: actual vs equilibrium and euro misalignment, 1991:1–2006:4

to 2006:4, the actual REERs remain close to stationary, with a very faint tendency to converge (the sign of the time trend variable is negative, but the variable itself is very small). In contrast, the equilibrium REERs clearly diverge, with the sign of the time trend variable positive and its size non-negligible.

These results indicate that whereas there are no openly visible divergent tendencies within the Eurozone, the impact of different dynamics of fundamentals on the dynamics of the 'equilibrium' REERs may be the cause for concern. The economic cohesion of the Eurozone is obviously not improving and some divergence trends are clearly indicated.

The actual and equilibrium REERs for the Eurozone as a whole are shown and compared in Figure 3.3. The figure shows that REER for the euro was undervalued (relative to the BEER model type of the equilibrium) from the euro's inception until the middle of 2002 and subsequently overvalued to the end of 2005. In 2006 we observe a mild tendency for an undervaluation, but basically REER for the euro was at the equilibrium. These results should surprise nobody. (However, it is still important to stress that the 'equilibrium' in the BEER model sense reflects the relationship between the REER and the 'medium'-term values of fundamentals – that is, the fundamentals' values minus shocks, measurement errors, short-term cyclical influences and so on. This concept does not reflect what is commonly understood as a macroeconomic equilibrium – that is, simultaneous internal and external equilibria. See Siregar and Rajan, 2006.)

Individual national REERs compared to the Eurozone's REER are shown in Figure 3.4. In the first few years of the euro's existence the four national REERs (Germany, Italy, Spain and France) were above the Eurozone-wide REER, indicating that initial euro 'undervaluation' was due to the remaining 'small' Eurozone members. A similar trend is observable subsequently, even if on a smaller scale. Both German and French REERs are below the Eurozone-wide value during the post-2002 period of 'overvaluation'. But Spain's REER remains consistently above the latter and Italy's differs from the Eurozone only marginally. Again, this indicates a strong influence of the smaller Eurozone members on the Eurozone-wide REER values.

Figure 3.5 compares national equilibrium REERs to the Eurozone-wide equilibrium REER. German equilibrium, initially somewhat above the Eurozone's subsequently dropped significantly below it. Italian equilibrium, initially below the Eurozone's, increased subsequently but then declined toward the Eurozone value. Spain's equilibrium was above the Eurozone's until the last year. French equilibrium started from significantly below the Eurozone value, increased steadily above the latter and declined somewhat recently, although still remaining above the Eurozone values. These dynamics obviously lack a common pattern, indicating both different reactions of the national economies to changing fundamentals and the different dynamics of fundamentals.

The relationships between actual national REERs and the Eurozone-wide equilibrium are in Figure 3.6. Except for the short period between 2002 and 2004, both German and French REERs appear to be undervalued relative to the Eurozone-wide equilibrium. Italy, initially experiencing real undervaluation relative to the Eurozone, went through a period of a strong relative overvaluation between 2002 and the beginning of 2006, before returning close to the Eurozone-wide equilibrium more recently. Spain experienced a strong relative overvaluation from 2001 onwards, even if this was declining recently.

Relative to national equilibria (Figure 3.7), German and Spanish REERs, after the initial undervaluation, became steadily overvalued from the end of 2002. Italy experienced overvaluation vis-à-vis the national equilibrium from the euro's inception, but this changed to undervaluation from 2005. French REER, after a short period of initial overvaluation relative to national equilibrium in 1999, experienced more or less equilibrium until 2003 and a relatively significant undervaluation recently.

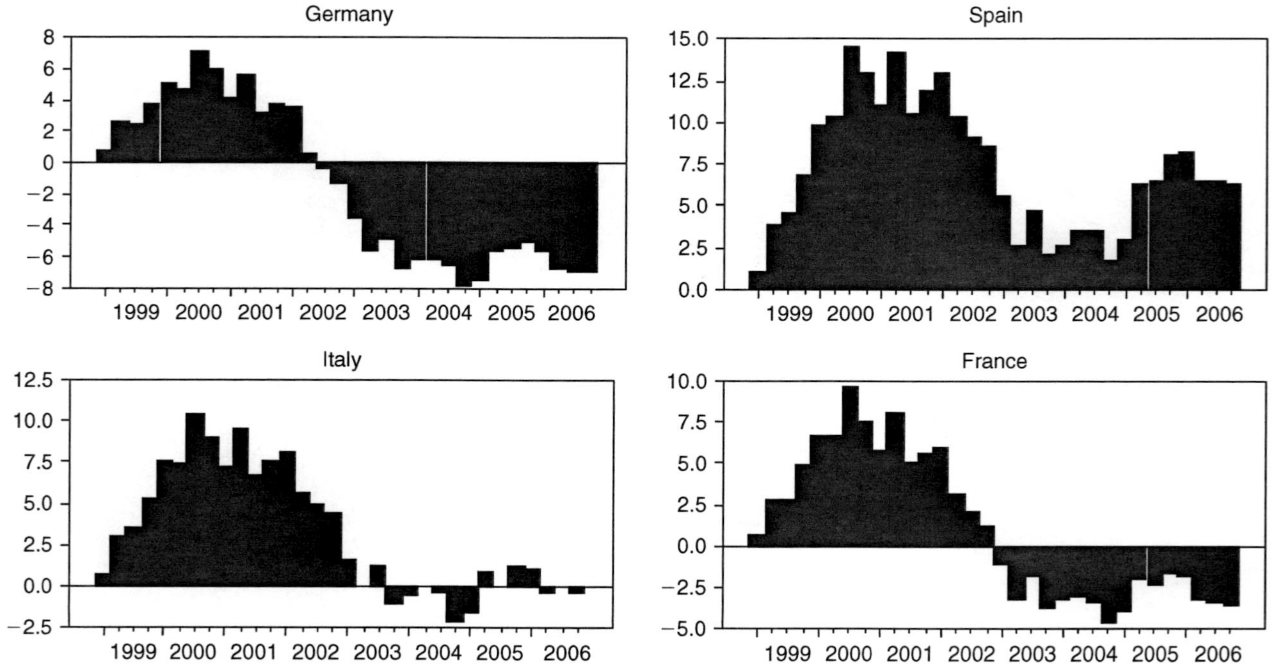

Figure 3.4 National REERs vs Eurozone, 1991:1–2006:4

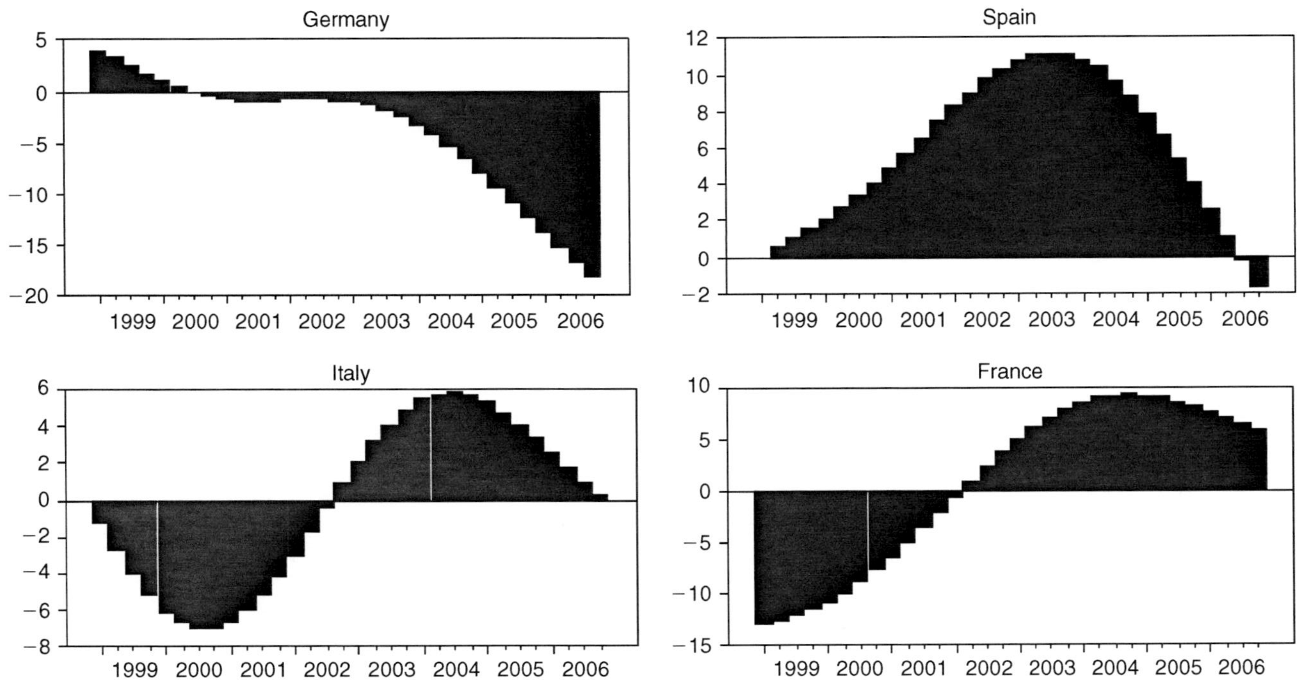

Figure 3.5 National equilibrium REERs vs Eurozone equilibrium, 1991:1–2006:4

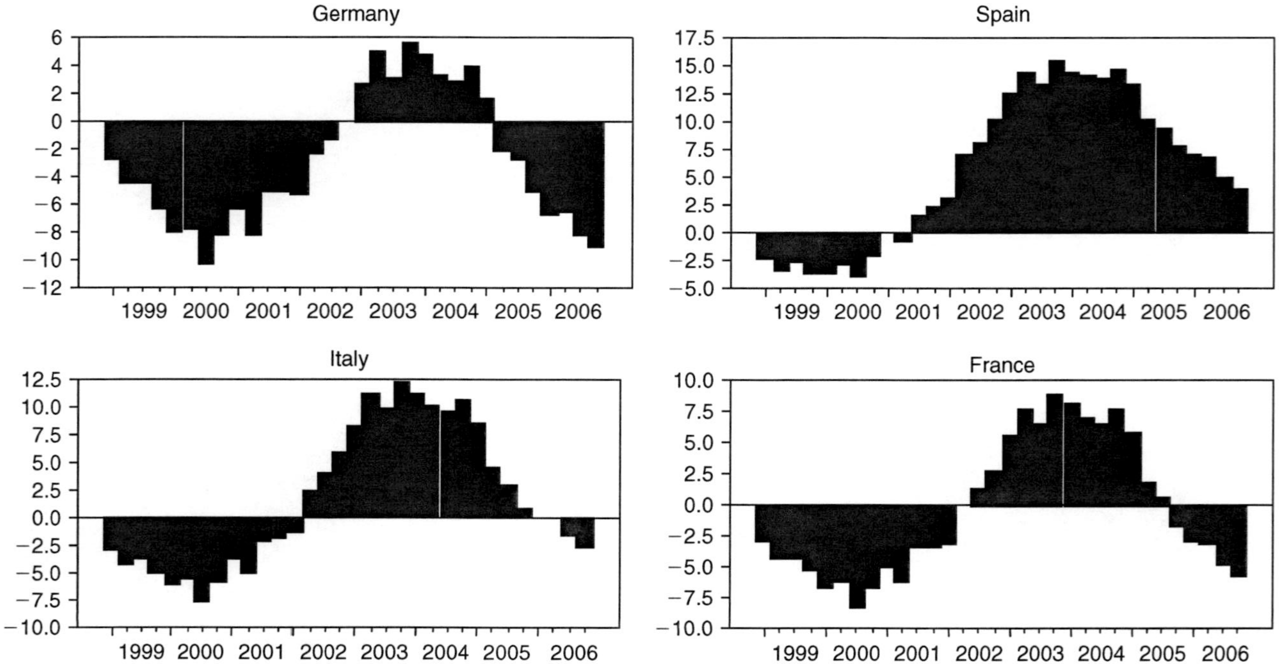

Figure 3.6 REERs: national actual vs Eurozone equilibrium, 1991:1–2006:4

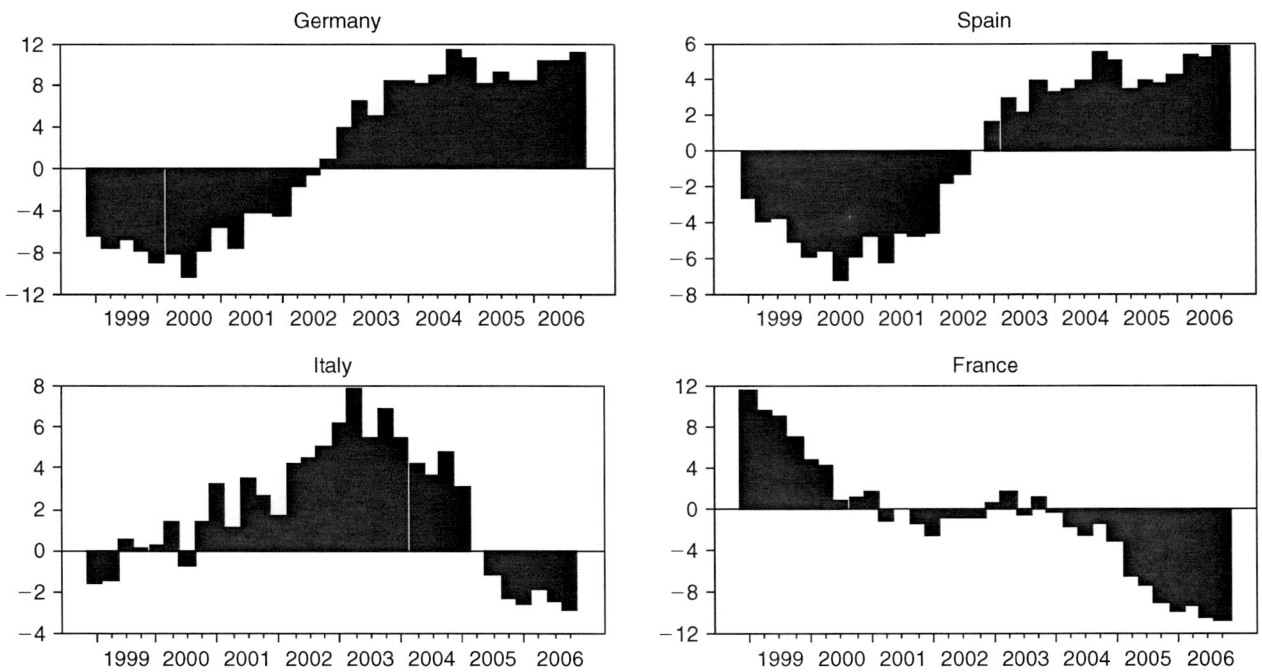

Figure 3.7 REERs: national actual vs national equilibrium, 1991:1–2006:4

3.6 Conclusions

The results represented in Tables 3.1 and 3.2 and Figures 3.1 to 3.7 certainly do not indicate any increased cohesion and convergence between the largest Eurozone member countries. But do they indicate a significant and growing divergence?

Comparing 'national' equilibria with the Eurozone-wide equilibrium indicates an affirmative answer. However, closer inspection of Figure 3.5 signals that for three of the four largest Eurozone members (Italy, Spain and France) the tendency in the last 8–10 quarters was for 'national' equilibrium REERs to move toward the Eurozone level. Only Germany indicates a growing divergence. (Of course, Germany is Eurozone's biggest economy.)

A similar result can be observed if we compare actual national REERs with the Eurozone equilibrium. Italy and Spain indicate a convergence toward the Eurozone equilibrium. France's REER indicates a growing, but still relatively minor undervaluation. Only in Germany does the actual 'national' REER indicate significant movement away from the Eurozone equilibrium and a growing overvaluation. However, when actual national REERs are compared to national equilibria, we see clear divergence. Germany and Spain show clear tendencies toward appreciation and overvaluation from the end of 2002, whereas Italy and France tend toward depreciation and a recent undervaluation.

We may therefore conclude that as far as REERs are concerned, the divergent tendencies among the four biggest Eurozone members remain unclear, even though they cannot be entirely denied.

Whether the REERs for the Eurozone and its four largest members converge or diverge cannot be convincingly answered at this stage. One would surmise that that at least part of the problem is in a relatively short time series, encompassing hardly more than one medium-term business cycle. Obviously, more research is needed when more data become available.

Appendix 3.1 Variables: definition and sources

s The real effective exchange rate, defined as a foreign currency per unit of the domestic currency times the domestic over foreign CPI price indexes. It is the weighted average of the Eurozone's (and individual countries) 41 largest trading partners. Source: Statistical base of ECB.

TOT Terms of Trade, defined as prices of exports over prices of imports in euros. The relevant price indexes for both the Eurozone and individual countries were obtained from Eurostat.

TNT Tradables to non-tradables price ratio, approximated here by the ratio of the producer to consumer price indexes. The relevant price indexes for both the Eurozone and individual countries were obtained from Eurostat.

r The domestic real interest rate, modelled as the nominal interest rate (3 month t-bill or the nominal money market rate) minus an expected consumer inflation (modelled as actual inflation four quarters ahead. The relevant data for both the Eurozone and individual countries were obtained from Eurostat.

*r** The world real interest rate, modelled in the same way as the domestic real interest rate. The weighted average of the US, Japan, the UK, Switzerland and Brazil was constructed. Data were obtained from the US Federal Reserve and IFS.

NFA Net foreign assets as the percentage of GDP. Data obtained from Eurostat (Eurozone) and the IFS (individual countries). In the case of individual countries, the RATS conversion program was applied to obtain quarterly approximations from annual data.

D Relative (domestic/world) public debt to GDP ratios. Data obtained from Eurostat.

Appendix 3.2 Unit root tests for variables in BEER models – ADF tests

	Eurozone	Germany	Italy	Spain	France
Log *s*	−0.96013	−2.83126	−0.80255	−0.04512	−1.05352
(critical value)	(−2.942)	(−2.953)	(−2.945)	(−2.945)	(−2.942)
Log *TOT*	−1.38742	−1.8672	−1.31887	−1.20597	−1.6089
(critical value)	(−2.942)	(2.945)	(−2.942)	(−2.953)	(−2.942)
Log *TNT*	−2.1774	−2.06705	−2.03061	−1.59505	−1.79528
(critical value)	(−2.945)	(−2.945)	(−2.950)	(−2.950)	(−2.945)
NFA	−2.23799	−1.4502	−1.49319	−0.87567	−2.85288
(critical value)	(−2.942)	(−2.947)	(−2.953)	(−2.945)	(−2.953)
r – *rt*	−2.55237	−2.9427	−2.46749	−2.13055	−1.45346
(critical value)	(−2.950)	(−2.950)	(−2.950)	(−2.947)	(−2.953)
Log *D*	−2.68751	−2.51455	−1.77638	−0.8961	−2.35553
(critical value)	(−2.953)	(−2.942)	(−2.945)	(−2.953)	(−2.953)
Log *sD*	−3.87357	−6.23613	−5.84816	−6.2743	−5.87181
(critical value)	(−2.945)	(−2.942)	(−2.942)	(−2.942)	(−2.942)
Log *TOTD*	−4.31998	−4.70603	−5.37953	−6.47898	−5.41979
(critical value)	(−2.942)	(−2.942)	(−2.942)	(−2.942)	(−2.942)
Log *TNTD*	−2.96615	−4.12089	−3.74267	−6.92235	−3.69045
(critical value)	(−2.942)	(−2.942)	(−2.942)	(−2.942)	(−2.942)
NFAD	−7.08564	−3.66516	−4.28052	−5.602	−4.29946
(critical value)	(−2.942)	(−2.947)	(−2.947)	(−2.942)	(−2.947)
(*r* – *rt*)*D*	−6.4357	−2.9853	−3.5154	−9.1649	−3.8711
(critical value)	(−2.942)	(−2.950)	(−2.950)	(−2.942)	(−2.950)
Log *DD*	−4.3053	−4.5435	−5.2274	−3.3225	−4.8482
(critical value)	(−2.942)	(−2.942)	(−2.942)	(−2.942)	(−2.942)

Notes: First 6 rows are variables in levels, next 6 rows are variables in 1st differences (with suffix *D*). The numbers in parenthesis are the 5% critical values for the ADF test. (They differ because of the optimal lag length – determined by the Autoselect procedure in the RATS program – differs for individual variables.)

References

Baffes, John, Ibrahim A. Elbadawi and Stephen A. O'Connell (1997). 'Single Equation Estimation of the Equilibrium Real Exchange Rate', Policy Research Working Paper 1800, The World Bank, Washington DC, August.

Bayoumi, Tamim, Hamid Faruqee and Jaewoo Lee (2005). 'A Fair Exchange? Theory and Practice of Calculating Equilibrium Exchange Rates', IMF Working Paper WP/05/229, Washington DC, December.

Clark, Peter B. and Ronald MacDonald (2000). 'Filtering the BEER: a Permanent and Transitory Decomposition', IMF Working Paper WP/00/144, Washington DC, August.

Clark, Peter B. and Ronald MacDonald (1998). 'Exchange Rates and Economic Fundamentals: a Methodological Comparison of BEERs and FEERs', IMF Working Paper WP/98/67, Washington DC, May.

Dias, Preethike and Ronald MacDonald (2007). 'BEER Estimates and Target Current Account Imbalances', mimeo, Petersen Institute of International Economics, Washington DC, March.

Feyzioglu, Tarhan (1997). 'Estimating the Equilibrium Real Exchange Rate: an Application to Finland', IMF Working Paper WP/97/109, Washington DC, September.

Frenkel, Jacob and Michael Mussa (1986). 'Asset Markets, Exchange Rates and the Balance of Payments', in E. Grossman and K. Rogoff (eds), *Handbook of International Economics*, vol. 2, Amsterdam: North Holland.

Gandolfo, Giancarlo and Alberto Felettigh (1998). 'The NATREX: an Alternative Approach. Theory and Empirical Verifications', Working Paper No. 52, CIDEI, University 'La Sapienza', Rome, November.

Johansen, S. (1988). 'Statistical Analysis of Cointegration Vectors', *Journal of Economic Dynamics and Control*, 12(2-3): 231–54.

MacDonald, Ronald (2000). 'Concepts to Calculate Equilibrium Exchange Rates: an Overview', Discussion Paper 300, Economic Research Group of the Deutsche Bundesbank, July.

MacDonald, Ronald (1999). 'Exchange Rates: do Fundamentals Matter?' *Economic Journal*, 109: F673–91.

MacDonald, Ronald (1997). 'What Determines Real Exchange Rates? The Long and Short of it', *Journal of International Financial Markets, Institutions and Money*, 8: 117–53.

Maeso-Fernandez, Francisco, Chiara Osbat and Bernd Snatz (2001). 'Determinants of the Euro Real Effective Exchange Rate', Working Paper No. 85, ECB, November.

Osbat, Chiara, Rasmus Rueffer and Bernd Schnatz (2003). 'The Rise of the Yen vis-à-vis the ("Synthetic") Euro: is it Supported by Economic Fundamentals?' Working Paper No. 224, ECB, April.

Siregar, Reza Y. and Ramkishen S. Rajan (2006). 'Model of Equilibrium Real Exchange Rates Revisited: a Selective Review of the Literature', Discussion Paper No. 0604, CIES, University of Adelaide, August.

Stein, Jerome (1999). 'The Evolution of the Real Value of the US Dollar Relative to the G7 Currencies', in R. MacDonald and J. Stein (eds), *Equilibrium Exchange Rates*, Amsterdam: Kluwer Academic Publishers.

Stein, Jerome (1994). 'The Natural Real Exchange Rate of the US Dollar and Determinants of Capital Flows', in J. Williamson (ed.), *Estimating Equilibrium Exchange Rates*, Washington DC: Institute of International Economics.

Tilford, Simon (2006). 'Will the Eurozone Crack?' Center for European Reform, London, September.

Wren, Simon (2003). 'Estimates of Equilibrium Exchange Rates for Sterling against the Euro', HM Treasury Printing Office, London.

Wren-Lewis, Simon, Rebecca Driver, John Williamson and Molly Mahar (1998). 'The Real Exchange Rates for the Year 2000', Policy Analyses in International Economics 54, Institute of International Economics, Washington DC.

Williamson, John (1994). 'Estimates of FEERs', in J. Williamson (ed.), *Estimating Equilibrium Exchange Rates*, Washington DC: Institute of International Economics.

4
Exchange Rate Policy Strategy in Large Currency Areas

Svatopluk Kapounek and Jitka Poměnková

4.1 Introduction

Monetary policy strategies are generally analysed in the context of the two models of central banking, the so-called Anglo-French model and the German model. These two models differ in the nature of their objectives and institutional designs and in the degree of political independence of central banks. In continental Europe, the German model prevails. There are two reasons for this. The first is the development of monetarist economic theory, the second is the strategic position of the German central bank in the European Monetary System. In the German model, price stability is considered to be the primary objective of the central bank. The pursuit of other objectives is subservient to this overriding goal (De Grauwe, 2007, pp. 162–3).

In this analysis we focus on the monetary policy characteristics of two central banks, the Czech National Bank (CNB) and the European Central Bank (ECB), both designed according to the German model. The primary goal of the CNB is defined in the statute (law Nr.6/1993, §2): 'the primary target of the Czech National Bank is maintaining price stability. Without prejudice to this primary target, the Czech national bank sustains the economic policy of the government which leads to sustainable economic growth.' The Constitution of the Czech Republic also states: 'the primary target of the Czech National Bank is to maintain price stability' (The Constitution of the Czech Republic, head 6, article 98). The primary objective of the ECB and its monetary policy, as defined in Article 105 of the Treaty Establishing the European Community, is also to maintain price stability. 'Without prejudice to the objective of price stability', the Eurosystem will also 'support the general economic policies in the Community with a view to contributing to the achievement of the objectives

Table 4.1 Consumer market size

	Domestic demand in the year 2006 (reference year 2000)		**Number of inhabitants in the year 2005**	
	mil.EUR	**% of Eurozone**		**% of Eurozone**
Czech Republic	78736.3	1	10235828	3
Eurozone	7294228.3	100	315789086	100
Belgium	268726.4	4	10478617	3
Germany	2055470.3	28	82469422	26
Ireland	120232.2	2	4159096	1
Greece	179707.9	2	11103965	4
Spain	834707.6	11	43398143	14
France	1619850.6	22	62818185	20
Italy	1263034.9	17	58607043	19
Luxembourg	20912.1	0	462043	0
Netherlands	423158.0	6	16319868	5
Austria	220545.4	3	8236225	3
Portugal	140049.3	2	10549424	3
Slovenia	27117.2	0	2000474	1
Finland	142355.0	2	5246096	2

Source: Eurostat.

of the Community.' These include a 'high level of employment' and 'sustainable and non-inflationary growth'.

It seems that the monetary policy character of these two central banks should be identical. Both banks' primary objective is price stability, with economic growth being important but distinctly secondary. However, the monetary policies of the ECB and the CNB impact different volumes of aggregate demand. Table 4.1 shows that the economic system of the Czech Republic (CR) comprises only 1 per cent of total domestic demand in the Eurozone and the population of the CR is only 3 per cent of the Eurozone total. We assume that the difference in size of economic systems affects the monetary policy character of central banks.

The reasoning is as follows: the relative size of domestic demand is directly related to the economy's degree of openness. The first reference to the relationship between the economy's openness and the size of domestic demand was formulated by John Stuart Mill in his reciprocal demand theory (Holman, 2001). From the role of the relative size of domestic demand it is possible to interpret the motives underlying the integration of small economies into international trade. Relationships between the economy's openness and domestic demand is illustrated in

Table 4.2 Exports of goods and services in percentage of GDP

	Euro area	Czech Republic	Slovakia	United States
1995	29.1	50.7	57.4	11.0
1996	30.0	51.4	52.9	11.5
1997	32.3	56.2	55.0	12.3
1998	33.7	62.5	61.8	12.1
1999	34.6	65.0	69.1	12.1
2000	37.3	73.1	74.8	12.7
2001	37.8	79.3	77.4	11.9
2002	38.1	79.5	77.8	11.4
2003	38.2	82.3	86.5	11.3
2004	40.0	94.9	88.6	12.0
2005	41.0	99.7	95.0	12.4
2006	43.2	*107.7	*106.0	13.1
2007	*45.0	*115.1	*116.2	*13.7
2008	*46.6	*121.0	*122.1	*14.3

Note: *Estimated values.
Source: Eurostat

Table 4.3 Imports of goods and services in percentage of GDP

	Euro area	Czech Republic	Slovakia	United States
1995	27.4	55.1	55.2	12.2
1996	27.9	59.3	60.6	12.8
1997	29.7	63.9	63.2	13.9
1998	31.9	69.7	71.0	14.9
1999	33.3	72.2	71.0	15.9
2000	35.6	81.0	76.3	17.4
2001	35.6	89.2	83.9	16.8
2002	35.4	91.9	84.3	17.1
2003	36.2	95.8	87.0	17.3
2004	37.9	108.0	89.9	18.6
2005	39.2	106.5	98.8	19.1
2006	41.1	*114.7	*107.5	19.7
2007	*42.9	*121.3	*114.7	*19.9
2008	*44.5	*127.2	*119.0	*20.4

Note: *Estimated values.
Source: Eurostat.

Tables 4.2 and 4.3. The tables show that small economies (Czech Republic and Slovakia) are more open than large economic systems (the Eurozone and the United States). The difference in openness between the Eurozone (large currency area) and CR (small open economy) is significant.

Table 4.4 Estimates of responses of real GDP and consumer prices to a 1 percentage point increase in the policy-controlled interest rates in the Eurozone

	Real GDP				**Consumer prices**			
	Year 1	**Year 2**	**Year 3**	**Year 4**	**Year 1**	**Year 2**	**Year 3**	**Year 4**
Model 1	−0.34	−0.71	−0.71	−0.63	−0.15	−0.30	−0.38	−0.49
Model 2	−0.22	−0.38	−0.31	−0.14	−0.09	−0.21	−0.31	−0.40
Model 3	−0.34	−0.47	−0.37	−0.28	−0.06	−0.10	−0.19	−0.31

Notes: Model 1 is the Area-Wide Model for the Euro Area (Fagan et al., 2001); Model 2 is the CNB Macroeconomic Model (Benes and Vavra, 2004); Model 3 is the NiGEM Model of the UK National Institute for Economic and Social Research.
Source: 'Recent Findings on Monetary Policy Transmission', ECB's Monthly Bulletin, October 2002.

The large degree of openness of small open economies is a robust argument for the integration of exchange rate movements into the monetary policy decision-making processes in these economies.

The target definition determines the monetary policy character of the central bank. The appreciation of the exchange rate, like a rise in the interest rate, dampens both economic growth and inflation. The real impact of monetary policy on interest rates movements, price stability and the exchange rate movement in the open economy is generally respected. But there is no theoretical or empirical consensus as to whether central banks are able to exert influence over economic growth. We assume a causality between interest rates and economic growth as described by the Keynesian transmission mechanism. The Keynesians assume that lower interest rates stimulate investment demand and autonomous consumption along with aggregate demand and output. These assumptions are consistent with the ECB policy pronouncements. Table 4.4 shows the responses of real GDP and consumer prices to a two-year increase of 100 basis points in the policy-controlled interest rates of the euro area. Figures are expressed in per cent from baseline. Simulations are performed using the ECB's area-wide model (AWM), the NCB's macroeconomic models (NCB) and the multi-country model of the NIESR (NiGEM). The impact of interest rates on consumer prices and on real GDP confirms the transmission mechanism assumptions. Subsequently, the transmission mechanism assumptions determine the decision-making process with respect to the monetary policy character and targeted interest rates.

The aim of this analysis is to identify the differences between the monetary policy decision-making processes of the central banks operating in a large currency area and a small open economy. The emphasis is placed on the impact of the exchange rate on the implementation of monetary policy. The significant variables that inspire the governing council members are identified for the ECB and the CNB by the Taylor rule. We assume that the difference in the monetary policy of large currency areas is important for Czech policymakers in the process of joining European Monetary Union. The empirical analysis tests the hypothesis that there is (or is not) a difference between the impact of exchange rate movements on short-term interest rates in the Eurozone and the CR.

4.2 Methodological approach

The central bank's monetary policy characteristics are determined by governing council decisions. The final decision is conditioned by practical compromises and affected by subjective factors.

Economists who deal with monetary policy decision-making process modelling use various monetary policy rules. These rules are based on economic theories that explain the impact of monetary policy on the real economy. The traditional monetary policy rule for modelling the causality between the short-term interest rate, inflation and economic growth is the Taylor rule, originally estimated for the US federal funds rate. Taylor rule type analysis was applied for the Eurozone by (among others) Gerlach-Kristen (2003).

Taylor (2001) defined a linear causality between interest rates, the price level and real output:

$$r = \pi + gy + h(\pi - \pi^*) + r^f, \tag{4.1}$$

where r represents short-term interest rates, π inflation (percentage change) and y the real output of the economy (percentage change). The variables g, h, π^* and r^f are constants. Romer (2006) used the Taylor rule in the formula:

$$i_t - \pi_t = \bar{r} + b(\pi_t - \pi^*) + c(\ln Y_t - \ln \overline{Y}_t), \tag{4.2}$$

where variable $\overline{Y}_t$ represents potential economic growth, i_t is the nominal short-term interest rate and $\bar{r}$ is the long-term safe interest rate. For the case of the Czech republic (a small open economy) formula (4.2) is expanded by adding the exchange rate movements e_t:

$$i_t - \pi_t = \bar{r} + b(\pi_t - \pi^*) + c(\ln Y_t - \ln \overline{Y}_t) + de_t. \tag{4.3}$$

The complexity of the transmission mechanism and the existence of lags in the impact of external shocks, financial market reactions and final effects on the macroeconomic indicators, especially on inflation and economic growth, complicate the implementation of monetary policy in the real economy. For this reason the model estimation is conditioned by different lag structures, especially when the forward lags are concerned.

In the process of an empirical analysis the vector autoregression approach (VAR) was considered (Greene, 2003). It is known that VAR models can be useful in the identification of relationships between variables in the Granger causality sense. It is, indeed, necessary to establish the lag length for the variables in the model.

However the requirement of equal lags for all variables in VAR models demonstrated that the VAR approach was inapplicable to this empirical study. Therefore the correlation analysis for the identification of variables lags is used. Note that the aim of this chapter is to identify significant variables from the given variables set.

The correlation analysis is used as a supporting method in the process of choosing variables for the multinomial regression. Correlation coefficients are calculated according to the formula (Anděl, 1978):

$$r_{YX} = \frac{s_{YX}}{s_Y \cdot s_X}, s_X^2 > 0, s_Y^2 > 0. \tag{4.4}$$

Multinomial regression model is used in the form:

$$y = X\beta + \varepsilon, \tag{4.5}$$

$$y_i = \beta_0 + \beta_1 x_{1i} + \cdots + \beta_k x_{1k} + \varepsilon_i, \quad i = 1, \ldots, n,$$

where

$y = (y_1, \ldots, y_n)$ dependent variable
$X = (\{x_{ij}\})$ a matrix of independent variables of the type $(n, k+1)$; $n < k$,
$\{x_{ij}\}$ value of the j'th observation of the variable x; $i = 1, \ldots, n, j = 1, \ldots, k$,
$\beta = (\beta_0, \ldots, \beta_k)^T$ vector of parameters,
$\varepsilon = (\varepsilon_1, \ldots, \varepsilon_n)^T$ vector of stochastic errors.

The OLS method is used for estimating the vector of parameters $\beta = (\beta_0, \ldots, \beta_k)^T$. Under the assumption that the stochastic error is normally distributed, the statistical significance of estimated parameters is tested according to the hypotheses:

$$H_0 : \beta_j = 0, \textit{ is not significant, } |t| < t_{1-\alpha/2}(n-p),$$
$$H_1 : \beta_j \neq 0, \textit{ is significant, } |t| \geq t_{1-\alpha/2}(n-p),$$

with testing statistic:

$$t = \frac{b_j}{SE(b_j)}, \quad SE(b_j) = \sqrt{\frac{RSS}{n-p} h_{j+1,j+1}}. \tag{4.6}$$

$b_j, j=1,\ldots,k$ is an estimate of the parameter β_j, $SE(b_j)$ is an estimate of corresponding parameter standard error, *RSS* is a residual sum of squares, p is a number of regression parameters, $h_{j+1,j+1}$ is $j+1$'th diagonal member of the matrix $H=(X'X)^{-1}$ (Hušek, 1995).

If the result of the testing process is that 'the null hypotheses is rejected', then the parameter is inconclusive. Thus, the corresponding variable is redundant and can be removed from the model. The model significance can be tested using the F-test. The corresponding hypotheses formulation for the F-test is:

$$H_0 : \beta_1 = \beta_2 = \ldots = \beta_k = 0, \textit{ is not significant, } F < F_c,$$
$$H_1 : \textit{at least one regression parameters } \beta_j \textit{ is not equal to zero, is significant,}$$
$$F \geq F_c,$$

where

$$F = \frac{ESS/(p-1)}{TSS/(n-p)} = \frac{\sum_{i=1}^{n} (est(y_i) - \bar{y})^2/(p-1)}{\sum_{i=1}^{n} (y_i - \bar{y})^2/(n-p)} \tag{4.7}$$

and critical value, $F_c = F_{1-\alpha}(p-1, n-p)$, is given by Fischer-Snedecor distribution (Hill et al., 2001).

4.3 Empirical analysis results

The empirical analysis uses the quarterly values for the period 1997:1–2007:1. The percentage changes on the corresponding period of the previous year are used. Price changes (P) are represented by the harmonized index of consumer prices, short-term interest rates (I) are day-to-day money market interest rates, economic growth (Y) is the gross domestic product at constant prices and exchange rate movements (RER) are the real effective exchange rates (deflator is unit labour costs in the total economy – 27 trading partners). The hypothesis is defined as:

H_0 : *monetary policies of the central banks in the large currency area (Eurozone) and small open economy (CR) are not determined by exchange rate movements.*

In the first step correlation analysis was utilized. The lag of the order $t-5, \ldots, t+5$ was chosen. The results are in Table 4.5.

The correlation analysis results enabled the multiple regression models to be designed. These models were tested by the t-test (statistical significance of parameters) and the F-test (statistical significance of the model). The chosen lags for the multiple regression analysis (in bold type in Table 4.5) define the monetary transmission mechanism.

In the case of interest rate (I) dependency on inflation (P), economic growth (Y), real exchange rate movements (RER) and with respect to the 4th lag order for all variables, two models were designed, Eurozone 1a and Eurozone 1b. As the t-test showed, model Eurozone 1a contains redundant variable RER. This redundant variable confirms the assumption about the monetary policy decision-making process in large currency areas. Thus, model Eurozone 1b contains the independent variables, inflation and economic growth, for the 4th lag of both variables, which are significant. Note that both models are statistically significant according to the F-test.

Model Eurozone 1a:

$$\begin{array}{lllll} \text{est}(I_t) & = & 1.2629P_{t+4} & -0.6125RER_{t+4} & +0.3486Y_{t+4} \\ & & (0.1935) & (6.8026) & (0.1968) \\ & & 6.5271 & -0.0900 & 1.7709 \\ \hline & & F=112.43 & R^2_{\text{adj}}=0.9030 & d=0.1833 \\ & & n=37 & & \end{array}$$

$$\begin{array}{lllll} \hat{I}_t & = & 1.2629P_{t+4} & -0.6125RER_{t+4} & +0.3486Y_{t+4} \\ & & (0.1935) & (6.8026) & (0.1968) \\ & & 6.5271 & -0.0900 & 1.7709 \\ \hline & & F=112.43 & \overline{R}^2=0.9030 & d=0.1833 \\ & & n=37 & & \end{array}$$

Table 4.5 Correlation analysis results for the Eurozone

Lag	**t − 5**	**t − 4**	**t − 3**	**t − 2**	**t − 1**	**t**	**t + 1**	**t + 2**	**t + 3**	**t + 4**	**t + 5**
	I(t)										
P	−0.3904	−0.4583	−0.4810	−0.4567	−0.3886	−0.2935	−0.1726	−0.0510	0.0948	**0.2132**	0.2715
Y	0.7057	0.7791	0.7989	0.7451	0.6062	0.4066	0.1847	−0.0333	−0.1766	**−0.2626**	−0.2941
RER	−0.4661	−0.6076	−0.6915	−0.6913	−0.6043	−0.4603	−0.2673	−0.0861	0.0983	**0.2059**	0.2688
	RER(t)										
I	0.2688	0.2059	0.0982	−0.0861	−0.2673	**−0.4603**	−0.6079	−0.6967	−0.6915	−0.6076	−0.4661
P	0.1953	0.3534	0.5437	0.7193	0.8013	**0.8239**	0.7603	0.5918	0.3954	0.1962	−0.0435
Y	−0.1173	−0.2137	−0.3600	−0.5280	−0.6563	**−0.6790**	−0.6789	−0.5219	−0.3259	−0.1802	−0.0619
	Y(t)										
I	−0.2942	−0.2626	−0.1766	−0.0333	0.1847	**0.4066**	0.6062	0.7451	0.7989	0.7791	0.7057
P	−0.2866	−0.3839	−0.4955	−0.5797	−0.6103	**−0.5246**	−0.4110	−0.2975	−0.1467	0.0444	0.1722
RER	−0.0619	−0.1802	−0.3259	−0.5140	−0.6605	**−0.6790**	−0.6563	−0.5280	−0.3600	−0.2137	−0.1173
	P(t)										
I	0.2715	0.2132	0.0949	−0.0510	−0.1727	**−0.2935**	−0.3886	−0.4568	−0.4810	−0.4583	−0.3904
Y	0.1722	0.0444	−0.1468	−0.2975	−0.4110	**−0.5246**	−0.6103	−0.5797	−0.4956	−0.3839	−0.2867
RER	−0.0435	0.1962	0.3954	0.5893	0.7513	**0.8239**	0.8013	0.7194	0.5437	0.3534	0.1954

Model Eurozone 1b:

$$\begin{array}{llll} \text{est}(I_t) & = & 1.2507P_{t+4} & +0.3634Y_{t+4} \\ & & (0.1356) & (0.1072) \\ & & 9.2223 & 3.3893 \\ \hline & & F=171.56 & d=0.1817 \\ & & n=37 & R^2_{\text{adj}}=0.9058 \end{array}$$

$$\begin{array}{lll} \hat{I}_t = & 1.2507P_{t+4} & +0.3634Y_{t+4} \\ & (0.1356) & (0.1072) \\ & 9.2223 & 3.3893 \\ \hline & F=171.56 & \overline{R}^2=0.9058 \\ & n=37 & d=0.1817 \end{array}$$

For real exchange rate movements (*RER*) the dependency on interest rate (*I*), inflation (*P*), economic growth (*Y*), and with respect to the 1st lag order for all variables, we designed model Eurozone 2. All variables were proved significant as well as the whole model.

Model Eurozone 2:

$$\begin{array}{lllll} \text{est}(RER_t) & = & -0.0134I_t & +0.0332P_t & -0.0166Y_t \\ & & (0.0039) & (0.0038) & (0.0042) \\ & & -3.4081 & 8.5982 & -3.9327 \\ \hline & & F=58.03 & R^2_{\text{adj}}=0.8114 & d=0.9923 \\ & & n=41 & & \end{array}$$

$$\begin{array}{llll} \widehat{RER}_t = & -0.0134I_t & +0.0332P_t & -0.0166Y_t \\ & (0.0039) & (0.0038) & (0.0042) \\ & -3.4081 & 8.5982 & -3.3927 \\ \hline & F=58.03 & \overline{R}^2=0.8114 & d=0.9923 \\ & n=41 & & \end{array}$$

For economic growth (*Y*) dependency on the interest rate (*I*), inflation (*P*), real exchange rate movements (*RER*) and with respect to the 1st lag order for all variables, we designed model Eurozone 3. The variable inflation (*P*) was redundant and was excluded from the model Eurozone 3. Note that that model is statistically significant according to the F-test.

Model Eurozone 3:

$$
\begin{array}{lll}
\text{est}(Y_t) = & 0.5964I_t & -11.2188RER_t \\
 & (0.0471) & (2.7022) \\
 & 12.6630 & -4.1516 \\
\hline
 & F=157.98 & R^2_{\text{adj}}=0.8898 \\
 & n=40 & d=0.3272
\end{array}
$$

$$
\begin{array}{lll}
\widehat{Y}_t = & 0.5964I_t & -11.2188RER_t \\
 & (0.0471) & (2.7022) \\
 & 12.6630 & -4.1516 \\
\hline
 & F=157.98 & \overline{R}^2=0.8898 \\
 & n=40 & d=0.3272
\end{array}
$$

In the case of inflation (P) dependency on the interest rate (I), economic growth (Y), real exchange rate movements (RER) and with respect to the 1st lag order for all variables we designed the model Eurozone 4. All variables and the model are statistically significant.

Model Eurozone 4:

$$
\begin{array}{llll}
\text{est}(P_t) = & 0.4820I_t & +19.8733RER_t & 0.2420Y_t \\
 & (0.0772) & (2.3113) & (0.1161) \\
 & 6.2411 & 8.5982 & 2.0846 \\
\hline
 & F=104.63 & R^2_{\text{adj}}=0.8863 & d=0.7587 \\
 & n=41 & &
\end{array}
$$

$$
\begin{array}{llll}
\widehat{P}_t = & 0.4820I_t & +19.8733RER_t & +0.2420Y_t \\
 & (0.0772) & (2.3113) & (0.1161) \\
 & 6.2411 & 8.5982 & 2.0846 \\
\hline
 & F=104.63 & \overline{R}^2=0.8863 & d=0.7582 \\
 & n=41 & &
\end{array}
$$

For the analysis of the situation in the Czech Republic the same process was repeated. Results for the correlation analysis with the same lags are shown in Table 4.6.

In accordance with the correlation analysis results multiple regression models were designed. These models were tested by the t-test (statistically significant parameters) and the F-test (statistical significance of the

Table 4.6 Correlation analysis results for CR

Lag	t − 5	t − 4	t − 3	t − 2	t − 1	t	t + 1	t + 2	t + 3	t + 4	t + 5
I(t)											
P	0.559556	0.631148	0.72464	0.806596	0.640068	0.657733	0.651499	0.640039	**0.664757**	0.664509	0.566121
Y	−0.6527	−0.71171	−0.77623	−0.80835	−0.59723	−0.6886	−0.74135	**−0.75099**	−0.74525	−0.72407	−0.67713
RER	−0.02358	−0.07352	−0.13171	−0.09042	0.180307	0.068633	−0.07654	−0.13958	**−0.19829**	−0.04001	0.133094
RER(t)											
I	0.133094	−0.04001	**−0.19829**	−0.13958	−0.07654	0.068633	0.180307	−0.09042	−0.13171	−0.07352	−0.02358
P	−0.06179	0.082712	0.194371	**0.250542**	0.201058	0.055886	−0.11655	−0.22784	−0.21882	−0.10576	0.016882
Y	0.057105	−0.00938	−0.02838	−0.03036	−0.05107	**−0.11656**	−0.15486	−0.18467	−0.17644	−0.16295	−0.1245
Y(t)											
I	−0.67713	−0.72407	−0.74525	**−0.75099**	−0.74135	−0.6886	−0.59723	−0.80835	−0.77623	−0.71171	−0.6527
P	−0.57953	−0.67143	−0.74319	−0.78225	**−0.80411**	−0.78821	−0.74806	−0.67131	−0.5636	−0.42875	−0.2977
RER	−0.1245	−0.16295	−0.17644	**−0.18467**	−0.15486	−0.11656	−0.05107	−0.03036	−0.02838	−0.00938	0.057105
P(t)											
I	0.566121	0.664509	0.664757	0.640039	0.651499	**0.657733**	0.640068	0.806596	0.72464	0.631148	0.559556
Y	−0.2977	−0.42875	−0.5636	−0.67131	−0.74806	**−0.78821**	−0.80411	−0.78225	−0.74319	−0.67143	−0.57953
RER	0.016882	−0.10576	−0.21882	**−0.22784**	−0.11655	0.055886	0.201058	0.250542	0.194371	0.082712	−0.06179

model). The chosen lags for the multiple regression analysis (in bold in Table 4.6) are consistent with the monetary transmission mechanism and economic theory.

In the case of the interest rate (*I*) dependency on inflation (*P*), economic growth (*Y*), real exchange rate movements (*RER*) and with respect to the chosen lag order for all the variables, two models were designed, model CR 1a and model CR 1b. As t-tests showed, model CR 1a contains redundant variables *RER* and *Y*. This result does not correspond to the theoretical assumption that the monetary policy character in a small open economy is determined not only by prices and economic growth but also by exchange rate movements. Model CR 1b contains inflation with the 3rd lag and is significant. Note however that the model is statistically significant according to the F-test.

Model CR 1a

$$\begin{array}{llll}
\widehat{I_t} = & 1.5121 p_{t+3} & -3.0156 RER_{t+3} & +0.02550 Y_{t+2} \\
 & (0.1943) & (14.8595) & (0.2522) \\
 & 7.7824 & -0.2029 & 0.1011 \\
\hline
 & F = 24.29 & \overline{R}^2 = 0.6519 & d = 1.5098 \\
 & n = 39 & &
\end{array}$$

Model CR 1b

$$\begin{array}{ll}
\widehat{I_t} & = 1.5121 p_{t+3} \\
 & \quad (0.1943) \\
 & \quad 7.7824 \\
\hline
F = 76.79 & \overline{R}^2 = 0.6689 \\
n = 39 & d = 1.500
\end{array}$$

For real exchange rate movements (*RER*) dependency on the interest rate (*I*), inflation (*P*), economic growth (*Y*), and with respect to the chosen lag orders for all variables, the model CR 2 was defined. All variables in this model are significant as is the whole model.

Model CR 2

$$\begin{array}{llll}
\widehat{RER_t} = & -0.0046 I_{t-3} & +0.0139 P_{t-2} & +0.0055 Y_t \\
 & (0.0016) & (0.0028) & (0.0021) \\
 & -2.9386 & 4.9604 & 2.6626 \\
\hline
 & F = 14.35 & \overline{R}^2 = 0.5259 & d = 0.4688 \\
 & n = 38 & &
\end{array}$$

For economic growth (Y) dependency on the interest rate (I), inflation (P), real exchange rate movements (RER) the model CR 3 was defined. Again, all variables in this model are significant as well as the whole model.

Model CR 3

$$
\begin{array}{llllll}
\widehat{Y}_t & = & 5.9727 & -0.1304I_{t-2} & -0.4217P_{t-1} & -9.9233RER_{t-2} \\
 & & & (0.0398) & (0.0752) & (3.4010) \\
 & & & -3.2724 & -5.6050 & -2.9177 \\
\hline
 & & & F=41.66 & \overline{R}^2=0.7624 & d=0.6245 \\
 & & & n=38 & &
\end{array}
$$

In the case of economic growth (Y) dependency on the interest rate (I), inflation (P), real exchange rate movements (RER) model CR 4 was designed. Note that the model is statistically significant according to the F-test.

Model CR 4

$$
\begin{array}{llllll}
\widehat{P}_t & = & 4.0032 & +0.4177I_t & -15.3730RER_t & -0.5811Y_t \\
 & & & (0.1604) & (5.4122) & (0.2549) \\
 & & & 2.6042 & -2.8404 & -2.2795 \\
\hline
 & & & F=42.73 & \overline{R}^2=0.7672 & d=0.4376 \\
 & & & n=38 & &
\end{array}
$$

Values of the Durbin-Watson d statistic are low for all models. This can indicate a positive autocorrelation of residuals. Because the aim of this chapter is to identify significant variables from a given variables set, we are not concerned with this.

The empirical analysis confirms the assumptions. The interest rate and the increase in economic growth and decrease in inflation cause the exchange rate appreciation in the Eurozone (model Eurozone 2). The causality between economic growth, the short-term interest rate and the exchange rate is related to business cycle fluctuations (model Eurozone 3). Inflation is increased by an exchange rate depreciation and an economic expansion. The interest rate reacts to the business cycle fluctuations (model Eurozone 4).

In the Czech Republic, the results are affected by structural changes in the post-transformation economy and the external balance crisis in 1997. The model CR 2 shows that exchange rate appreciation is caused by an increase in the interest rate and a decrease in inflation. Economic growth has a negative impact on the exchange rate appreciation. Economic growth in the Czech Republic (model CR 3) is negatively influenced by interest rates and prices. An exchange rate depreciation impacts positively on economic growth. But the estimation of the model of inflation is not consistent with economic theory. The assumption that the positive causality between the inflation and the interest rate is related to business cycle fluctuations is rejected by the negative impact of economic growth. Only the exchange rate depreciation and inflation increases are consistent with the theory assumptions in model CR 4.

However, for the purposes of this analysis the most important are models 1 for Eurozone and CR. The empirical analysis does not reject the hypothesis that the short-term interest rate (controlled by ECB monetary policy) is not determined by the real effective exchange rate of the euro (model Eurozone 1). This result corresponds to our assumption for the monetary policy decision-making process in large currency areas.

The model estimates of the Taylor rule for the Czech Republic with the 3rd forward lag identified only inflation as a significant factor determining short-term interest rates (controlled by the CNB). Economic growth and exchange rate movements were not statistically significant.

4.4 Conclusions

Many economists have demonstrated that the monetary policy rule models for open economies with exchange rate movements have a significant impact not only on exchange rates and inflation but also on real output. Ball (2001, p. 142) concludes: 'In a closed economy, inflation targeting and Taylor rules perform well in stabilizing both output and inflation. In an open economy, however, these policies perform poorly unless they are modified. Specifically, if policymakers minimize a weighted sum of output and inflation variances, their policy instrument should be an MCI based on both the interest rate and the exchange rate.' Bofinger (2001, p. 412) argues that central banks in the large currency areas are able to stabilize exchange rate movements without losing control over domestic interest rates.

Consistently with the introduction above, monetary policy strategy in small open economies is more complex than in the large currency areas. The share of international trade in GDP is the basic reason why central banks in small open economies focus not only on price stability and economic growth but also on exchange rate movements and the balance of payments. Conversely, in the Eurozone (a large currency area and a relatively closed economy) exchange rate movements do not have a significant impact on the monetary policy of the central bank. If the domestic interest rate changes (caused by a monetary policy reaction on the exchange rate movements) have no impact on aggregate demand and economic growth, the monetary policy authorities in large currency areas do not lose control over the domestic interest rates and, consequently, monetary policy implementation is more effective. Therefore, joining or creating a currency area are attractive options for small open economies that participate in international trade.

The empirical analysis in this chapter did not reject the hypothesis that exchange rate movements have no statistically significant impact on short-term interest rates in the Eurozone. Indeed, the theoretical economic assumptions of the authors were not confirmed for the Czech Republic. The model estimated for the Czech Republic identifies only inflation as impacting the short-term interest rates. This conclusion corresponds with the main monetary policy target of the CNB. The monetary policy decision-making process contains the effects of international trade participation by way of the law of one price.

References

Anděl, J. (1978). *Matematická statistika*, Praha: SNTL/ALFA.

Ball, L. (2001). 'Policy Rules for Open Economies', in J.B. Taylor (ed.), *Monetary Policy Rules*, Chicago: NBER, University of Chicago Press, pp. 127–56.

Benes, J. and D. Vavra (2004). 'SDGE Models to Support Monetary Policy', CNB/CERGE-EI Macro Workshop, Prague, May.

Bofinger, P. (2001). *Monetary Policy. Goals, Institutions, Strategies, and Instruments*, New York: Oxford University Press.

De Grauwe, P. (2007). *Economics of Monetary Union*, Seventh Edition, Oxford: Oxford University Press.

ECB (2002). 'Recent Findings on Monetary Policy Transmission', ECB's Monthly Bulletin, October.

Fagan, G., J. Henry and R. Mestre (2001). 'An Area-Wide Model (AWM) for the Euro Area', ECB Working Paper No. 42, Frankfurt, January.

Gerlach-Kristen, P. (2003). 'Interest Rate Reaction Function and the Taylor Rule in the Euro Area', ECB Working Paper No. 258, September.

Greene, W. H. (2003). *Econometric Analysis*, Fifth Edition, New Jersey: Prentice Hall.

Hill, C.R., W.E. Griffiths and G.G. Judge (2001). *Undergraduate Econometrics*, New York: John Wiley & Sons.

Holman, R. et al. (2000). *Dějiny ekonomického myšlení*, Praha: C.H. Beck.

Hušek, R. (1995). *Ekonometricka Analyza*, Prague: Ekopress Publishing.

Romer, D. (2006). *Advanced Macroeconomics*, Third Edition. London: McGraw-Hill/Irwin.

Taylor, J.B. (2001). 'A Historical Analysis of Monetary Policy Rules', in J.B. Taylor (ed.), *Monetary Policy Rules*, Chicago: NBER, The University of Chicago Press.

UK National Institute of Economic and Social Research, http://nimodel.niesr.ac.uk/.

5
Euro Area Enlargement and European Central Bank Reform

David Howarth

5.1 Introduction

On 19 December 2002, in preparation for the coming into force of the Treaty of Nice, the European Central Bank (ECB) Governing Council adopted a recommendation on new Governing Council voting procedures following the enlargement of the Eurozone (formally approved on 3 February 2003).[1] Prior to this agreement, there was a growing literature on the manner in which enlargement should/might affect ECB decision-making institutionally, including Berger (2002), Buiter (1999), Baldwin (2001), Baldwin et al. (2001), Bjorksten (2000), Eichengreen and Ghironi (2001), Fatum (2000) and de Grauwe (2000). This work contributes to the literature focusing on the efficiency of monetary policymaking and the coherence of monetary policymaking for economically diverse states – including Deutsche Bundesbank (2001), de Grauwe (2000), European Parliament (2001) and Gros and Hefeker (2000). To this can be added the literature on the legitimacy of the existing decision-making structures of the ECB, including Buiter (1999), Haan and Eijffinger (2000), Haan et al. (2005), ECB (2002), Issing (1999) and Leino (2001). Heisenberg (2003) attempts to bridge discussions about efficiency, transparency, enlargement and democratic legitimacy.

This chapter analyses the recent agreement on ECB Governing Council reform in terms of national economy size reflected in the bargaining power of the Governing Council members and macroeconomic preference. The reform was subject to consensual decision-making in the Governing Council and subsequently met the unanimous approval of national finance ministers in the Economics and Finance Council (Ecofin). While acting in an *ad personam* (that is, independent and personal[2]) capacity, the twelve NCB governors and six Executive Board members of the Governing Council agreed upon a reform that reflects national macroeconomic policy interests and particularly the interests of the member states with the largest economies. The reform conforms *barely* to the principles of *ad personam* participation,[3] equality[4] ('one governor, one vote') and representativeness[5] (all the Eurozone is represented) set out in the Protocol to the TEC on the Statute of the European System of Central Banks (ESCB) and of the ECB. The reform also *inadequately* addresses concerns about Governing Council decision-making inefficiency. In order to prevent enlargement from contributing significantly to decision-making inefficiency, the principles of 'equality' and 'representativeness' were distorted. Yet the reform was a 'fudge', stopping far short of the kinds of changes sought by many monetary economists and central bankers. Ultimately, the reform might also reflect the recognition by Governing Council members of the ECB's problematic legitimacy.

This chapter in effect presents a loose intergovernmentalist explanation – 'intergovernmentalism without governments' – of the agreement on Governing Council reform. Not only does the reform adopted suggest that Governing Council members defended the macroeconomic interests of their home member states but also that the individual members had bargaining power that reflected the size of their home economies which likewise contradicts their *ad personam* status. Despite the official requirement that the ECB targets Eurozone-wide inflation there is suspicion – albeit not yet proven – that the ECB is also particularly preoccupied with the effect of its monetary policy on the largest national economies (Heinemann and Huefner, 2004; Howarth and Loedel, 2005).

The ECB reform process lacked transparency. The argument presented in this chapter about Governing Council member and member state government preferences is thus speculative. The argument is based on an analysis of the preoccupations about monetary (and specifically ECB Governing Council) decision-making that have been outlined by monetary economists and central bankers over the past decade. A small number of ECB officials involved either directly or indirectly with the reform have been interviewed and official justifications of the reform considered. The reform adopted is examined in relation to major reform alternatives that have been presented over the years as more effectively addressing particular concerns (efficiency and/or representation) than others. Critiques of the reform by monetary economists and central bankers are also considered. Based on this analysis, the reform adopted appears to be a trade-off that reflects both 'intergovernmentalism without governments' and legitimacy concerns.

5.2 The difficulties posed by enlargement: size matters but so too does representation

The 2000 Intergovernmental Conference which preceded the Nice Summit agreed upon the reform of several EU institutions to cope with a considerable increase in member state numbers yet largely ignored the impact of enlargement upon the operation of the ECB. Article 10.6 was introduced in the Statute of the ESCB and of the ECB calling upon the ECB Governing Council to present a recommendation 'as soon as possible' following the entry into force of the Treaty of Nice on the necessary institutional reforms in the bank to cope with enlargement. While the new EU member states were expected to respect most of the convergence criteria and, following accession, could potentially include their currencies in the Exchange Rate Mechanism (ERM) II, they could only participate in the Eurozone at a later stage. By January 2007 six of the new member states had become ERM II members: Cyprus, Estonia, Latvia, Lithuania, Malta and Slovakia. On 1 January 2007, Slovenia became the thirteenth Eurozone member and the Governing Council expanded to 19 members.

The impact of Eurozone enlargement looms large for the ECB principally because it highlights existing problems with the operation of the Governing Council – problems that reflect the uneasy balance between equality, representativeness and decision-making efficiency and effectiveness. The ECB Governing Council is already the largest monetary policy committee of any central bank (the voting contingent of the Federal Open Market Committee (FOMC) of the US Federal Reserve has only twelve members). There is a growing body of work on optimal monetary policy committee (MPC) size to best ensure decision-making efficiency and effectiveness (see Blinder, 2004; Sibert, 2003, 2006). Sibert (2006) examines the economics literature on monetary policymaking by committee and the literature on groups in the other social sciences – especially social psychology – focusing on the effect of size on group performance and decision outcomes. She concludes that the optimal number of MPC members is at least five and not much beyond this. On the basis of such studies, personal experience and observation, many other observers argue that the ECB Governing Council is too large. At 18 (now 19) members it is conducive neither to maximum efficiency nor to effectiveness in monetary policymaking – in particular on technical as opposed to political aspects (notably, the specification of the ECB's operational goals) (see for example, Haan et al., 2005; Eijffinger, 2006; Sibert, 2006). The prospect of future enlargements exacerbate such concerns.

Amongst others, Willem Buiter, a former member of the Monetary Policy Committee of the Bank of England, complains of the Governing Council's size prior to Greek accession:

> A group of 17 is already too large for the serious and productive exchange of views, discussion and group decision making ... A squad of 21 will be quite unwieldy. Thirty would be a mob ... Based on my own limited experience, a policy making body with seven members would probably be optimal.
>
> (Buiter, 1999, p. 200)

The Governing Council was empowered to change (by unanimity) its own practices if it found problems or potential problems in its decision-making subject to the approval of the Council. There is much scope for its procedures to evolve – such as the creation of more working groups – and the work of the Governing Council can involve more activity at the ECB level or through the NCBs. However, the size problem still matters. Some monetary economists have argued that the problem could be resolved by more centralized policymaking along the lines of the FOMC of the US Federal Reserve. In the ECB this would involve increasing the power of the Executive Board in relation to the NCB governors and rotating a smaller number of Governing Council places among the governors (Haan et al., 2005; Eijffinger 2006; Favero et al., 2000). Others see an entirely centralized system – the creation of a Monetary Board detached from the member state NCBs – as the only effective way to resolve the efficiency problem (Baldwin, 2001; Baldwin et al., 2001).

Such recommendations ignore the unique character of both the Eurosystem as a 'federal' banking system and the EU as a political entity. First, the centre (the ECB) is considerably less dominant in the Eurosystem than in the American system. The NCBs retain considerably more power than the US Federal Reserve District Banks and the governors have final say – thanks to their majority in the Governing Council – over the allocation of functions. Any reform to strengthen the Executive Board at the expense of the NCB governors would be challenged on grounds of legitimacy: despite their *ad personam* status (and *not* as national representatives), the strong presence of the NCB governors on the Governing Council was considered vital to selling the EMU project to sceptical national publics (Haan et al., 2005; Howarth and Loedel, 2005). The arrangements of the US Federal Reserve Board were developed just over 60 years ago, around 160 years after the creation of the United States as a country and long after the conclusion of the Civil War successfully asserted federal government authority. There is obviously no parallel situation in the EU. The legitimacy concerns that the principles of equality and representativeness seek to address require a decentralized form of Eurozone monetary policymaking.

Verdun and Christiansen (2000) and Dyson (2000) argue that the independence of the ECB and the specific objectives assigned to it in the TEC and the Statute of the ESCB and of the ECB place importance upon 'output' rather than 'input' legitimacy. The 'output' legitimacy of the ECB and the EMU project involves providing low inflationary economic growth. The focus of most monetary economists and central bankers on improving the efficiency and effectiveness of ECB monetary policy directly concerns this form of EMU legitimacy. Although of secondary importance to overall ECB and EMU legitimacy, 'input' legitimacy is nonetheless of some relevance. The ECB's goal setting and operational independence means that democratic control via elected representatives is unable to provide this 'input' (apart from the unlikely possibility of treaty reform). Without direct democratic control, the make-up of the membership of the Governing Council assumes greater importance in providing 'input' legitimacy. The technocratic expertise of the members provides some (Dyson, 2000). It is argued here that the presence of national representatives (even in an *ad personam* capacity) provides further 'input' legitimacy. EMU has normally been presented by the governments of member states participating in the Eurozone as the pooling and sharing of monetary policymaking powers. EMU is rarely presented as the transfer or loss of these powers. The presence of national representatives in the ECB confirms the former. The absence suggests the latter. The limited forms of interaction between the ECB and various EU institutions – the European Parliament, the European Commission, the Council of Ministers (Ecofin and the Eurogroup) and the Economic and Financial Committee – further reinforces the importance of the bank's link to the member states. The ECB is poorly embedded in the contested political system of the EU which is, at present, unable to provide 'input' legitimacy (Amtenbrink, 1999, 2004; Banchoff and Smith, 1999; Beetham and Lord, 1998; Wincott 2004). The importance of 'input' legitimacy as a consideration was strongly suggested by the explicit emphasis placed upon 'decentralization' as a 'core principle' by members of the Governing Council guiding their consideration of reform alternatives (Mersch, 2003). A practical dimension to this emphasis on 'decentralization' should also be mentioned. The continued importance of national macroeconomic policymaking and the weakness of EU-level economic governance provides an additional reason to maintain the direct link with member states and member state governments via NCB governors.

Calls to restrict the total number of NCB governors in the Governing Council are thus problematic.[6] No other EU institution[7] currently denies member states representation (although the Treaty of Nice creates this possibility for the European Commission once the number of EU member states exceeds 27).[8] Officially, each NCB governor participates in the Governing Council in a personal capacity as an experienced expert on central banking not as a national representative per se. In theory, therefore, a rotation of governors (either all or only the less populated member states) would be an adequate resolution of the size problem: a particular group of them should be as representative of informed opinion as all of them. However, it would be difficult for the governors to present the perspectives of other member states as effectively as their own and thus highly problematic to exclude certain member states from voting on a permanent, let alone regular, basis. Moreover, the governors are de facto national representatives because they each come from one of the member states and are most familiar with their own national economies and banking systems. De Grauwe et al. (1999) also note that there is nothing in the treaties to prevent NCB governors from prioritizing the economic interests of their own member states (although it is unlikely that they would do so overtly as this would undermine the credibility of their commitment to the ECB's operational goals which target the entire Eurozone).[9]

5.3 Alternative reform proposals

In addition to variants of the rotation system (discussed below), five alternative reform proposals were considered and rejected by Governing Council members: a constituency model, a system of weighted voting, a double majority system, the creation of a Monetary Board and an election system (Berger et al., 2004; Haan et al., 2005; ECB, 2003; Mersch, 2003; interviews with ECB officials in 2004). A constituency model, based on regional groupings as in the World Bank and the IMF, was rejected. Officially (ECB, 2003; Mersch, 2003) it was argued that this would violate the principle of independence of the individual NCB governors in that they would become *de jure* representatives of a specific constituency rather than operating on an *ad personam* basis (in a personal capacity). The extension of the system of weighted voting was deemed contrary to the 'one member, one vote' principle established in Article

10.2 of the Protocol to the TEC on the Statute of the ESCB and ECB. This Statute allows weighted voting (excluding EB members) only on matters pertaining to shareholdership, that is, NCB capital. Governing Council members also rejected the kind of double majority system (number, population and/or GDP to be considered) adopted in the Nice Treaty for the Council which, 'concerning an intergovernmental body', was not seen to be a relevant precedent for Governing Council reform (Mersch, 2003). The NCB governors from the smaller member states were concerned that the need for a double majority would result in a kind of *directoire* dominated by the largest member states. One variant of this model required a majority vote including at least three of the six Executive Board members, with any Governing Council member possessing the right to verify that a pre-set GDP level was represented, thus (if based on current figures) giving the French and German NCB governors the possibility of blockage if that level was set at 62 per cent. Another rejected model was a Governing Council consisting of a preponderance of Executive Board members and a few rotating NCB governors (akin to the FOMC of the American Federal Reserve). This model was seen as contradicting the 'core principles of decentralisation and representation' (Mersch, 2003). Finally, an 'election system' in which NCB governors would elect a limited number of their colleagues to the Governing Council was rejected on several grounds: an unrestricted election might infringe the representativeness criteria, result in the creation of a 'market' for votes and undermine cooperation between Governing Council members.

5.4 Rotation system

The rotation system for voting in the Governing Council is impressively complex for the uninitiated. The lack of transparency in the preparation of the proposed reform – itself suggestive that considerations beyond the core principles and efficiency goals were influential in determining the system agreed upon – has been criticized by several ECB watchers, notably the well-known German monetary economist Daniel Gros (2003). According to the reform agreement, the number of NCB governors exercising a voting right would be capped at 15, while all governors would continue to attend meetings. When the number of NCB governors in the Governing Council exceeded 15, voting rights would be exercised on the basis of a rotation system, designed to ensure that the NCB governors with the right to vote would be from member states which, taken together, were representative of the Eurozone's economy as a whole.

Consequently, the NCB governors would exercise a voting right with different frequencies depending on an indicator of the relative size of the economies of their member states within the Eurozone. Based on this indicator, NCB governors would be allocated to different groups.

Initially, there would be two groups. The governors from the five member states with the largest economies (currently, Germany, France, Italy, Spain and the Netherlands) would form one rotating group possessing four votes (thus only four of these five governors would have the right to vote at any one time with a voting frequency of 80 per cent). The governors from the other member states (numbering eleven to seventeen) would form the second rotating group, sharing eleven votes. Once the total number of member states in the Eurozone increased beyond 22 (up to 27, that is, the current EU member states and the 12 accession countries listed in the Protocol on enlargement annexed to the Treaty of Nice), three groups would be established. The first would remain the same. The second group would consist of the NCB governors from the countries with the next largest economies, sharing eight votes on a rotational basis. The size of this group would equal the total number of governors divided by two (then rounded up to a full number if necessary). The third group would consist of the governors from the countries with the smallest economies sharing three votes on a rotational basis. The members of the Executive Board would preserve their permanent voting rights.

The division of member states into the two/three groups would reflect their share in the Eurozone according to a composite indicator of 'representativeness' consisting of principally the member states' GDP at market prices (five-sixths weight in the indicator) and its total assets of the aggregated balance sheet of monetary financial institutions (TABS-MFI) (one-sixth weight). The data on GDP would be provided by the European Commission, while the rules for the calculation of the key for subscription of the ECB's capital would apply (article 29.2 Statute of the ESCB). The data on TABS-MFI would be defined on the basis of an existing Council Regulation (No. 2533/98 of 23 November 1998) concerning the collection of statistical information by the ECB. This data would be updated every five years. The Governing Council proposed that a two-thirds majority of *all* its members would be required to decide on the initial adaptation of the voting rights in the two-group system as the number of Eurozone member states increased. The same procedure of a two-thirds majority of *all* members would apply to the definition of the precise implementing provisions for the rotation of voting rights within each group (for example, the time interval between the rotation of voting rights).

5.5 The official justification

The agreement on the rotation system reflects the concern of many Governing Council members (especially Executive Board members and NCB governors from the larger participating member states) with regard to the potential inefficiencies of an excessively large Governing Council. A principal concern was that one form of representativeness (namely, one member, one vote) would override representation of the actual Eurozone economy as simple majority voting could (see also Berger, 2002; Haan et al., 2005; Eijffinger, 2006). Such a possibility currently exists in the system of representation and voting in the Governing Council. However, the possibility would increase considerably if all the accession NCB governors obtained voting rights. The official ECB position was that a system of rotation with varying voting rights on the basis of reasonable economic criteria ensured the true equal treatment of the NCB governors and 'sufficient' levels of representativeness. The design of the rotation system was, according to the ECB, guided by the following principles (ECB, 2002b):[10]

- The *'equality'* of NCB governors ('one member, one vote' principle) is maintained in three ways. Even though all the governors do not vote all the time, the votes all carry the same weight regardless of the size of national economies. No NCB governor retains a permanent vote. Furthermore, all governors are allowed to attend all Governing Council meetings.
- The principle of *'ad personam'* participation (allowing all Governing Council members to attend all meetings in a personal and independent capacity rather than as representatives of a specific member state per se or constituency) is preserved.
- *Representativeness* is preserved in the sense that voting NCB governors will be representative of the entire Eurozone (even though some NCB governors are not voting) yet there is no 'renationalization' in the sense of governors being required to represent specific regions.
- *Consistency* is to be maintained during the transition from two to three phases by avoiding the danger that governors of certain NCBs move randomly up and down between certain groups.

The rotation system was also defended in terms of not discriminating against the NCB governors of countries acceding to the Eurozone in the future. Four of the new member states were expected to enter the second rotating group – assuming the continued non-participation of the UK,

Sweden and Denmark – while the strong possibility exists that several of the other new member states would move eventually from the third to the second group because of their relatively strong economic growth (on average much higher than the Eurozone 12).[11]

5.6 Debates on the number and composition of rotating groups, voting rights, composite indicator and representativeness

Two or three rotating group models. The number of rotating groups was debated at length in the Governing Council. Numerous alternative proposals of two-group models of different sizes were proposed (interviews; ECB 2004). These were likely rejected because of the concerns expressed by several of the current NCB governors of being placed in a rotating group with governors from member states with much smaller economies. The NCB governors from the largest member states also sought to create a small group with relatively high voting frequency. Thus the three-group model – with NCB governors from large, medium and small member states respectively – was the preferred option from the start of discussions, with the intermediary phase of a two-group model.

18 versus 21 votes. The concern for decision-making efficiency encouraged the governors from the largest member states to favour maintaining the existing 18 votes, while several governors from the smaller member states defended a higher number of voting members to ensure greater voting frequency in the second and third groups. The compromise reached was 21 votes: 6 permanent votes for the Executive Board members and up to 15 rotating votes for the governors.

Representativeness indicator. The NCB governors from several of the member states (notably the Netherlands) preferred to avoid the use of population criteria given that this would allow several of the NCB governors from Central and Eastern European Countries (CEECs) to replace existing member state governors in the second group and allow Poland to replace the Netherlands in the first group. The official logic for excluding the population criterion (ECB, 2003; Mersch, 2003) is curious: this was seen as inappropriate as the ECB is 'an economic and not a political body', even though the population criterion is already used in addition to GDP for determining member state capital contributions to the ECB and voting on these contributions. Most NCB governors and member states preferred just using the GDP criterion. However, the NCB governors from some of the Eurozone member states (notably Luxembourg) also sought to include recognition of the financial sector. This was defended (ECB, 2003; Mersch, 2003) on the grounds that central banks are charged (de jure and/or de facto) with observing financial sector stability. The bankers also made explicit reference (ECB, 2003) to the experience of the American Federal Reserve System which takes into consideration financial sector size by granting only one Federal Reserve District Bank president – the president of the New York Federal Reserve Bank – permanent voting rights in the Federal Open Market Committee (FOMC).[12] TABS-MFI was adopted on the grounds that it was the broadest measure of the financial sector, with an existing definition in EU law and an established and consistent statistical framework.

5.7 Compromising representativeness and efficiency

The reform proposed by the ECB Governing Council has been widely criticized by academics, journalists, non-Eurozone central bank officials and politicians. Gros (2003, p. 1) has been particularly outspoken in his criticism arguing that 'the solution proposed by the ECB is worse than the status quo. It is inefficient, opaque, internally inconsistent and arbitrary'[13] (see also Bofinger, 2003). After several debates and expressions of expert opinion, the reform proposals were rejected by the European Parliament's Committee on Economics and Monetary Affairs on the grounds of their 'complexity' – although this rejection was not binding upon the Council. The parliamentary committee voted to retain the 'status quo', that is the preservation of votes for all NCB governors, with an enlarged Executive Board of nine members, thus challenging the validity of claims of a size–efficiency trade-off. However, if rotation were to be adopted, the parliamentary committee accepted the use of a composite indicator, based on the criteria of economy and financial market size *but also* population, thus challenging the legitimacy of the ECB's more restricted criteria (EC, 2004).

On efficiency grounds, the proposed reform does not address the concerns that the ECB Governing Council is already too big: the Governing Council is set to grow to 21 members from the present 18. Preventing some NCB governors from voting is not the same as preventing them from speaking and they will continue to attend all Governing Council meetings. Thus the potential for cacophony that concerns Buiter (1999) and others remains. The nod in favour of efficiency was managed only in the context of a great distortion of the principle 'one member, one vote', with the new rotation system reflecting national economic size.

The reform – in order to ensure representativeness – moves in the opposite direction to the preference of those observers who advocate a more centre-heavy US Federal Reserve model (Haan et al., 2005; Eijffinger 2006; Favero et al., 2000) or the Monetary Board proposed by Baldwin et al. (2001). The reform places increased emphasis on representation of the Eurozone economy rather than member states but all NCB governors can continue to attend Governing Council meetings and there is an increased number of voting members.

The new form of representativeness reflected in the rotation system and the failure to meet efficiency objectives reflects the macroeconomic preferences of the five Eurozone member states with the biggest economies more than the other current and future member states. The establishment of two/three groups for rotation, with the NCB governors from the five member states with the biggest economies assured more frequent voting rights than the other governors seems to contradict the *ad personam* status of the NCB governors. The reform officially recognizes that the status of the NCB governors should vary and this in turn suggests that the governors are not to be treated as truly independent people operating in a personal capacity. The reform demonstrates that the governors' home member state is of relevance and determines their status, at least by guaranteeing governors from member states with larger economies a more frequent vote than governors from member states with smaller economies.

Of course, one might see the proposed reform as 'politically reasonable' and legitimate in that it appears that the governors have recognized that economy and financial market size do in fact matter: if there must be rotation why should the governors of the banks of Malta and Slovenia be treated the same as the Bundesbank president? Clearly, the member states with the biggest economies have already lost out in terms of a 'representativeness' that reflects economic size. Officially, their central bank governors possess the same vote as the others on all decisions except those having to do with the capital of the ECB. The adoption of the new rotational scheme is a way of potentially strengthening this kind of 'representativeness', if only to a limited degree. Put another way, the 'representativeness' of one governor one vote has been qualified by a 'politically reasonable' 'representativeness' that accepts the relevance of economy size. This qualification reflects the reality that most Eurozone citizens are preoccupied, first and foremost, with conditions in their national economy rather than the Eurozone economy as a whole. While this qualification no doubt reflects the power concerns of NCB governors from the largest member states, it might also reflect a concern with regard to public perception in these member states of the legitimacy of Eurozone monetary policymaking.

Crucially, the two/three rotating group system and the agreed cap of 21 for Governing Council voting members reflects the macroeconomic preferences of the largest member states (especially Germany and France). The voice of the five largest member states is hardly diminished by the proposed reform, dropping from five out of eighteen to four out of twenty-one (in a Eurozone of 22 member states or more). It might also be argued that de facto over-representation of the large member states in the Governing Council is set to continue. Howarth and Loedel (2005) show that the underlying objective of equal national representation was undermined with the first appointment of the Executive Board in 1998 and the (almost) constant representation of the four largest member states on the Executive Board.[14] These Executive Board members are expected to maintain a focus on the entire Eurozone, as required by the Statute of the ESCB and of the ECB. Nonetheless, the over-representation of large member states does challenge the principles of equality and representativeness. At the very least, it can be argued that having served most, if not all, of their career in their member states of origin, the Executive Board members are more familiar with their home economy than other national economies. As explained below, this familiarity can have an impact on monetary policymaking preferences. If Executive Board members are to be considered potential national representatives in disguise, the twenty-one maximum membership of the Governing Council established in 2003 only slightly diminishes the weight of the largest five member states from the current nine out of eighteen to eight out of twenty-one. It is very likely (interviews; ECB, 2004) that the French and German NCB governors (and perhaps even the Italian and Spanish ones) preferred a double majority system of GDP size and voting members – or a voting system weighted according to GDP – which would have given two or three of these governors an effective veto on all monetary policymaking. Clearly, such a system would have been unacceptable to the large majority of NCB governors. It would also have posed considerable risks for the public's perception of the legitimacy of Eurozone monetary policymaking – especially, in the event of a future move to greater transparency in the Governing Council.[15]

5.8 The economic danger of 'equality'

In the context of enlargement, one principal consideration linked to the different economies and economic needs of the future Eurozone member states likely contributed to the reform preferences of the largest member state NCB governors (interviews; ECB, 2004). Given the more rapid expansion of their economies over the medium to long term, the future member states would have much higher inflation on average than existing member states and considerably higher inflation than France and Germany (and even Italy and Spain). Completely equal member state NCB governor representation on the Governing Council in an enlarged Eurozone would result in the over-representation of inflation-prone member states and the possible establishment of an entrenched bias in favour of higher interest rates. This over-representation arguably already exists in the current Governing Council, where inflation differentials between the member states have spilled over to private and public differences between ECB Governing Council members on interest rate changes, and vociferous criticism by certain Executive Board members of certain member states with higher inflation (Howarth and Loedel, 2005).

The fear of over-representation is linked to two related concerns. The first is the extent to which national policy preferences shape the governors' (and even the Executive Board members') positions. The second is in regard to the structural differences of the national economies. Regarding the first concern – as already noted – no explicit provision in the TEC and the Statute of the ESCB and of the ECB prevents an NCB governor from presenting policy positions based on domestic data and national needs (de Grauwe et al., 1999; Meade and Sheets, 2002). There have been a small number of studies which attempt to differentiate between policymaking on the basis of national preferences and policymaking on the basis of Eurozone-wide preferences and the low inflation target of the ECB (for example, de Grauwe et al., 1999; Heinemann and Huefner, 2004; Sanchez-Santos and Varela, 2003). The jury is out on whether or not national preferences have had a 'distorting' effect on ECB monetary policymaking and this chapter does not attempt to enter into this debate. However, it is important to emphasize that the presence of a much larger number of NCB governors from small and medium-sized national economies with relatively high inflation creates additional pressure for a monetary policy which focuses less on the interests of the biggest member state economies (Heinemann and Huefner, 2004).[16]

The likelihood of a considerable inflation differential in the future enlarged Eurozone is due to the Balassa-Samuelson effect: inflation rates in the poorer ten CEECs will be systematically higher than in wealthier current member states and will likely remain so for some time (Baldwin, 2001b; Bjorksten, 2000; Égert et al., 2003; Égert, 2005; Eichengreen and

Ghironi, 2001). In 2004, for example, there was an inflation rate of 3.7 per cent for the ten future member states and 4.4 per cent for the twelve (the ten, Romania and Bulgaria) versus an average of 2 per cent for the current Eurozone (ECB, 2005). If we are to assume that all NCB governors view inflation risks similarly – despite the ECB's overall inflation target of or close to 2 per cent over the medium term – those governors from the future member states would tend to prefer tighter monetary policy while those from many of the old member states would prefer a looser policy. Baldwin et al. (2001) thus complain of a strong potential for a disjuncture between the requirements of the economy of the entire Eurozone (more than 70 per cent of which is made up of the five largest member states) and the preferences of the smallest 14 (16) member states, which will form a majority of members in the Governing Council of an enlarged Eurozone of 22 (24) member states. The economic situation of the 10 (12) accession countries thus creates difficulties for the entire Eurozone and problems for monetary policymaking. Without the 2003 reform to Governing Council voting procedures, member states with only 6 per cent of the Eurozone GDP (2000 figures) (but 35 per cent of the population) would have controlled 10 voting positions on the Governing Council. In the future enlarged Eurozone of 24 member states, Germany, France and Italy would comprise 67 per cent of the GDP, yet – according to the old voting system – would have held only three of the NCB governors' 24 votes or 12.5 per cent (assuming Sweden, Denmark and the UK stay out but all the new accession countries, Romania and Bulgaria come in). In a monetary union of 27 member states, the smallest 17 would represent only 10 per cent of the Eurozone's economy yet would form a majority of votes in the Governing Council (Berger, 2002). Without reform, all newcomers to the Eurozone – with the exception of the United Kingdom – will have greater political than economic weight.

In addition to the concern about inflation differentials between the larger and future poorer member states, the largest member states also had other economic reasons to seek to preserve their relative voting power in the Governing Council. The differences in monetary transmission mechanisms due to national economic structural differences and different national banking systems – see Angeloni et al. (2003), Bank of England (1999), Corsetti and Pesenti (1999), de Grauwe (2000) and EP (2001) – can result in different monetary policy preferences. Interest rate changes have significantly different effects on the national economies of the Eurozone (although understanding the precise impact is an inexact science given the complexity of variables in the national economies). Therefore, while NCB governors might agree on the need for an interest rate change, a consideration of the impact of the change on national economies might encourage them to push for varying levels of change. Several variables can be mentioned. There are different levels of consumer and public debt: thus interest rate changes will have a considerably different impact on consumer and public spending in different member states. The maturities of debt also vary considerably: for example, because firms in Italy and France have shorter-term loans than the firms in other Eurozone member states, they are more affected by ECB interest rate changes. Furthermore, the degree to which interest rate changes are buffered by national banks varies (Angeloni et al., 2003). The economic structures of the future new member states of the Eurozone will likely vary as much as the current member states. Thus, the concern of the current large member state NCB governors regarding new member state voting is not only related to their economic differences as a group but also to the further dilution of large member state concerns regarding the impact of interest changes.

5.9 Conclusions

Disenfranchising a significant number of the smaller member states was thus not only considered vital to the preservation of the macroeconomic preferences of the largest member states but also to the perception of the legitimacy of Eurozone monetary policymaking for the citizens of these member states. However, the only way that the NCB governors from the existing smaller member states would agree to this reduction of total votes was if rotation was to apply to all the member states and if the established principles of equality ('one member, one vote') and representativeness were respected officially. These treaty-based principles were distorted to become, in effect: 'one member, one vote only some of the time with varying frequency determined by economy and financial market size'.[17] For the full Eurozone of 27 members including all current EU member states, Romania and Bulgaria, the total number of votes and frequency of voting will vary considerably: 4 out of 5 and 80 per cent frequency for the first group; 8 out of 14 or 57 per cent for the second; and 3 out of 8 or 37 per cent for the third. Even with fewer Eurozone members, the preferences of the smallest (and crucially the future poorer) member states are much less likely to prevail and those of the larger member states are more likely to be asserted. The insistence that economy and financial market size matter over population size (however reasonable from the perspective of monetary policymaking) was also reflected in the preferences of the smallest of the current large member states (notably the Netherlands) and other current small member states, few of which would end up in the third rotating group. With the possibility (however remote) of future Turkish entry into the Eurozone, even German, French and Italian NCB governors had a clear interest in establishing group selection by economy and financial market size as opposed to GDP and population size.

Given the lack of transparency surrounding the intra-ECB discussions and negotiations on Governing Council reform, the precise policy positions of the different NCB governors and the precise nature of internal debates are impossible to determine for the time being. However, the reform agreed upon suggests that the NCB governors of the largest member states defended policy positions conforming to national macroeconomic interests, even though compromise was necessary that took on board the concerns of other current Eurozone NCB governors and respected – albeit only in a highly distorted manner – treaty-based principles and legitimacy concerns. The distortion reflects possible efforts to weaken the representation of the NCB governors from the future CEEC member states in order to diminish a structurally determined bias in favour of higher interest rates. The distortion also reflects the interests of the NCB governors of the largest member states in maintaining their disproportionate representation in the Governing Council in order to ensure their relatively strong influence on interest rate changes affecting their economies in a particular way due to specific national economic structures. The reform of Governing Council voting procedures transforms the underlying concept of 'representativeness' in the Eurozone. It undermines the principle of member state representation that has been (and remains) vital to the legitimacy of ECB policy-making (and EMU more generally), while strengthening the relevance of national economic size and the representation of the entire economy of the Eurozone (rather than its member states and their populations). The official ambition to avoid enlargement contributing *significantly* to decision-making inefficiency can arguably be said to have been met. However, inefficiency was, nonetheless, potentially worsened and the core concerns about size raised by many monetary economists were not addressed.

Some monetary economists have granted qualified praise to the agreed reform of the ECB Governing Council and the creation of the three rotating groups. They do so on the grounds that this reform moves in the right direction towards a truly desirable voting system that aligns the 'political power and economic weight' of national central bank governors as closely as possible (Hann et al., 2005; Eijffinger, 2006; see also

Berger et al., 2004). Such a system is, according to these authors, 'the best way' – short of the centralization of operational policymaking in the Executive Board – 'to ensure that national interests will not unduly influence ECB policy-making' (Eijffinger, 2006, p. 97). Their argument doubts the *ad personam* participation of NCB governors and the possibility that they can make monetary policy decisions without specific reference to their own national economies. If NCB governors can in effect represent national economic concerns over those of the Eurozone as a whole, the alignment of voting power in the Governing Council with economic weight negates the possibility of reflecting this bias in ECB monetary policy. These observers are concerned with the policymaking inefficiencies created by emphasizing NCB governor equality and member state representativeness. They also believe that treating NCB governors equally in terms of voting rights in the Governing Council results in the over-representation of the smaller national economies of the Eurozone which in turn damages effective ECB monetary policy. The problem will worsen with enlargement.

The analysis adopted in this chapter accepts that these considerations might well have influenced the reform agreed by the Governing Council members. However, it is argued here that the move in the direction of aligning political (voting) weight and economic weight runs contrary to the 'equality' and 'representativeness' principles in a manner which undermines ECB and EMU legitimacy. The argument that political weight should reflect economic weight responds to the legitimacy and power concerns of the governments of the largest Eurozone national economies. However, the way in which this argument denies the equality and *ad personam* participation of NCB governors – by emphasizing that they represent member state economies – undermines the legitimacy of the ECB and in turn the EMU project. Rooted in a contested EU political system, ECB and EMU legitimacy relies to an unclear extent on equal member state representation, however indirect and qualified by the principle of *ad personam* participation. The agreed Governing Council reform of December 2002 and February 2003 fudges the principles of equality, representativeness and *ad personam* participation of the Governing Council members. Yet the reform does not entirely discard these principles. The reform is potentially damaging to ECB and EMU legitimacy but it is considerably less so than the reform proposals driven solely by either efficiency concerns or the recognition of member state economic weight or both. The monetary economists who advocate such proposals would do well to consider 'input' as well as 'output' legitimacy.

Notes

1. This ECB recommendation, under Article 10.6 of the Statute of the European System of Central Banks and of the European Central Bank, for a Council Decision on an amendment to Article 10.2 of the Statute of the European System of Central Banks and of the European Central Bank (ECB/2003/1; 2003/C29/07) was submitted by the European Central Bank to the Council on 3 February 2003. The decision of the Council, meeting in the composition of the Heads of State or Government, was taken on 21 March 2003 (Council 2003/223/EC) after taking into consideration the opinions of the European Commission and the European Parliament. The agreed amendment was then recommended to the member states for ratification in accordance with their respective constitutional requirements.
2. Article 108 TEC and Article 7 of the Statute of the ESCB and of the ECB establish the independence of Governing Council members. They cannot 'seek or take instructions from Community institutions or bodies, from any government of a member state or from any other body'.
3. See note 2 above. Governing Council members are also officially committed to Eurozone goals (Article 2 of the Statute of the ESCB and of the ECB) which suggests that these goals override specifically national concerns. However, it should be noted that no TEC or Statute provisions explicitly prevent an NCB Governor from representing specifically national concerns.
4. The 'one member, one vote' principle is established in Article 10.2 of the Protocol to the TEC on the Statute of the ESCB and ECB: '... each member of the Governing Council shall have one vote' except on a limited range of matters concerning the capital of the ECB where votes are weighted according to the national central banks' shares in the subscribed capital of the ECB (Art. 10.3) and the terms and conditions of employment of the members of the Executive Board (on which Executive Board members have no right to vote (Art. 11.3)).
5. The principle of 'representativeness' can be said to be established in TEC Article III-382 and Article 10.1 of the Protocol to the TEC on the Statute of the ESCB and ECB which confirm that 'the Governing Council of the European Central Bank shall comprise ... the Governors of the national central banks of the Member States'. This provision is further reinforced by the equality provision of Article 10.2 of the Protocol to establish 'representativeness'.
6. Buiter (1999) for example recommends – even without Eurozone enlargement – restricting the size of the Governing Council to nine members and the Executive Board to four.
7. The ECB enjoys a special status and is not a Community institution in the legal sense.
8. The Nice Treaty (Article 4(2)) requires the Council to adopt a rotation of European Commission places totalling below the number of member states once this number exceeds 27. The Draft Treaty Establishing a Constitution for Europe (Article I-26(6)) specifies this further, allowing – after one full Commission term under existing rules – for the number of Commissioners to equal two-thirds the number of member states (subject to possible modification by the European Council acting unanimously).
9. In terms of the ECB's operational goals, the Eurozone-wide inflation target should effectively force individual governors to disguise specifically national

concerns. Furthermore, to adopt an explicitly national perspective in the Governing Council would discredit an NCB governor as an 'objective' analyst of Eurozone-wide inflation.

10. The fifth principle was transparency (of the wording of the text outlining the rotation system) (ECB, 2002).
11. See Section 5.8 below on 'The economic danger of equality'.
12. The other eleven presidents of the Federal Reserve District Banks rotate into four voting positions on the FOMC. The US Federal Reserve Act makes no reference to the relative weight of Federal Reserve districts, while section 2 of the Act establishes the criteria of convenience and 'customary course of business' to determine voting weights.
13. Gros also challenges the lack of clarity and the arbitrariness surrounding the rotation of NCB governors with voting rights. He provides an alternative for the reform of the ECB developed by the CEPS Macroeconomic Policy Group – which involves the Governing Council meeting less often and setting the guidelines for monetary policy, while the Executive Board assumes more control over the execution of monetary policy – and urges the European Commission to propose an alternative reform for adoption by the Council.
14. Three replacements since June 2004 demonstrate the continuity of large member state representation: the Spanish Executive Board member, Eugenio Domingo Solans, was replaced by another Spaniard, Jose Manuel Gonzalez-Paramo; the Italian Tommaso Padoa-Schioppa by Lorenzo Bini Smaghi; and the German Ottmar Issing by Jürgen Stark. France was not represented on the Executive Board for only a brief period following the replacement of Christian Noyer as ECB Vice President and the accession of Jean-Claude Trichet as President. However, this was an inevitable interruption given that Noyer's departure was part of the controversial compromise allowing Trichet to take office. The extent to which the French President went in 1998 to ensure the appointment of the Bank of France Governor, Trichet, as the ECB president, further suggests the importance attached to securing Executive Board places by the largest member states.
15. There is disagreement among legal scholars as to whether primary Community law prohibits the publication of minutes of the meetings of the Governing Council. It has been argued by some that Article 10.4 of the Statute of the ESCB and of the ECB limits transparency in this regard (Amtenbrink, 1999). Article 10.4 states: 'The proceedings of the meetings shall be confidential. The Governing Council may decide to make the outcome of its deliberations public.' Although no provision in the TEC (and specifically Article VII or the Protocol on the Statute of the ESCB and of the ECB) necessarily blocks transparency, the ECB Governing Council members justified their 1998 decision to prevent disclosure of Governing Council minutes as a necessary evil to prevent the exertion of domestic political pressures on national central bankers (ECB, 1999). In effect, non-transparency might also decrease the appearance of NCB governors advocating monetary policy changes that conform to national preferences (Howarth and Loedel, 2005).
16. Heinemann and Huefner (2004) apply different economic approaches to determine if national preferences rather than a Eurozone focus determine ECB interest rate decisions. Using the ordered probit approach, these authors conclude that national preferences (based on controlling national inflation rates

rather than the Eurozone inflation rate) do affect monetary policy – although they accept clear limitations to their study. Given the increased divergence between economies and inflation rates in member states in a future enlarged Eurozone, these authors argue that 'If for EMU-12 there is some evidence that divergence is not irrelevant in the Governing Council this should be even more pronounced for EMU-27. In this sense our first results back the case for adjusting the representation and/or voting weights in the Governing Council in favour of the countries with large GDP shares as recommended by the ECB' (ibid., p. 556).

17. Author's own words.

References

Amtenbrink, F. (1999). *The Democratic Accountability of Central Banks: a Comparative Study of the European Central Bank*, Oxford: Hart Publishing.

Amtenbrink, F. (2004). 'On the Legitimacy and Democratic Accountability of the European Central Bank: Legal Arrangements and Practical Experiences', in Anthony Arnull and Daniel Wincott (eds), *Accountability and Legitimacy in the European Union*, Oxford Studies in European Law, Oxford: Oxford University Press, pp. 147–64.

Angeloni, I., A. Kashyap, B. Mojon and D. Terlizzese (2003). 'Monetary Transmission in the Euro Area: Where Do We Stand?', in I. Angelino, A. Kashyap and B. Mojon (eds), *Monetary Policy in the Euro Area*, Cambridge: Cambridge University Press, pp. 383–407.

Baldwin, R. (2001). 'Preparing the ECB for Enlargement', CEPR Discussion Paper, no. 6.

Baldwin, R., E. Berglof, F. Giavazzi and M. Widgren (2001). *Nice Try: Should the Treaty of Nice be Ratified?* Washington, DC: Brookings.

Banchoff, Thomas and Mitchell P. Smith (1999). 'Conceptualizing Legitimacy in a Contested Polity', in T. Banchoff and M.P. Smith (eds), *Legitimacy and the European Union*, London: Routledge, pp. 1–23.

Bank of England (1999). 'The Transmission Mechanism of Monetary Policy', *Bank of England Quarterly Bulletin*, 39(2): 3–12.

Beetham, D. and C. Lord (1998). *Legitimacy and the EU*, Boston: Addison Wesley.

Berger, H. (2002). 'The ECB and Euro-Area Enlargement', IMF Working Paper No. 02/175.

Berger, H., J. de Haan and R. Inklaar (2004). 'Restructuring the ECB', in H. Berger and T. Moutos, (eds), *Managing European Union Enlargement*, Cambridge, MA: MIT Press, pp. 29–66.

Blinder, A. (2004). *The Quiet Revolution: Central Banking Goes Modern*, New Haven, CT: Yale University Press.

Bofinger, P. (2003). 'Consequences of the Modification of the Governing Council Rules', Briefing Paper for the Committee on Economic and Monetary Affairs of the European Parliament, February.

Bjorksten, N. (2000). 'Economic Catching up in the Enlarged Euro Area: Implications for the Common Monetary Policy', EUI Working Papers, RSC, No. 2000/52; see http://www.ieu.it/RSC/WP-Texts/00_52.pdf.

Buiter, W. (1999). 'Alice in Euroland', *Journal of Common Market Studies*, 37(2): 181–209.
Corsetti, G. and P. Pesenti (1999). 'Stability, Asymmetry and Discontinuity: the Outset of European Monetary Union', Brookings Papers on Economic Activity, Brookings Institution, Washington DC.
Council (2003). 'Decision of the Council, meeting in the composition of the Heads of State or Government of 21 March 2003 on an amendment to Article 10.2 of the Statute of the European System of Central Banks and of the European Central Bank (2003/223/EC)'; see http://ec.europa.eu/economy_finance/publications/euro_related/2005/compendium/pdfs/a06_en.pdf.
De Grauwe, P. (2000). 'Monetary Policies in the Presence of Asymmetries', *Journal of Common Market Studies*, 38(4): 593–612.
De Grauwe, P., H. Dewachter and Y. Aksoy (1999). 'The ECB Decision Rules and Macroeconomic Performance', CEPR Discussion Paper No. 2067.
Deutsche Bundesbank (2001). 'Monetary Aspect of the Enlargement of the EU', Monthly Report, October, Frankfurt: Deutsche Bundesbank; see http://www.bundesbank.de/en/monatsbericht/textteil/bericht10/01/mb1001ges_e.pdf.
Dyson, K. (2000). *The Politics of the Euro-Zone: Stability or Breakdown?* Oxford: Oxford University Press.
EC (2004). Economic and Monetary Affairs Committee, 20 February.
ECB (1999). *Annual Report 1998*, Frankfurt: ECB.
ECB (2002). Press Statement, 20 December.
ECB (2003). *Annual Report 2002*, Frankfurt: ECB.
ECB (2005). *Annual Report 2004*, Frankfurt: ECB.
Égert, B. (2005). 'Balassa-Samuelson Meets South Eastern Europe, the CIS and Turkey: a Close Encounter of the Third Kind?' *European Journal of Comparative Economics*, 2(2): 221–43.
Égert, B., I. Drine, K. Lommatzsch and C. Rault (2003). 'The Balassa-Samuelson Effect in Central and Eastern Europe: Myth or Reality?' *Journal of Comparative Economics*, 31(3): 552–72.
Eichengreen, B. and F. Ghironi (2001). 'EMU and Enlargement', unpublished manuscript; see http://fmwww.bc.edu/ec-p/WP481.pdf.
Eijffinger, S.C.W. (2006). 'Change at the ECB Executive Board', *Intereconomics*, 41(2) March/April: 93–9.
European Parliament (EP) (2001). 'Monetary Policy Transmission in the Euro Area', Luxembourg: Directorate-General for Research; see http://www.europarl.eu.int/workingpapers/econ/pdf/110rev_en.pdf.
Fatum, R. (2000). 'Economical and Political Implications of Bargaining versus Voting in a Monetary Union', Santa Cruz Center for International Economics, Working Paper No. 00-16; see http://sccie.ucsc.edu/papers/workingpapers/2000/sccie-00-16.pdf.
Favero, C., X. Freixias, T. Persson and C. Wyplosz (2000). *One Money, Many Countries: Monitoring the European Central Bank 2*, London: CEPR.
Gros, D. (2003). 'Reforming the Composition of the ECB Governing Council in View of Enlargement. How Not To Do It!' briefing paper for the Monetary Committee of the European Parliament, Brussels: CEPS, February; see http://www.europarl.eu.int/comparl/econ/pdf/emu/speeches/20030217/gross.pdf.
Gros, D. and C. Hefeker (2000). 'One Size Fits All: National Divergences in a Monetary Union', CEPS Working Paper, No. 149, July.

Haan, J. de and S.C.W. Eijffinger (2000). 'The Democratic Accountability of the European Central Bank: a Comment on Two Fairy-Tales', *Journal of Common Market Studies*, 38(3): 393–407.

Haan, J. de, S.C.W. Eijffinger and S. Waller (2005). *The European Central Bank: Credibility, Transparency, and Centralization*, Boston, MA: MIT Press.

Heinemann, F. and F. Huefner (2004). 'Is the View from the Eurotower Purely European? National Divergence and ECB Interest Rate Policy', *Scottish Journal of Political Economy*, 51(4): 544–58.

Heisenberg, D. (2003). 'Cutting the Bank Down to Size: Efficient and Legitimate Decision-Making in the European Central Bank after Enlargement', *Journal of Common Market Studies*, 41(3): 397–420.

Howarth, D. and P. Loedel, P. (2005). *The European Central Bank: the New European Leviathan?* Second (revised) Edition, Basingstoke: Palgrave.

Interviews (2004). Interviews with seven ECB officials on the subject of the proposed ECB Governing Council reform, Frankfurt am Main, 7–11 June 2004.

Issing, O. (1999). 'The Eurosystem: Transparent and Accountable of "Willem in Euroland"', *Journal of Common Market Studies*, 37(3): 503–19.

Leino, P. (2001). 'The European Central Bank and Legitimacy: is the ECB a Modification of or an Exception to the Principle of Democracy?', Harvard Jean Monnet Working Paper, 1/01; see http://www.jeanmonnetprogram.org/papers/00/001101.html.

Meade, E. and N. Sheets (1999). 'Regional Influences on US Monetary Policy: Some Implications for Europe', London: Centre for Economic Performance Working Paper; see http://cep.lse.ac.uk/pubs/download/dp0523.pdf.

Mersch, Y. (2003). 'The reform of the Governing Council of the ECB', panel statement, Central Bankers' Panel, European Banking and Financial Forum, Prague, 25 March. Reproduced in *BIS Review*, 16/2003.

Sanchez-Santos, J. and D. Varela (2003). 'Representative or Independent? A Rational Choice Model of Interest Rate Decision-Making by the European Central Bank', paper presented at the UACES Annual Research Conference, 2–4 September, Newcastle, UK; see http://www.udc.es/rrii/ajm/papers/ECBpaper 08.pdf.

Sibert, Anne C. (2003). 'Monetary Policy Committees: Individual and Collective Reputations', *Review of Economic Studies*, 70(3): 649–65.

Sibert, Anne C. (2006). 'Central Banking by Committee', *International Finance*, 9(2) Summer: pp. 145–68.

Verdun, A. and T. Christiansen (2000). 'Policies, Institutions and the Euro: Dilemmas of Legitimacy', in C. Crouch (ed.), *After the Euro: Shaping Institutions for Governance in the Wake of European Monetary Union*. Oxford: Oxford University Press, pp. 162–78.

Wincott, D. (2004). 'National State and European Union and Changing Dynamics in the Quest for Legitimacy', in Anthony Arnull and Daniel Wincott (eds), *Accountability and Legitimacy in the European Union*, Oxford Studies in European Law, Oxford: Oxford University Press, pp. 487–96.

Part II
EU Expansion: New Members in the EU Environment

6

Fiscal Convergence in Monetary Union: are the New Member Countries Better Disciplined than Eurozone Members?

Evžen Kočenda, Ali M. Kutan and Taner M. Yigit

6.1 Introduction

In this chapter we analyse the fiscal discipline of the ten EU newcomers and comparable performance in the Eurozone by using alternative measures of fiscal discipline and employing vastly flexible tests, which allow for structural breaks, to assess the state of fiscal discipline in the enlarged European Union (EU). Our general measure of fiscal discipline is based on satisfying Maastricht fiscal criteria. Since the idea underlying the fiscal rules of the EU is debt sustainability, this chapter is related to other recent studies on debt sustainability in developed and developing countries (for example, Uctum et al., 2006; Uctum and Wickens, 2000). However, we are more interested in the question of how the EU countries are developing in terms of the heterogeneity (rather than the sustainability) of their fiscal performance on their path to a monetary union. Our results suggest generally poor fiscal discipline. More importantly, we find that the new members are as undisciplined as the EU-15, if not more so. Since the outcome of the estimations imply that monetary unions need not provide fiscal discipline, we also offer ideas for the EU newcomers on improving their fiscal performance in order to meet the Maastricht criteria.

Our study is important for several reasons. First, fiscal discipline in the EU has been receiving increasing attention since the formulation of the convergence criteria under the Maastricht Treaty.[1] The two fiscal criteria limiting the deficit and debt ratios within a percentage of GDP have come under sharp scrutiny.[2] These conditions were set to allow qualifying countries to form the Economic and Monetary Union (EMU) in 1999. After this formation, empirical literature has turned to analysing the new EU fiscal framework under the Stability and Growth Pact and its reform.[3] Our study provides a different perspective on fiscal discipline via an explicit comparison of the fiscal convergence during accession, membership and the Stability and Growth Pact.

Second, in May 2004, ten new members joined the EU.[4] All of these countries must join the Eurozone once they satisfy the Maastricht criteria. Although EU accession leaves new members some freedom to select how to link their national currencies to the euro, policymakers in the new member countries appear to be inclined to adopt the euro sooner rather than later (McKinnon, 1999; Buiter and Grafe, 2002; Buiter, 2004). The sooner the new EU countries complete their restructuring process and become more like the core EU members in terms of a broad range of macroeconomic indicators, the more likely and faster they are to unilaterally adopt the euro (for example, Salvatore, 2004). Understandably, several observers have raised concerns about the fiscal indiscipline of some new members.[5] Many of the new EU members have therefore been put under the Excessive Deficit Programme (EDP) since their entry in 2004. In this respect, our empirical study of fiscal discipline also offers a way to evaluate the effectiveness of the EDP.

Third, although the analysis of the fiscal discipline of the 10 new members is understudied in comparison to the core EU-15, a comparison of the fiscal performance of the new 10 members against the core EU-15 is missing in the literature.

Fourth, studying fiscal sustainability in a monetary union is itself important for several reasons. First of all, evidence indicates a direct relationship between fiscal policy and macroeconomic performance. In their study of discretionary fiscal policy for 91 countries, Fatás and Mihov (2003) conclude that 'governments that use fiscal policy aggressively induce significant macroeconomic instability' in the form of output volatility.[6] Second, there is ample evidence that a fiscal convergence is systematically associated with an enhanced business cycle synchronization as it eliminates idiosyncratic fiscal shocks. And finally, there is the proof of reduced primary fiscal deficits (or higher surpluses) increasing the coherence of business cycles across countries (Darvas et al., 2005). Therefore, since both the Maastricht convergence criteria and the Stability and Growth Act require fiscal discipline before entry to the EMU, they indirectly move the EU closer to an optimum currency area in the sense of Mundell (1961). Thus, it is argued that the increased business cycle coherence due to fiscal discipline makes countries within the region better candidates for a currency union (Darvas et al., 2005). Further, reducing or even removing independence in fiscal policy means removing a source of asymmetric shocks, hence moving more quickly towards monetary integration.

In the next section, we briefly summarize the existing theoretical and empirical studies. In Sections 6.3 and 6.4, we describe our methodology and data. Empirical results are reported in Section 6.5. Section 6.6 concludes.

6.2 Related studies and our contribution

6.2.1 Theoretical and empirical studies

Based on a simple game theoretical framework where agents agree on long-term goals, Onorante (2004) shows that fiscal constraints lead to an implicit coordination characterized by lower deficits, low interest rates and controlled inflation. Further, fiscal activism is always increased by entry into a monetary union, in which the capacity of a central bank to keep inflation close to targets is much smaller than in the one-country case. Finally, a strategy of convergence in public finances prior to entry into a monetary union may be preferable both for the acceding country and the stability of the existing monetary union. To sum up, the model provides an argument for the benefits of fiscal discipline with respect to the integration and existence of a monetary union, and helps us to extend the conclusions we can derive from our empirical findings.

As with theoretical studies, there are scant empirical analyses on fiscal policy coordination in the EU countries. Sanz and Velázquez (2003) test whether the convergence of the composition of government expenditures is greater for EU member states than in the non-EU countries of the OECD. Using data from 1970 to 1997, they find that EU member states are converging towards a different steady state composition of government expenditures and their convergence is faster than the non-EU countries of the OECD. However, they also report that the margin for future convergence seems to be limited because the functional distribution of government expenditures appears to be close to the steady state. Finding different steady states for each country suggests that each country has its own individual functional distribution of public expenditure in the long term, driven by preferences and historical and institutional factors of individual countries, indicating the lack of a common, sustainable fiscal policy.

Arestis et al. (2002) suggest that a sustainable fiscal arrangement is a must for a viable monetary union. In their comparison of the Eurozone deficit with the US federal deficit, they find (i) fiscal discipline, measured by fiscal convergence in most of the countries and by the achievement of 3 per cent criteria by all Eurozone countries immediately before the launch of the euro; (ii) similar magnitudes and variability of deficit in the EU and the US; and (iii) that the Eurozone is subject to smaller fiscal shocks than the US. Our research may also be considered as extending their results as we compare the new member countries against the core EU members.

Faini (2006) investigated the link between fiscal policy and interest rates in the European context and found that an expansionary fiscal policy in one EMU member will have an effect both on its spreads and on the overall level of interest rates for the currency union as a whole. Finding that the second effect is quantitatively much more significant Faini suggests that there are substantial spillovers, through the interest rate channel, among the fiscal policies of member countries. To limit countries' incentives to run expansionary fiscal policies, a set of rules, like those embedded in the Stability and Growth Pact, is needed.

6.2.2 Our contribution

Given limited studies on fiscal discipline, in particular in relation to the new EU states, and its importance for EU policymakers, we provide a comprehensive empirical study on fiscal discipline based on fiscal convergence between the new EU members and the EU-15. We relate fiscal discipline to progress in managing public finances and the specific risks that policymakers in the new member states must overcome in the process of joining the Eurozone. To measure fiscal discipline based on fiscal convergence (to different benchmarks), we employ beta- and sigma-convergence tests, allowing for structural breaks. Towards this end, we use a test developed by Vogelsang (1998) which is particularly suitable for analysing absolute convergence.[7] In this approach we are confronted with the existing empirical evidence on structural breaks in many economic indicators during the transition and pre-accession process in the Central and Eastern European (CEE) countries.[8] Since such structural breaks in economic series may distort the findings, we employ the modified version of the Vogelsang test that allows for structural breaks (see Section 6.3 'Methodology' for details). Since this method not only allows for structural breaks but is also flexible enough to allow researchers to derive convergence estimates reliably, it yields more reliable inferences about fiscal convergence than those found in earlier studies.

One of the ways to test for the fiscal discipline of the new member states in relation to the EU is to compare their distance from convergence criteria as established in the Maastricht Treaty: (1) fiscal deficit up to 3 per cent of GDP and (2) national debt up to 60 per cent of GDP.

In this respect we do not dispute or discuss the choice of the two ratio-values.[9] Instead we complement the previous criteria with an alternative way of measuring fiscal discipline in the EU newcomers with respect to two synthetic benchmarks: (1) the EU core, represented by Austria, Belgium, France, Germany and the Netherlands, and (2) the EU periphery represented by Greece, Portugal and Spain. This alternative measure of fiscal discipline is in the spirit of the Stability and Growth Pact since we test whether any of the new EU members have been performing like the old EU countries (EU-15). This tells us whether the new EU members are as fiscally disciplined as the EU-15 countries.[10]

6.3 Methodology

The analysis of convergence used in this chapter to draw inferences about fiscal discipline has been an active as well as a challenging field of interest since the late 1980s.[11] Numerous methods have been used to analyse different measures of convergence, namely absolute or conditional beta-convergence, sigma-convergence, and stochastic convergence. While the former two types analysed the issue of catching up, the latter and more recent approach focused on the synchronization of shocks and cross-sectional units moving together in time. The enlargement of the EU has refocused interest in the issue of the 'catching up' of the new entrants to the core EU members. Cross-sectional tests mostly used to analyse beta-convergence were criticized on the grounds of their rejection of the null hypothesis of no convergence (Quah, 1996; Bernard and Durlauf, 1996). These criticisms pushed researchers to apply time series (or panel data) methodologies to introduce a second dimension to beta-convergence.

A new test introduced by Vogelsang (1998, 1999) deals with the beta-convergence issue by relying on time-series methodology. Following this literature, we consider a simple model of convergence towards a benchmark as:

$$y_t = \mu + \delta t + u_t \tag{6.1}$$

where y_t is the difference of the natural logarithm of a variable minus a benchmark; in our case for example, the budget deficit-to-GDP ratio of country i minus the Maastricht (or other) benchmark at time t would be the y_t variable, while μ is an intercept to capture the initial level of the deviation, t is a deterministic time trend, and u_t is the residual term. In such a set-up, beta-convergence requires that for countries where μ is initially significantly negative, so the country is lagging behind, the trend coefficient δ should have the opposite sign (positive) and be statistically significant. Carlino and Mills (1993) developed this test with a very restricted form of serial correlation for the residual term, namely AR(2). Vogelsang (1998) extended the analysis of this specification to u_t with an unknown form of serial correlation, allowing for specifications ranging from integration of order zero, $I(0)$, to order one, $I(1)$. Since the possibility of no convergence implies non-stationarity of the error terms, one can draw a false inference on the trend coefficient when the errors are assumed to be stationary AR(2).[12] Vogelsang's (1998) methodology, in the spirit of equation (6.1), considers the following partial sums with J correction (PSW) test statistic that helps to alleviate the above problems.[13] It is defined as:

$$PSW_T = T^{-1}(R\hat{\beta} - r)'[R(X'X)^{-1}R']^{-1}(R\hat{\beta} - r)/(100T^{-1}s_z^2 \exp(bJ_T(m))) \tag{6.2}$$

where X and β consist of $[1 \;\; t]$ and $[\mu \;\; \delta]$ respectively, s_z^2 is the standard deviation of the partial cumulated sum of y_t and J_T is the Park and Choi (1988) unit root test statistic obtained from the following regression:

$$y_t = X_t\beta + \sum_{i=2}^{m} c_i t^i + u_t$$

$$J_T(m) = (RSS_y - RSS_J)/RSS_J \tag{6.3}$$

In other words, J_T is the Wald statistic that tests the joint hypothesis of $c_2 = c_3 = \cdots = c_m = 0$. In Monte Carlo simulations, Vogelsang (1998) finds the values of b and m for which the above tests would be comparable and valid for every type of serial correlation form, including unit roots.

Despite the great flexibility of these tests in deriving the mean and trend coefficient estimates in time series with varying stationarity properties, one needs to be careful in using this methodology in the analysis of post-transition economies. This is because of the volatile nature of these economies and the presence of structural shifts that are documented in the empirical literature. The problem of structural breaks during the transition process is given serious empirical consideration in Fidrmuc and Tichit (2004) who provide evidence of significant breaks for macroeconomic data. They argue that empirical analyses of transition economies must account for the possibility of structural changes, otherwise inferences are misleading. However, only a few papers consider the structural breaks on transition issues (see, for example, Dibooglu and Kutan, 2001; and Kočenda, 2005).

We obtain robust results by using Vogelsang's (1999) methodology that allows for structural breaks in the modification of the statistics by including the possibility of shifts in the trend function. The test has been designed in two versions: one with predetermined breaks and the other with endogenous break selection. We favour the latter. First, we estimate the break date using the optimal tests of Andrews and Ploberger (1994). Then, using the estimated break date, normalized critical values are obtained using the following altered version of equation (6.1):

$$y_t = \mu_1 DU_{1t} + \mu_2 DU_{2t} + \delta_1 DT_{1t} + \delta_2 DT_{2t} + u_t \tag{6.4}$$

where $DU_{1t} = 1$ if $t \leq T_b$ (the break date) and zero otherwise, $DU_{2t} = 1$ if $t > T_b$ and zero otherwise, $DT_{1t} = t$ if $t \leq T_b$ and zero otherwise, and finally $DT_{2t} = t - T_b$ if $t > T_b$ and zero otherwise.

To derive inferences on fiscal discipline we test the significance and the opposite signs in the pair of coefficients, μ_1, δ_1 and μ_2, δ_2. The null hypothesis is that trend coefficients are equal to zero, which in our framework translates to no trend in developments of budget deficit or debt. An alternative hypothesis of trend coefficients being statistically different from zero indicates the existence of positive or negative trends in developments of both measures, depending on the sign. In particular, the finding of (statistically significant) mean and trend coefficients with opposite signs indicates how countries with different starting positions approach the benchmark. As an example consider the dependent variable being the budget deficit (surplus) to GDP ratio in country i minus the 3 per cent deficit benchmark. Then a positive intercept indicates a surplus or a deficit ratio below 3 per cent since the negative 3 per cent benchmark subtracted from a less negative deficit ratio yields positive value. Accordingly, a positive trend coefficient indicates improving comparative fiscal stance. The reverse follows for the opposite combination of signs. We supplement these results by tests of sigma-convergence[14] since confirmation of absolute convergence requires both beta- and sigma-convergence.

Granted that the Vogelsang (1999) methodology allows for only a single break, and it is desirable to use methodologies allowing for more breaks – such as Bai and Perron (1998, henceforth BP) – the data availability and the performance of BP under $I(1)$ errors prevent us from pursuing alternative methodologies. Uctum et al. (2006) analyse the mean reversion of the debt of developed and developing countries to examine sustainability by using a combination of the BP and Zivot and Andrews (1992) tests. These tests revolve around the same idea, testing for the mean reverting trends and temporary fluctuations around them (stationarity) in the existence of breaks. We prefer the Vogelsang methodology since it provides more accurate inferences on the trend functions (and breaks in them) regardless of the (non-)stationarity of the data series.[15] This way, one does not have to test for the stationarity of the series around the trend values to evaluate convergence to benchmarks (or debt sustainability in the case of Uctum et al., 2006). Finally, we complement our analysis with a panel study of long-term interest rates to show the potential cost of fiscal indiscipline.

6.4 Data and sample period

We assess the fiscal discipline of the CEE8, Cyprus and Malta using the official Maastricht criteria of the deficit-to-GDP and debt-to-GDP ratios. We further examine the fiscal discipline of these countries with respect to two naturally produced benchmarks. These are deficit and debt ratios achieved in the core of the EU, represented by the average values in Austria, Belgium, France, Germany and the Netherlands, and the EU periphery, represented by average values from Greece, Portugal and Spain. An analysis of the deficit and debt ratios is also consistent with testing the theoretical implications of the disciplining effects of monetary unions.

We use quarterly data from 1995:1 through 2005:4 for variables under research. The time span was chosen because: (1) official EU membership applications started in 1995; (2) Eurostat began using the harmonized time series on macroeconomic variables at that time; and (3) consistent data are available for all countries up to the end of 2005. In addition, the post-1995 period excludes the major transition-related shocks observed in the early 1990s. The data are obtained primarily from the Eurostat database and checked for consistency against the International Financial Statistics of the IMF. In case of missing or incomplete observations, data are gathered from individual central banks and finance ministries.[16] We also annualize the quarterly debt and deficit data by summing the four quarters and then using this sum to obtain the deficit-to-GDP and debt-to-GDP ratios. We should reiterate at this point that the serial correlation generated by the methodology used for de-seasonalizing the data is of little concern here since the Vogelsang test is able to handle broad forms of serial correlation.

6.5 Empirical findings

The Vogelsang test results are displayed in Tables 6.1 and 6.2 below. They display the results for *PSW* (partial sums with *J* correction) tests, given by the specification in equation (6.2). The last column in each table contains the estimated break date using the maximum $T^{-1}W_T$ statistic of Andrews and Ploberger (1994). Following the theoretical grounds of the methodology employed, we apply a 10 per cent trimming from each end of the sample since the break dates close to the endpoints are unreliable and should mostly be disregarded. We display the test statistics below the coefficient estimates and the asymptotic critical values for the endogenous break option of the *PSW* tests on the bottom rows of each table.

When interpreting results, the reader should note that positive trend coefficients represent *improvements* of fiscal position in comparison to the Union, suggesting that newcomers are better disciplined than the old EU members. For instance, a positive trend coefficient shows new members' fiscal position is improving further, away from the 3 per cent deficit benchmark. In short, a positive trend coefficient is always good. We supplement this brief explanation at the bottom of each table by indicating the dependent variable and providing a brief guideline to enable the results to be easily interpreted.

The dependent variables in the analyses are the ratio of the budget deficit (surplus) to GDP and total debt to GDP in a new member country minus the benchmarks, 3 per cent for deficit and 60 per cent for total debt. Since all deficits (debt) are indicated by a negative number (for example, −2 per cent stands for a 2 per cent deficit), all mean values that are positive indicate surplus or deficit (debt) ratios below (less negative than) 3 per cent (60 per cent), values that are zero indicate deficit (debt) of exactly 3 per cent (60 per cent), and values that are negative indicate deficit (debt) ratios greater than 3 per cent (60 per cent). Accordingly, negative trend coefficients depict deficit (debt) increases (or declining budget surpluses) with respect to the benchmark, suggesting fiscal indiscipline relative to the benchmark, and positive coefficients suggest just the opposite (fiscal discipline)

As a complementary measure of fiscal discipline, we also report the sigma-convergence tests to be able to test whether the fiscal position of the newcomers are diverging or converging towards the core and periphery EU members. We illustrate the sigma-convergence levels graphically. One should note that since the sigma (standard deviation in our case) is calculated cross-sectionally, then the choice of benchmark does not alter the results.

Table 6.1 Budget deficit convergence to Maastricht benchmark as well as the core and the periphery

	PSW test with endogenous break selection (regression of y_t with J_T correction)				
Countries	μ_1	δ_1	μ_2	δ_2	**Break**
Cyprus – bench.	3.31*(1.46)	−0.49*(−1.70)	−0.93(−0.66)	−0.02(−0.20)	1998Q3
Cyprus – core	3.18*(1.38)	−0.34(−0.74)	−2.60**(−2.59)	−0.01(−0.29)	1996Q3*
Cyprus – perip.	7.94**(2.15)	−0.64(−0.88)	−1.10(−0.68)	−0.07(−0.86)	1996Q4**
Czech – bench.	3.91**(2.83)	−0.24**(−3.42)	−4.74*(−1.89)	0.57(1.53)	2003Q1*
Czech – core	4.64**(2.99)	−0.36**(−3.96)	−6.04**(−2.73)	0.32(1.31)	2002Q1**
Czech – perip.	9.65**(3.05)	−0.61(−1.43)	−2.22(−1.19)	−0.04(−0.46)	1997Q4**
Estonia – bench.	1.03(0.63)	0.21(1.24)	0.41(0.34)	0.19**(2.67)	1998Q4
Estonia – core	1.83(0.96)	0.09(0.43)	−1.26(−0.89)	0.19**(2.25)	1998Q4
Estonia – perip.	6.25**(3.27)	−0.14(−0.68)	−0.14(−0.10)	0.13*(1.69)	1998Q3*
Hungary – bench.	2.61(1.07)	−0.41**(−1.92)	−0.94(−0.44)	−0.11(−0.79)	1999Q3
Hungary – core	1.30(0.36)	−0.04(−0.07)	−4.33**(−2.34)	−0.01(−0.06)	1997Q2
Hungary – perip.	8.24**(3.16)	−0.83**(−3.46)	−1.87(−0.88)	−0.14(−1.04)	1999Q2
Latvia – bench.	0.46(0.56)	0.25**(2.94)	−0.30(−0.50)	0.12**(3.21)	1998Q4*
Latvia – core	1.58*(1.39)	0.07(0.66)	−2.25**(−2.53)	0.14**(2.48)	1999Q1*
Latvia – perip.	5.96**(6.34)	−0.15(−1.55)	−0.98(−1.40)	0.07*(1.67)	1998Q4**
Lithuania – bench.	3.20**(2.65)	−0.22**(−2.35)	0.50(0.42)	0.08(0.86)	2002Q2**
Lithuania. – core	3.16**(1.96)	−0.21(−1.26)	−3.10**(−2.59)	0.15**(2.05)	1998Q4**
Lithuania – perip.	8.14**(8.42)	−0.54**(−7.31)	−0.19(−0.19)	0.01(0.16)	2000Q2**

(continued)

Table 6.1 (Continued)

Countries	PSW test with endogenous break selection (regression of y_t with J_T correction)				
	μ_1	δ_1	μ_2	δ_2	Break
Malta – bench.	−8.86**(−5.68)	0.19**(2.35)	−7.89**(−2.79)	0.73*(1.74)	2003Q1
Malta – core	−8.40**(−4.64)	0.10(1.10)	−8.92**(−2.53)	0.71(1.24)	2003Q2
Malta – perip.	−2.18(−1.10)	−0.36**(−1.98)	−5.48**(−3.37)	0.04(0.36)	1999Q2
Poland – bench.	−0.07(−0.18)	0.13**(4.79)	−1.55**(−2.84)	0.00(0.06)	2001Q3**
Poland – core	0.78*(1.37)	0.00(0.00)	−2.75**(−3.78)	−0.04(−0.52)	2001Q3*
Poland – perip.	4.23**(2.89)	−0.12(−1.33)	−2.38(−1.27)	−0.08(−0.45)	2001Q3
Slovak – bench.	0.03(0.01)	−0.19(−1.12)	−8.34**(−4.16)	0.43**(2.93)	2000Q1*
Slovak – core	0.74(0.33)	−0.30*(−1.66)	−10.37**(−4.82)	0.45**(2.86)	2000Q1*
Slovak – perip.	5.60**(2.88)	−0.59**(−4.51)	−6.52**(−2.90)	0.28(1.44)	2001Q1**
Slovenia – bench.	3.02**(7.63)	−0.07**(−2.95)	3.45**(5.77)	−0.06(−0.79)	2002Q2
Slovenia – core	3.70**(7.02)	−0.18**(−5.92)	2.81**(3.53)	−0.17**(−1.81)	2002Q2**
Slovenia – perip.	8.19**(6.09)	−0.38**(−1.94)	1.06(1.43)	0.00(−0.11)	1997Q3**
Crit. val.					
5%	1.51	1.88	1.92	1.81	
10%	1.21	1.58	1.65	1.54	

Notes: The first dependent variable is the budget deficit (surplus) to GDP ratio in country *i* minus the 3% deficit benchmark (a positive number indicates a surplus or a deficit ratio below 3% since the negative 3% benchmark subtracted from a less negative deficit ratio yields positive values). For the core (periphery), it is the deficit to GDP ratio in country *i* minus the core (periphery) deficit ratio (that is, a negative number indicates a deficit ratio worse than that of the core (periphery) and a positive trend indicates lowering comparative deficit ratios). Hence, a positive trend coefficient indicates improving comparative fiscal stance. The numbers in parentheses for Tables 6.1 and 6.2 indicate the test statistic associated with the coefficient estimate and are to be compared with the critical values at the bottom of the table. ** indicates 95%; * indicates 90% significance. Significance levels of breaks are determined using the critical values in Andrews and Ploberger (1994).

6.5.1 Fiscal discipline: budget deficit results

Table 6.1 examines whether the mean and trend coefficients of equation (6.4) are (i) statistically different from zero, implying that there is a positive or negative trend in budget deficits and (ii) have opposite signs, indicating that countries with higher (or more negative) deficits approach the benchmark or each other. Initially, one becomes aware of the fact that the coefficients are quite often not significant, which means that these countries are not showing a significant change in their deficit in one particular direction. Although the lack of statistical significance in the deficit analysis precludes an unambiguous judgement (see also Figure 6.1), the following pattern emerges for the Maastricht benchmark: most of the countries start with surplus or low deficit ratios and some of them reduce the surplus during the pre-break period; in fact only three countries with statistically significant surplus coefficients proceeded with a reduction in surplus, while four of them experienced deepening in their deficits. In the post-break period, the statistically insignificant coefficients preclude a qualified judgement, but Estonia, Latvia, Malta and the Slovak Republic show more fiscal discipline than the others, who maintain the status quo. A strict pattern does not emerge as a result of the estimations, but one notices that countries with large deficits tend to act more prudently (except the Czech Republic) than the others.

The deficit-to-GDP ratio with respect to the benchmark of the core shows in essence a clearer picture than that of the 3 per cent benchmark (Table 6.1). The large negative post-break mean values (μ_2) indicate less fiscal prudence than the EU core countries. Observing that most of these countries start out with much better fiscal positions compared to the core implies that their attention was focused elsewhere. Despite this fact, only a few of the new members try to improve their fiscal position in the post-break period. This finding is confirmed when we compare the new members with the periphery. The drastic difference in fiscal position between the new members and the periphery at the beginning of the sample period had not only been closed in all countries, but it reverses direction in some countries, including the Slovak Republic, later on. In short, the difference between the new members and the core and periphery regressions point towards more fiscal indiscipline in the EU-15 than among the ten new members.

Inspecting Figure 6.2a for sigma-convergence, one notices that the older EU members are generally in conjunction with one another while the 10 new members show a very slow decline in their cross-sectional standard deviation. Accounting for the average mean deficit of each group (Figure 6.2b) confirms this finding with the deficit condition of

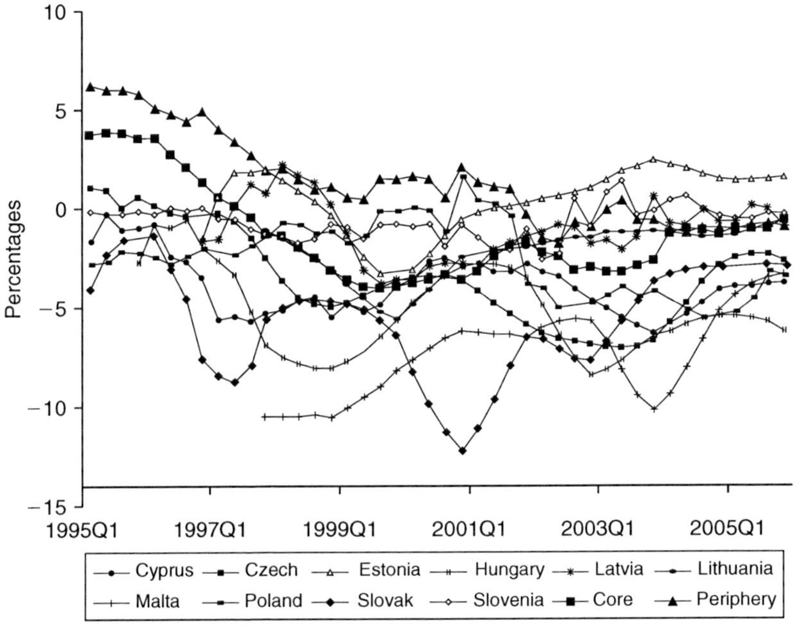

Figure 6.1 Budget deficit to GDP ratios

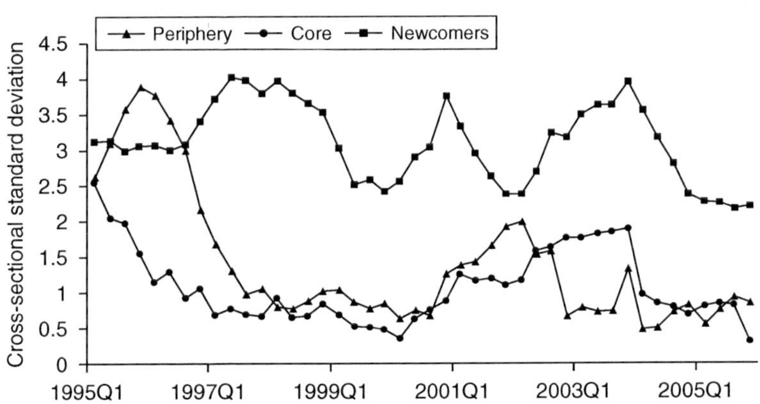

Figure 6.2a Deficit (sigma)-convergence

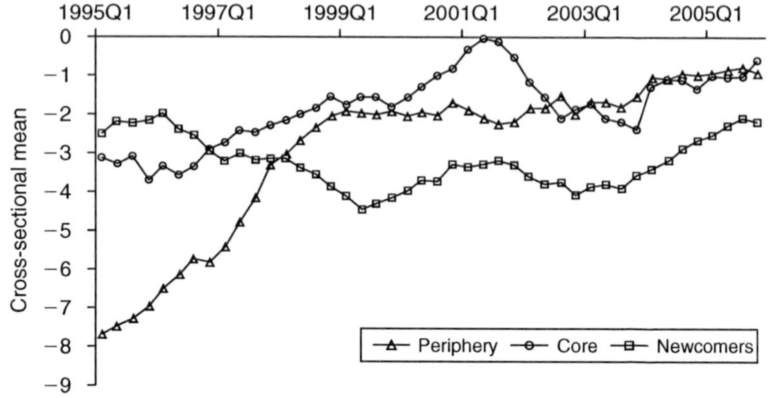

Figure 6.2b Average deficit levels

the new members exhibiting an inferior trend when compared to the older members. The periphery countries seem to be the best performers with their constant decline in the mean and standard deviation of the deficit ratio while the core countries seem to lose focus after 2001. The mean ratio of the newcomers shows no improvement (or decline) with a flat trend during the period under research. The old members seem to be converging to a higher than desired equilibrium. From this perspective, convergence of the newcomers in terms of deficit-to-GDP ratio towards either the core or the periphery looks like a dubious enterprise, casting doubts on the stability of the Eurozone.

6.5.2 Fiscal discipline: debt results

Convergence of the general government debt-to-GDP ratio towards the Maastricht benchmark of 60 per cent as well as towards the core and periphery is displayed in Table 6.2 and Figure 6.3, in a similar fashion as with the budget deficit. The key dependent variable in Table 6.2 is the consolidated debt-to-GDP ratio in a new member country minus the 60 per cent benchmark. A positive number indicates a debt ratio below 60 per cent since the negative 60 per cent benchmark subtracted from a less negative debt ratio yields positive values; thus, for example, a mean value of 40 means a 20 per cent debt-to-GDP ratio. All countries, except Hungary, start with a debt-to-GDP ratio lower than the Maastricht benchmark of 60 per cent since the mean coefficients are all positive. The few positive trend coefficients observed in the pre-break period either reverse direction or lose significance in the post-break period, suggesting that the new member countries are increasing their debt-to-GDP ratio or showing

Table 6.2 Consolidated debt/GDP convergence to Maastricht benchmark as well as the core and the periphery

	PSW test with endogenous break selection (regression of y_t with J_T correction)				
Countries	μ_1	δ_1	μ_2	δ_2	**Break**
Cyp – bench.	8.81**(3.99)	−0.46**(−2.04)	6.51**(3.99)	−0.75**(−7.61)	1998Q4
Cyp – core	4.05**(1.77)	−0.64**(−2.70)	−2.57(−1.52)	−0.70**(−6.82)	1998Q4
Cyp – perip.	32.61**(17.72)	−0.83**(−8.83)	−0.26(−0.08)	0.09(0.18)	2003Q1
Cze – bench.	51.50**(12.45)	−0.26(−1.33)	25.19**(2.66)	0.27(0.14)	2003Q4**
Cze – core	46.11**(12.45)	−0.38**(−2.17)	18.08**(2.13)	0.23(0.13)	2003Q4**
Cze – perip.	67.59**(10.66)	0.69(0.55)	73.55**(26.56)	−1.00**(−7.66)	1996Q4
Est – bench.	50.32**(92.52)	0.19**(5.76)	53.89**(73.38)	0.06(0.83)	2001Q4**
Est – core	45.69**(58.02)	0.00(0.08)	44.50**(44.10)	0.21**(2.17)	2001Q3
Est – perip.	74.86**(42.90)	−0.33**(−4.03)	67.43**(16.88)	−0.06(−0.08)	2003Q4
Hun – bench.	−18.65**(−3.87)	1.05**(3.11)	8.53(1.60)	−0.44(−1.00)	2000Q4*
Hun – core	−27.21**(−4.65)	1.38*(1.60)	−6.20**(−1.92)	0.05(0.28)	1997Q3*
Hun – perip.	−0.21(−0.04)	**1.51****(2.46)	16.50**(5.41)	−0.09(−0.56)	1998Q1*
Lat – bench.	49.12**(50.80)	0.00(0.03)	45.83**(60.75)	0.02(0.45)	1999Q1
Lat – core	44.84**(50.76)	−0.24**(−3.30)	35.41**(44.20)	0.18**(3.14)	1999Q4**
Lat – perip.	73.88**(28.88)	−0.60**(−4.94)	58.09**(9.92)	0.22(0.19)	2003Q4*
Lit – bench.	36.68**(23.38)	0.01(0.05)	26.96**(19.90)	0.58**(6.34)	1999Q3**
Lit – core	31.74**(17.77)	−0.14(−0.89)	17.10**(11.09)	0.69**(6.62)	1999Q3**
Lit – perip.	62.12**(17.18)	−0.63**(−2.09)	38.29**(11.67)	0.62**(2.70)	1999Q4**

(continued)

Table 6.2 (*Continued*)

Countries	PSW test with endogenous break selection (regression of y_t with J_T correction)				Break
	μ_1	δ_1	μ_2	δ_2	
Mal – bench.	24.97**(11.23)	−1.19**(−7.65)	1.92(0.79)	−1.05**(−5.12)	2000Q4
Mal – core	20.31**(9.98)	−1.37**(−9.63)	−8.20**(−3.65)	−0.87**(−4.67)	2000Q4
Mal – perip.	49.12**(11.76)	−1.60**(−3.48)	19.16**(6.54)	−0.88**(−5.18)	1998Q3
Pol – bench.	8.93**(3.43)	0.81**(3.00)	20.82**(10.81)	−0.23**(−1.95)	1998Q4**
Pol – core	4.36**(3.35)	0.60**(4.74)	11.29**(11.11)	−0.16**(−2.48)	1999Q1*
Pol – perip.	33.28**(11.91)	0.33(1.16)	33.51**(16.20)	−0.29**(−2.32)	1998Q4
Slov – bench.	40.38**(17.98)	−0.16(−1.02)	23.95**(9.67)	−0.15(−0.74)	2000Q4
Slov – core	35.72**(15.84)	−0.34**(−2.16)	13.83**(5.56)	0.02(0.10)	2000Q4
Slov – perip.	65.28**(22.05)	−0.72**(−3.48)	34.57**(10.59)	−0.09(−0.33)	2000Q4*
Slovak – bench.	48.68**(54.04)	−0.77**(−9.74)	36.03**(46.32)	−0.22**(−4.26)	1999Q3**
Slovak – core	43.92**(33.29)	−0.94**(−7.73)	26.52**(24.48)	−0.13*(−1.80)	1999Q2**
Slovak – perip.	73.25**(40.31)	−1.28**(−8.45)	47.10**(28.58)	−0.21**(−1.86)	1999Q4**
Crit. val.					
5%	1.51	1.88	1.92	1.81	
10%	1.21	1.58	1.65	1.54	

Notes: Values are in percentages. The dependent variable for the benchmark is the consolidated debt to GDP ratio in country *i* minus the 60% benchmark (a positive number indicates a debt ratio below 60% since the negative 60% benchmark subtracted from a less negative debt ratio yields positive values). For the core (periphery), it is the consolidated debt to GDP ratio in country *i* minus the core (periphery) debt ratio (hence a negative number indicates a debt ratio worse than that of the core (periphery) and a positive trend indicates lowering comparative debt ratios). Therefore, a positive trend coefficient indicates improving comparative debt position. (See also note to previous table.) **indicates 95%; * indicates 90% significance. Significance levels of breaks are determined using the critical values in Andrews and Ploberger (1994).

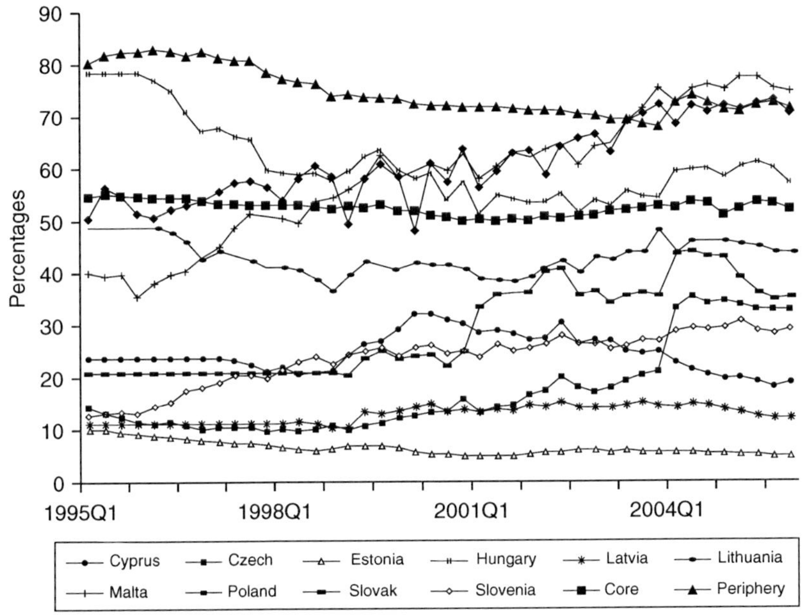

Figure 6.3 Debt-to-GDP ratio

lack of fiscal discipline. Malta and the Czech Republic stand out with the large deterioration of their indebtedness towards the benchmark.

A similar tendency and a clearer picture are observed when the 60 per cent benchmark is replaced by the actual debt-to-GDP ratio in the core and the periphery. Again the big debt position difference at the beginning of the sample period narrows down in the second half due to the fiscal indiscipline of the new members. Only Hungary stands out as consistently prudent among the new members. The other more disciplined countries, Estonia and Poland, seem to adopt fiscal discipline post- and pre-2000, respectively, displaying a less consistent picture than Hungary. A quick glance at Figure 6.3 shows a slight decline in the core's debt situation, while the high debt of the periphery keeps the new members within comparatively acceptable debt positions. However, we can hardly call it a success story because their indebtedness increases in general and its dynamics are discomforting.

Both the results from Table 6.2 and the sigma-convergence results in Figure 6.4a support the theoretical argument presented in Restoy (1996), as we observe that the 10 new members outperformed the

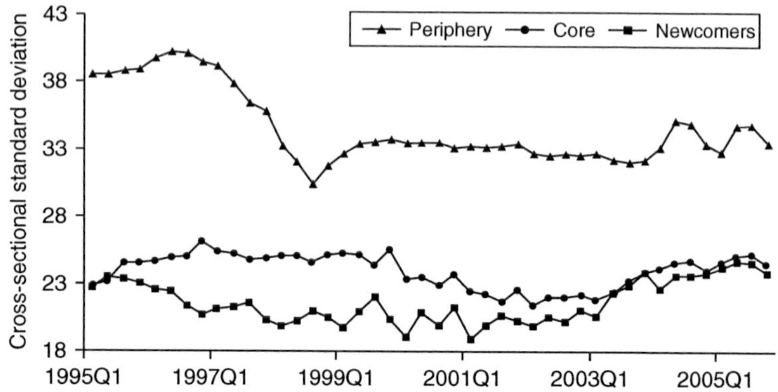

Figure 6.4a Debt (sigma)- convergence

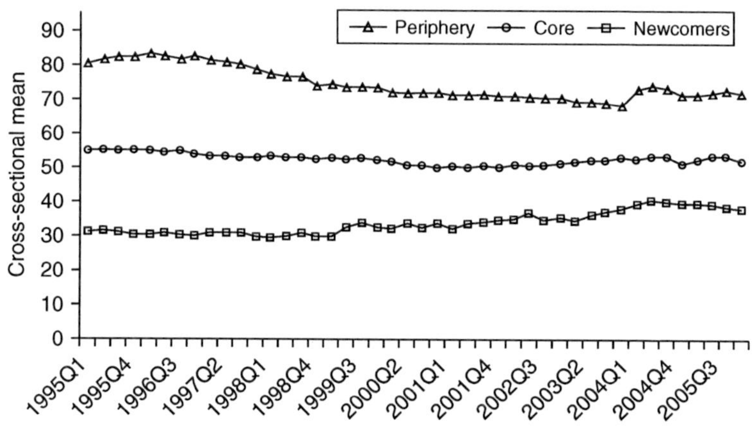

Figure 6.4b Average debt levels

EU-15, especially before 2001. Afterwards, their fiscal discipline loses some of its momentum as the variation of the debt positions of the 10 new members evolves at par with the core after 2003. Fiscal discipline of the periphery starts to improve after 1996 but loses its original dynamics in 1998, further worsening in the more recent period. The average debt ratios in Figure 6.4b confirm this finding since the periphery as well as the core shows worse debt positions than the newcomers. On the other hand, its dynamics point at slowly diminishing debt position over time. The results of the sigma-convergence thus support better performance by the new members than the older ones but this finding is confronted with the worsening dynamics of their debt position.

6.5.3 Recommendations for achieving fiscal discipline

Our results indicate that the ongoing reform of the public finance systems in the EU-25 as a whole is an agenda that is not to be underestimated. In the new EU member states, this issue is even more important, because neglect of public finance reforms and lack of fiscal discipline could lead to serious consequences for these countries, well beyond the satisfaction of the Maastricht criteria and the consideration of entry into the Eurozone.

Another implication is for the need for the authorities in the new EU and old core members to better coordinate fiscal and monetary policies to improve fiscal discipline.[17] Such a claim is supported by our empirical evidence and is consistent with Gleich (2003) who shows that countries with institutional structures that are more conducive to strengthening coordination and cooperation in budget decision-making have been associated with lower budget deficits and reduced debt levels. Consequently, our results are consistent with the notion that countries with weak budget institutions tend to have a lower level of fiscal discipline. Hence, further and more serious reforms in the areas of budget preparation and legislation are necessary to improve fiscal discipline.

Another recommendation is that policymakers need to design policies to improve fiscal consolidation.[18] It is widely observed in the literature that most EU countries have been lowering both direct and indirect taxes and, although such trends are sensitive to the economic cycles experienced by the countries, lowering taxes is consistent with the recommendations of many observers (for example, von Hagen et al., 2002).

EU policymakers may also consider adopting fiscal policy rules, rather than a counter-cyclical fiscal policy.[19] Some countries, such as Poland and the Netherlands, have already introduced fiscal rules into the laws and constitutions (Tanzi, 2005). Of course, the fact that the member states have different fiscal positions certainly creates implementation problems, at least initially. Tanzi (2005, p. 63) suggests that 'flexibility is required as to the time needed to conform to the rule, but the rule should not be relaxed to the point of making sinning more acceptable for everyone'.

6.6 Conclusions

Our study examines the fiscal discipline of the new EU members with respect to EU-15, using alternative measures of fiscal convergence and employing vastly flexible tests of convergence, allowing for structural breaks, and hence providing enhanced inference. We observe an extent of heterogeneity in fiscal convergence and a lack of discipline in general, raising warning signals for the old and new members. However, the findings comparing the difference between the new members and the core and periphery regressions point towards more fiscal indiscipline in EU-15 than among the 10 new members, especially prior to their joining the EU in 2004. However, the newcomers lose their momentum in fiscal discipline after 2004. This finding may raise concerns about the ability of a monetary union to provide fiscal discipline for its new members.

Notes

1. See, for example, Glick and Hutchison (1993), Hutchison and Kletzer (1995) and Watson (1997).
2. Influential studies include, among others, Buiter et al. (1993), Corsetti and Roubini (1995) and Holzmann et al. (1996).
3. Buti and Giudice (2002), Orban and Szapary (2004), Tanzi (2004), Eichengreen (2005), Eijffinger (2005), Feldstein (2005) and Schuknecht (2005).
4. Eight were Central and Eastern European countries (hereafter the CEE8), namely the Czech Republic, Estonia, Hungary, Latvia, Lithuania, Poland, the Slovak Republic and Slovenia. The other new members were Cyprus and Malta.
5. Berger et al. (2004) point out that deteriorating fiscal performance, especially in Central European countries, may constrain these members from satisfying the Maastricht criteria because continuing large fiscal deficits can create inflationary pressures. Further arguments in the same spirit are voiced by De Grauwe and Schnabl (2004). Buiter and Sibert (2006, p. 18) state that 'it is frequently believed that a country's actual or threatened insolvency might jeopardize the entire Eurozone financial system or destabilize common currency by forcing the European Central Bank into a bail-out'.
6. In a similar spirit in a study based on data from the US states, Fatás and Mihov (2004) state that 'fiscal policy is a significant source of business cycle volatility among the U.S. states, and, as a result, constraints on politicians lead to less volatile economic fluctuations'.
7. Until recently, the cross-sectional tests used in analysing absolute convergence were criticized for their rejection of the null hypothesis of no convergence (Bernard and Durlauf, 1996), shifting the emphasis to conditional and stochastic convergence. However, the need to meet the EU criteria for full EMU membership has regenerated interest in absolute convergence.
8. See Dibooglu and Kutan (2001), Fidrmuc and Tichit (2004), and Kočenda (2005), among others. Further, it has to be recognized that the transition alone by definition represented a massive structural shift.
9. Buiter and Grafe (2004) find the existing criteria to be seriously flawed and propose an alternative rule, the Permanent Balance Rule, based on a strong form of tax smoothing.
10. Fiscal prudence is the key issue since governments tend towards deficits even under the Growth and Stability Pact. This behaviour is in accordance with

classical arguments by Kydland and Prescott (1977) or Buchanan and Wagner (1977).

11. For more recent discussions, see Taylor (1999) and de la Fuente (2002).
12. When u_t is $I(1)$, the estimate of β obtained from the above regression is not related to the true trend, and information on β must be obtained from the estimate of the intercept in the autoregressive representation of y_t.
13. See Vogelsang (1998) for further test statistics and a deeper elaboration of the tests.
14. Sigma-convergence occurs when the cross-sectional standard deviation of a variable for a group of economies decreases in time.
15. The determination of the structural break date in Uctum et al. (2006) and in this chapter is quite similar.
16. In some cases, quadratic interpolation of annual data was necessary to fill some missing data points because the empirical methodology we use relies on uninterrupted data. Quadratic interpolation of annual data was used for debt in the case of Austria, Estonia, France, Germany and the Netherlands, and for the Portuguese deficit and the second half of the Greek deficit.
17. See Dixit (2001) and Dixit and Lambertini (2001) for a review of the literature on the interaction of monetary and fiscal policies in a monetary union. For supporting empirical evidence, see Darnaut and Kutos (2005).
18. Daviddi and Ilzkovitz (1997) provide a discussion of this and other related issues.
19. For an important early treatment of this issue, see Kydland and Prescott (1977).

References

Andrews, Donald W. K. and Werner Ploberger (1994). 'Optimal Tests when a Nuisance Parameter is Present only under the Alternative', *Econometrica*, 62(6): 1383–414.

Arestis, Philip, Mosahid Khan and Kul B. Luintel (2002). 'Fiscal Deficits in Monetary Unions: a Comparison of EMU and United States', *Eastern Economic Journal*, 28(1): 89–103.

Bai, Jushan and Pierre Perron (1998). 'Estimating and Testing Linear Models with Multiple Structural Changes', *Econometrica*, 66: 47–78.

Berger, Helge, George Kopits and István Szekély (2004). 'Fiscal Indulgence in Central Europe: Loss of the External Anchor?' IMF Working Paper WP 04/62.

Bernard, Andrew B. and Steven N. Durlauf (1996). 'Interpreting Tests of the Convergence Hypothesis', *Journal of Econometrics*, 71: 161–73.

Buchanan, J.M. and R.F. Wagner (1977). *Democracy in Deficit: the Political Legacy of Lord Keynes*, New York: Academic Press.

Buiter, Willem H. (2004). 'The Purgatory and Beyond: When and How Should the Accession Countries from Central and Eastern Europe Become Full Members of EMU?' CEPR Discussion Paper No. 4342.

Buiter, Willem H. and Clemens Grafe (2002). 'Anchor, Float or Abandon Ship: Exchange Rate Regimes for Accession Countries', *Banca Nazionale del Lavoro Quarterly Review*, 221: 1–32.

Buiter, Willem H. and Clemens Grafe (2004). 'Patching up the Pact: Suggestions for Enhancing Fiscal Sustainability and Macroeconomic Stability in an Enlarged European Union', *Economics of Transition*, 12(1): 67–102.
Buiter, Willem H. and Anne C. Sibert (2006). 'Eurozone Entry of New EU Member States from Central Europe', *Development and Transition*, 04/2006, 16–19.
Buiter, Willem H., Giancarlo Corsetti and Nouriel Roubini (1993). 'Excessive Deficits: Sense and Nonsense in the Treaty of Maastricht', *Economic Policy*, 8(16): 57–100.
Buti, Marco and Gabriele Giudice (2002). 'Maastricht's Fiscal Rules at Ten: an Assessment', *Journal of Common Market Studies*, 40(5): 823–48.
Carlino, G.A. and L.O. Mills (1993). 'Are US Regional Incomes Converging?' *Journal of Monetary Economics*, 32: 335–46.
Corsetti, Giancarlo and Nouriel Roubini (1995). 'Political Biases in Fiscal Policy: Reconsidering the Case for the Maastricht Fiscal Criteria', in B. Eichengreen, J. Frieden and J. von Hagen (eds), *Monetary and Fiscal Policy in an Integrated Europe*, European and Transatlantic Studies, London: Springer, pp. 118–37.
Darnaut, Nathalie and Paul Kutos (2005). 'Poland's Policy Mix: Fiscal or Monetary Leadership', *ECFIN Country Focus*, 2(1): 1–6.
Darvas, Zsolt, Andrew K. Rose and György Szapáry (2005). 'Fiscal Divergence and Business Cycles Synchronization: Irresponsibility is Idiosyncratic', NBER Working Paper No. 11580.
Daviddi, Renzo and Fabienne Ilzkovitz (1997). 'The Eastern Enlargement of the European Union: Major Challenges for Macro-economic Policies and Institutions of Central and East European Countries', *European Economic Review*, 41: 671–80.
de Grauwe, P. and G. Schnabl (2004). 'Nominal versus Real Convergence with Respect to EMU Accession. How to Cope with the Balassa-Samuelson Dilemma', European University Institute Discussion Paper RSCAS No. 2004/20.
de la Fuente, Angel (2002). 'On the Sources of Convergence: a Close Look at the Spanish Regions', *European Economic Review*, 46: 569–99.
Dibooglu, Selahattin and Ali M. Kutan (20010. 'Sources of Real Exchange Rate Fluctuations in Transition Economies: the Case of Poland and Hungary', *Journal of Comparative Economics*, 29: 257–75.
Dixit, Avinash (2001). 'Games of Monetary and Fiscal Interactions in the EMU', *European Economic Review*, 45: 589–613.
Dixit, Avinash and Luisa Lambertini (2001). 'Monetary and Fiscal Policy Interactions and Commitment versus Discretion in a Monetary Union', *European Economic Review*, 45: 977–87.
Eichengreen, Barry (2005). 'Europe, the Euro and the ECB: Monetary Success, Fiscal Failure', *Journal of Policy Modeling*, 27(4): 427–39.
Eijffinger, Sylvester C.W. (2005). 'On a Reformed Stability and Growth Pact', *Intereconomics/Review of European Economic Policy*, 40(3): 141–7.
Faini, Riccardo (2006). 'Fiscal Policy and Interest Rates in Europe', *Economic Policy*, 21(47): 443–89
Fatás, Antonio and Ilian Mihov (2003). 'The Case for Restricting Fiscal Policy Discretion', *Quarterly Journal of Economics*, 118(4): 1419–47.
Fatás, Antonio and Ilian Mihov (2004). 'The Macroeconomic Effects of Fiscal Rules in the US States', CEPR Discussion Paper No. 4372.

Feldstein, Martin (2005). 'The Euro and the Stability Pact', *Journal of Policy Modeling*, 27(4): 421–6.

Fidrmuc, Jan and Ariane Tichit (2004). 'Mind the Break! Accounting for Changing Patterns of Growth during Transition', William Davidson Institute Working Paper No 643.

Gleich, H. (2003). 'Budget Institutions and Fiscal Performance in Central and Eastern European Countries', European Central Bank Working Paper No. 215.

Glick, Reuven and Michael Hutchison (1993). 'Fiscal Policy in Monetary Unions: Implications for Europe', *Open Economies Review*, 4(1): 39–65.

Holzmann, Robert, Yves Herve and Roland Demmel (1996). 'The Maastricht Fiscal Criteria: Required but Ineffective?' *Empirica*, 23(1): 25–58.

Hutchison, Michael M. and Kenneth M. Kletzer (1995). 'Fiscal Convergence Criteria, Factor Mobility, and Credibility in Transition to Monetary Union in Europe', in Eichengreen, Frieden, and von Hagen (eds), *Monetary and Fiscal Policy in an Integrated Europe*, European and Transatlantic Studies, London: Springer, pp. 138–65.

Kočenda, Evžen (2005). 'Beware of Breaks in Exchange Rates: Evidence from European Transition Countries', *Economic Systems*, 29(3): 307–24.

Kydland, F.E. and E.C. Prescott (1977). 'Rules Rather than Discretion: the Inconsistency of Optimal Plans', *Journal of Political Economy*, 85(3): 473–92.

McKinnon, Ronald I. (1999). 'Toward Virtual Exchange-Rate Stability in Western and Eastern Europe with the Advent of EMU', in Mario I. Blejer and Marko Skreb (eds), *Balance of Payments, Exchange Rates, and Competitiveness in Transition Economies*, Boston: Kluwer, pp. 131–58.

Mundell, Robert (1961). 'A Theory of Optimum Currency Area', *American Economic Review*, 51: 657–65.

Onorante, Luca (2004). 'Fiscal Convergence before Entering EMU', in K. Liebscher et al. (eds), *The Economic Potential of a Larger Europe*, Cheltenham, UK and Northampton, MA: Edward Elgar, pp. 245–59.

Orban, Gabor and Gyorgy Szapary (2004). 'The Stability and Growth Pact from the Perspective of the New Member States', *Journal of Policy Modeling*, 26(7): 839–64.

Park, J.Y. and B. Choi (1988). 'A New Approach to Testing for a Unit Root', Working Paper No. 88–23, Department of Economics, Cornell University.

Quah, D.T. (1996). 'Empirics for Economic Growth and Convergence', *European Economic Review*, 40(6): 1353–75.

Salvatore, Dominick (2004). 'Restructuring and Euroization in Accession Countries', *Journal of Policy Modeling*, 26: 889–902.

Sanz, Ismael and Francisco J. Velázquez (2003). 'Has the European Integration Approximated the Composition of Government Expenditures? A Comparative Analysis between the EU and Non-EU Countries of the OECD', Research Paper 2003/09, Leverhulme Centre for Research on Globalization and Economic Policy, University of Nottingham.

Schuknecht, Ludger (2005). 'Stability and Growth Pact: Issues and Lessons from Political Economy', *International Economics and Economic Policy*, 2(1): 65–89.

Tanzi, Vito (2004). 'The Stability and Growth Pact: its Role and Future', *Cato Journal*, 24(1–2): 57–69.

Tanzi, Vito (2005). 'Fiscal Policy and Fiscal Rules in the European Union', *CESIfo Forum*, 3: 57–64.

Taylor, Alan M. (1999). 'Sources of Convergence in the Late Nineteenth Century', *European Economic Review*, 43: 1621–45.

Uctum, Merih and Michael Wickens (2000). 'Debt and Deficit Ceilings, and Sustainability of Fiscal Policies: an Intertemporal Analysis', *Oxford Bulletin of Economics and Statistics*, 62(2): 197–222.

Uctum, Merih, Thom Thurston and Remzi Uctum (2006). 'Public Debt, the Unit Root Hypothesis and Structural Breaks: a Multi-Country Analysis', *Economica*, 73(289): 129–56.

Vogelsang, T.J. (1998). 'Trend Function Hypothesis Testing in the Presence of Serial Correlation', *Econometrica*, 66: 123–48.

Vogelsang, T.J. (1999). 'Testing for a Shift in Trend when Serial Correlation is of Unknown Form', Tinbergen Institute Discussion Paper No. 99-016/4 (last version: Cornell Department of Economics, 2001).

von Hagen, Jürgen, Andrew Hughes Hallett and Rolf Strauch (2002). 'Budgetary Consolidation in Europe: Quality, Economic Conditions, and Persistence', *Journal of the Japanese and International Economies*, 16: 512–35.

Watson, Alison M.S. (1997). *Aspects of European Monetary Integration: the Politics of Convergence*, New York: St Martin's Press; London: Macmillan Press.

7

Business Cycles Similarity and EMU Enlargement: the Concordance Index for Central and Eastern European Countries

Petr Rozmahel

7.1 Introduction

The Central and Eastern European Countries (CEECs) that acceded to the European Union in 2004 are facing the question of appropriate timing for joining the Eurozone. The adoption of the euro is an integral and also obligatory strand of Economic and Monetary Union membership. Joining the Eurozone is conditional on fulfilling the Maastricht criteria assessing the level of nominal convergence. Moreover, the preparedness of the candidate countries to adopt the euro is assessed by alternative measures.

Any discussion on the suitable moment for the adoption of the euro involves a great deal of empirical study, focusing on the assessment of various indicators of the structural and cyclical similarities between the candidate and member economies. A vast majority of such academic studies and convergence reports are based on the theoretical and methodological foundations of the theory of optimum currency areas (OCA). This theory was proposed by the Nobel Laureate Robert Mundell in his classic article of 1961. The characteristics of optimum currency areas, which determine the effective formation of a common currency area, are classified and characterized in that paper. Besides Mundell, the list of original OCA characteristics is defined by the other authors and pioneers of this theory such as McKinnon (1963), Kenen (1969) or Ingram (1962). The criteria of labour mobility, the openness of an economy, commodity diversification of production and consumption, fiscal integration, similarity in inflation rates and the integration of financial markets are all included on the classical OCA list. A later approach to

OCA theory called the 'New Optimum Currency Areas Theory' (Mongelli, 2002) introduces other characteristics, among them business cycles similarity, and the asymmetry or symmetry of shocks occurring within the acceding economies.

The similarity of business cycles is one of the characteristics defined in the frame of the new OCA theory. From the perspective of OCA theory synchronized business cycles[1] minimize the risk of the occurrence of asymmetric shocks that do not affect the member countries equally. Similar cycles also reduce the necessity for national autonomous monetary policies.

The current approach to the measurement of the similarity of business cycles mainly uses the correlation analysis method. Individual analytical reports assessing the correlation of the cycles usually differ only in selection of the input data and the way in which data are stylized (the filtering technique). However, these methods actually measure the correlation of the cyclical path of the selected indicator (gross domestic product, industrial production and so on) approximating the overall economic activity of a nation. The correlation method does not include identification of the business cycle itself. Such identification would consist of the indication of turning points and different phases of a cycle.

The main aim of this chapter is to assess the level of similarity of business cycles in the economies of the selected Central and Eastern European countries and the Eurozone member states by the application of the concordance index technique. The chapter is composed of four main parts. In Section 7.2, the data and methodology are explained. Section 7.3 includes the application of the traditional correlation analysis approach on a sample of selected candidate and member countries. The concordance index technique is applied in Section 7.4, and Section 7.5 concludes.

7.2 Data and methodology

The aim of the chapter is to evaluate the similarity between actual business cycles in the Eurozone member states and the Central and Eastern European countries applying for full membership of EMU. Two different indicators of aggregate economic activity approximating the business cycles – gross domestic product (GDP) and the industrial production index (IP) – are used for the measurement of business cycles similarity.

Two alternative approaches are also applied to the identification of business cycles. These approaches are currently considered to be the predominant identification techniques in economic theory. The classical approach defines business cycles as a cyclical fluctuation covering the decline and growth in an absolute level of a nation's aggregate economic activity (Burns and Mitchell, 1946). The growth cycle approach is an alternative to the classical cycle. The growth (deviation) cycle specifies business cycles as cyclical fluctuations in the cyclical component of an economic variable around its trend (Lucas, 1977). The later approach therefore needs the application of selected time series detrending techniques. Growth cycles are often identified in recent economic literature, together with subsequent correlation analysis.

The alternative methods of measuring the similarity of business cycles are used in the analytical part of the chapter below. Traditional correlation analysis and the concordance index technique, including the identification of the turning points and individual phases of the cycle, were applied to assess the current similarity of the sample.

Input data include seasonally adjusted time series of quarterly GDP and the monthly IP index for the selected EMU member and candidate countries. Eurostat and International Monetary Fund (IMF) international financial statistics (IFS) were the key data sources.[2] The selection of candidate countries – Hungary, Poland, Slovakia and the Czech Republic – was made with reference to earlier intensive economic and political relations as well as to a similar position at the beginning of the transformation period in the 1990s. Slovenia is also a part of the analysis. Although Slovenia has only been a member of the Eurozone since 2007, it was a candidate country during the analysed time period. Selected Eurozone members include the dominant economies of Germany and France and peripheral economies with relatively lower GDP per capita, such as Spain, Portugal and Greece. The sample of EMU member countries finally includes Austria, which is structurally similar to the majority of selected CEECs, and the dynamically growing Ireland. The economic data of the Eurozone (average), United States and Russia were also analysed as alternative benchmarks.

The input data comprise the natural logarithms of indicators, which are subsequently stylized by the first order differences procedure, which is partially in line with the presumptions of the classical approach to business cycle identification. The data were also detrended by the Hodrick-Prescott Filter (HP) applying parameters $\lambda = 1600$ for quarterly data and $\lambda = 14\,400$ for monthly data.[3] The final detrending technique was the Baxter-King band-pass filter (BK) that passes through components of the time series with periodic fluctuations between 6 and 32 quarters, while removing components at higher and lower frequencies.[4] The MATLAB program was used for both filter calculations. The similarity of results reached in the case of both input indicators as well as the application of described methods increases the robustness of the conclusions. Potential dissimilarities in results, when different methods are applied to the same data, may indicate the influence of alternative business cycles identification and detrending methods on the final shape and character of identified cycles.

7.3 The traditional approach: correlation of business cycles

The resultant correlation coefficients[5] indicate the intensity of association between the aggregate activity indicators time series of the compared economies within a whole analysed time period. Values in Table 7.1 characterize cross-correlation between all researched countries and describe the actual similarity of the business cycles. Thus the results in the table describe the model situation of cycles similarity assessment in the case of Eurozone enlargement at the end of 2004 and the beginning of 2005. The north-eastern part of the table indicates cross-correlation coefficients of quarterly GDP series stylized by the first order differences procedure (FOD). The south-western part of the table shows cross-correlation of the growth cycles of the same indicator stylized by the Hodrick-Prescott Filter ($\lambda = 1600$). The Baxter-King band-pass filtering technique was not applied because of the relatively short available time series.

The values of cross-correlation in Table 7.1 indicate very low or negative association of the Czech economy business cycle with the Eurozone member economies as well as with the candidate countries, even with structurally similar Hungary. Relatively high values of correlation coefficients illustrate mutual performing structural similarity among the EMU member countries. This similarity increases when the non-linear trend component in the analysed time series is extracted. Candidate countries show low mutual correlation. Particularly Hungary and Slovenia (which became a member of the Eurozone in 2007) show very good results in business cycles similarity with Germany as well as with the Eurozone. Such identified cycles similarity increases when the non-linear trend is eliminated. A similar relation between the FOD and growth cycles is also observable in the case of the Czech Republic.

When considering the cross-correlation results of GDP time series we can generally conclude that the correlation (the direction of cycle components varying in the time series) identified by the FOD procedure was confirmed by the correlation results of the detrended time series. We can also observe prevailing higher values of correlation coefficients when the HP filter is used, which indicates the existing influence of the business

Table 7.1 Cross-correlation of GDP cycles, 1995–2004

	CR	HU	SLO	AT	GER	FRA	ESP	POR	IRL	GRE	EUR	USA
CR		−0.213	0.002	−0.104	−0.051	−0.052	−0.312	−0.166	−0.172	0.072	−0.166	−0.033
HU	−0.474		0.157	0.264	0.180	0.582	0.359	−0.007	0.227	−0.025	0.481	0.241
SLO	0.005	0.422		0.183	0.004	0.258	0.041	0.038	−0.146	−0.207	0.177	0.208
AT	−0.132	0.585	0.571		0.204	0.445	0.413	0.379	0.299	0.011	0.558	0.389
GER	0.094	0.617	0.501	0.599		0.235	0.281	0.105	0.549	−0.201	0.760	0.328
FRA	−0.168	0.825	0.548	0.811	0.754		0.314	0.093	0.330	−0.044	0.701	0.219
ESP	−0.381	0.826	0.473	0.786	0.659	0.818		0.163	0.130	0.267	0.482	0.245
POR	−0.274	0.472	0.455	0.641	0.493	0.623	0.614		0.130	0.041	0.264	−0.004
IRL	0.025	0.662	0.413	0.641	0.746	0.714	0.613	0.526		−0.172	0.499	0.110
GRE	0.104	0.061	−0.139	0.016	−0.044	0.062	0.128	0.009	−0.022		0.020	−0.067
EUR	−0.128	0.824	0.595	0.824	0.899	0.940	0.845	0.640	0.766	0.047		0.380
USA	−0.140	0.309	0.421	0.619	0.243	0.340	0.479	0.275	0.187	−0.084	0.396	

Note: Data for Ireland available for the period of 1997Q1–2004Q4.
Source: Eurostat, author's calculations.

cycle identification approach option upon the final results of measured business cycles similarity.

Using the IP index as an indicator of aggregate economic activity allows the application of the third filtering technique of the Baxter-King band-pass filter. Considering the higher number of countries taken into account in the IP cycles analysis Table 7.2 includes the cross-correlation results of all analysed countries with four selected benchmarks – Eurozone (total), Germany, the United States and Russia.[6] The United States is considered a traditional partner of all Eurozone members and an increasingly important economic partner of the candidate countries, whereas Russia was economically and politically strongly related with the CEECs.

The results of the IP cycles cross-correlation broadly confirm the tendency of generally higher values of correlation coefficients of data stylized with a non-linear filtering technique compared to classical FOD cycles observable in GDP cycle analysis. Except for Portugal (and Greece which was not included in the analysis because comparable data were not available) the Eurozone member countries show high cycles similarity with Germany and the Eurozone (total). Relatively high synchronization of business cycles among the EMU member economies is determined by a higher structural similarity and also a lower volatility in IP cycles, in comparison to currently growing and thus volatile (in terms of IP development) candidate economies catching up with the EMU standard. The influence of the trend is apparent in the case of BK filtered data. However, we must look at the data stylized by the BK filter with some criticism because the final correlation is measured on time series half the length of those used in the FOD and HP filtering procedures. Accordingly, the results are more robust in the case of the HP filter technique. However, in spite of the limitations of the BK filter, the application of the filter is useful because a potential similarity in results to the HP filtering technique increases the robustness of the final indicated direction between identified variation of business cycles.[7]

Among the candidate countries, Hungary, Slovenia (a former candidate) and (partially) Poland show the highest similarity with the IP cycles of Germany and the Eurozone (similarly in the case of GDP cycles). The Czech Republic, as well as Slovakia, also demonstrates a positive but somehow lower correlation with the Eurozone IP cycle. In the case of the Czech Republic, the indicated IP cycles similarity is higher than in the case of business cycles approximated by a GDP indicator. We cannot observe the profiling European business cycle because the values of the correlation with the US cycle in the analysed period are comparable to the

Table 7.2 Cross-correlation of IP cycles, 1993–2004

	FOD				HP 14400				BK			
	EUR	GER	USA	RUS	EUR	GER	USA	RUS	EUR	GER	USA	RUS
CR	0.210	0.114	0.078	0.007	0.427	0.365	0.167	−0.008	0.161	0.137	−0.198	0.074
HU	0.181	−0.049	0.068	0.137	0.656	0.570	0.563	0.026	0.951	0.945	0.675	0.319
POL	0.227	0.026	−0.009	0.070	0.460	0.375	0.417	0.167	0.452	0.435	0.499	0.435
SVK	0.194	0.108	−0.101	0.050	0.376	0.296	0.032	0.079	0.156	0.180	−0.380	0.011
SLO	0.135	0.209	0.106	−0.082	0.516	0.530	0.276	−0.143	0.610	0.652	−0.009	0.391
AT	0.286	0.080	0.011	−0.069	0.689	0.580	0.517	0.020	0.941	0.934	0.673	0.278
GER	0.584	1.000	0.172	0.065	0.851	1.000	0.596	0.005	0.979	1.000	0.637	0.284
FRA	0.582	0.109	−0.037	−0.069	0.846	0.642	0.498	0.051	0.935	0.881	0.567	0.394
ESP	0.531	0.200	0.179	0.055	0.739	0.555	0.552	−0.087	0.783	0.728	0.891	0.058
POR	0.176	−0.015	−0.013	0.093	−0.072	−0.172	−0.250	0.068	−0.077	−0.119	−0.505	−0.355
IRL	0.323	0.288	0.087	−0.014	0.410	0.303	0.132	−0.037	0.860	0.825	0.496	0.065
EUR	1.000	0.584	0.162	0.022	1.000	0.851	0.636	0.027	1.000	0.979	0.647	0.326
USA	−0.080	0.172	1.000	−0.022	0.636	0.596	1.000	0.124	0.647	0.637	1.000	0.012
RUS	0.047	0.065	−0.022	1.000	0.027	0.005	0.124	1.000	0.326	0.284	0.012	1.000

Source: IMF, author's calculations.

values of correlation with the Eurozone. Finally, we can state that none of the analysed Eurozone member or candidate economies show a significant synchronicity to the IP cycle of Russia. This can provide evidence of the weakening economic relations between Russia and the CEECs in comparison with the time period before economic transformation.

7.4 The concordance index technique

In comparison with the traditionally used correlation method to assess the similarity of business cycles, the concordance index technique is a rarely used approach. However, this technique is slowly being taken into account by an increasing number of authors.[8]

The concordance index represents a simple empirical measure of a similarity which '...basically indicates the proportion of time for which the countries have shared the same cycle phase' (Artis, 2003, p. 8). The resultant values range between (0;1) or (0%;100%) as an indication of the fraction (percentage) of the whole time period that the countries have gone through for the same phases of their business cycles. Although the measure was mainly applied on the classical cycles, the growth cycles application has recently become more popular. The precondition of the concordance technique is the identification of the turning points and related phases of the cycle in the analysed time period. The identified phases are modified into a binary series (1;0) subsequently. The binary indicators suggest the identified phases of recession (1) or expansion (0) in the cycle. Harding and Pagan (2002, 2006) propose a simple measure of concordance through the following equation:

$$I_{ij} = \frac{1}{T}\sum_{t=1}^{T} [S_{it}S_{jt} + (1 - S_{it})(1 - S_{jt})], \tag{7.1}$$

where $S_{it} = 1$ (for $t = 1, \ldots, T$ *and* $i = 1, \ldots, N$) indicates that the country i is experiencing a recession in the time period t, whereas $S_{it} = 0$ indicates an expansion).

Inadequate time series of the indicators available at the official statistical authorities are likely the reason for the rare use of the concordance index technique. Lower harmonization of statistical methods (collection, processing and stylizing the data) in the CEECs is also considered a problem. As far as the short available time periods are concerned, it is the classical cycles in the CEECs that are especially difficult to indicate. Artis et al. (2004) state that post-communist countries went through maximally one completed classical business cycle in the transformation

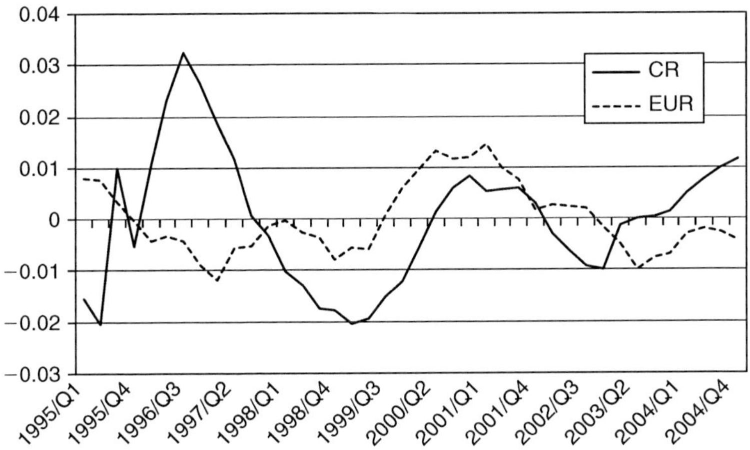

Figure 7.1 The growth cycles of the Czech Republic and the Eurozone, 1995–2004 (GDP)
Source: Eurostat, author's calculations.

period. The authors suggest analysing solely the similarity of the growth cycles with respect to the dominant growth trend within the time series. Regarding the transformation process the results become more reliable the longer the time series available from the official statistics. Accordingly, a wider use of the concordance technique, even applied on the classical cycles of the CEECs, might be expected in the future.

Figure 7.1 illustrates the growth cycles of the Eurozone and the Czech Republic identified by the Hodrick-Prescott filter. The data of natural logarithms of quarterly GDP were used for the analysis. The rules characterized in Canova (1999) were applied for the identification of the business cycles. According to these rules, the peak of the cycle is identified by two rises in the cyclical component of the time series c (identified by the Hodrick-Prescott filter) followed by at least two declines in quarterly GDP, which could be written as $c_{t+1} < c_t > c_{t-1} > c_{t-2}$. The bottom (trough) of the cycle is defined by two consecutive decreases in the cyclical component followed by its rise – written in symbols $c_{t+1} > c_t < c_{t-1} < c_{t-2}$. For the identification of peaks and troughs the condition of intersecting the trend $c_t < (>) 0$ *and* $c_{t-1} < (>) 0$ or $c_{t+1} < (>) 0$ *and* $c_t < (>) 0$ must also be fulfilled. Finally the minimum length of a cycle phase of 6 months and a total cycle of 15 months is also required.

An increasing similarity between the growth cycles of the Eurozone and the Czech Republic in the second part of the analysed time period

Table 7.3 The concordance index of the candidate and member countries of Eurozone, 1995–2004

CR	CR										
HU	0.43	HU									
SLO	0.75	0.58	SLO								
AT	0.65	0.58	0.80	AT							
GER	0.48	0.90	0.53	0.53	GER						
FRA	0.45	0.78	0.70	0.80	0.73	FRA					
ESP	0.38	0.85	0.63	0.63	0.80	0.93	ESP				
POR	0.40	0.83	0.65	0.75	0.78	0.95	0.98	POR			
IRL	0.58	0.65	0.48	0.68	0.78	0.78	0.75	0.78	IRL		
GRE	0.60	0.18	0.60	0.55	0.13	0.40	0.33	0.35	0.38	GRE	
EUR	0.43	0.75	0.68	0.78	0.70	0.98	0.90	0.93	0.94	0.43	EUR

Note: Data for Ireland available for the period of 1997Q1–2004Q4.
Source: Eurostat, author's calculations.

can be seen in Figure 7.1. Different cycles in the beginning of the period likely resulted from an intensive transformation process in the Czech economy at the beginning of the 1990s. This included price and trade liberalization, industrial restructuring, the privatization of state factories, high foreign capital inflows and so on. All these factors contributed to the formation of the Czech national economy in the transformation period and influenced trends in inflation, unemployment and GDP growth as well as affecting the business cycle. A higher similarity in the second part of the time period is in line with a continuous integration process and more intensive economic and trade links between the Czech Republic and the rest of the European Union.

The cross-concordance indices of selected candidate and member countries of the Eurozone are included in Table 7.3. The input data consisted of quarterly GDP statistically adjusted (detrended) by the Hodrick-Prescott filter. When analysing the concordance of the classical cycles Artis's (2003) precondition was confirmed. The majority of the transforming economies had not completed a business cycle in the analysed period (1995–2004). Therefore only a concordance of the growth cycles is analysed.

In the case of Germany and France, as well as the peripheral member states, Spain, Portugal and Ireland, relatively high concordance coefficients were indicated. Austria is also relatively synchronized regarding the values of concordance higher than 0.5 in connection with all EU countries. A divergent business cycle was indicated in Greece.

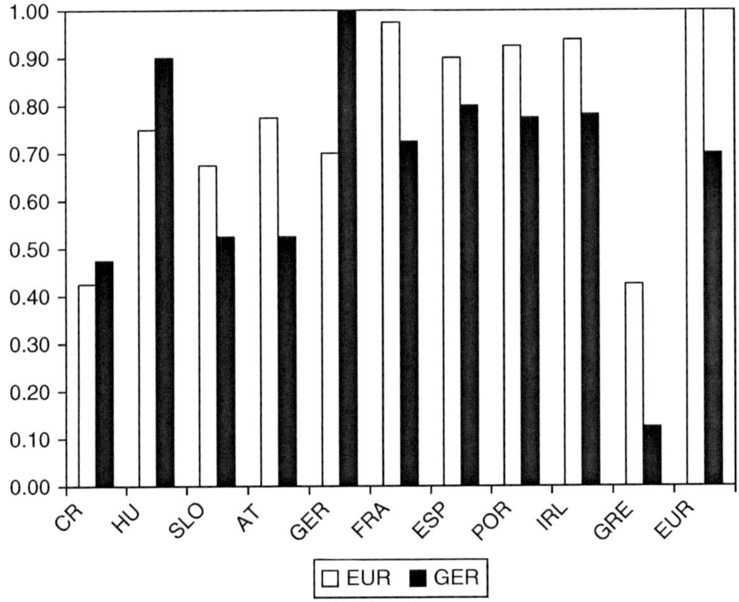

Figure 7.2 The concordance index of the selected candidate states with respect to the German and Eurozone average, 1995–2004 (GDP)
Source: Eurostat, author's calculations.

As for the acceding countries, Hungarian and Slovenian cycles could be considered highly similar in the selected period. The Slovenian results are also interesting, particularly with respect to the Slovenian adoption of the euro in January 2007, which is considered an example of successful and smooth Eurozone enlargement. The cycles of Hungary and Slovenia are also similar to the Eurozone members, whereas in the case of the Czech business cycle more divergent tendencies were indicated. The value of the concordance index is less then 50 per cent which implies that the Czech cycle has gone through different phases in comparison to members of the Eurozone. An illustrated comparison of the concordance indices of the analysed countries, with respect to the Eurozone average cycle and the German cycle, is shown in Figure 7.2.

From the OCA theory perspective the results suggest that the Czech Republic is not an appropriate candidate for joining the Eurozone at the moment. Hungary and Slovenia, on the other hand, might be considered more suitable adepts for euro adoption. The risk of the occurrence of an asymmetric shock increases in line with the long-standing divergent business cycles of the countries. Supposing that alternative mechanisms such as labour mobility or the level of fiscal integration are not sufficiently well developed, the solution would demand an autonomous monetary policy device. However, such actions will not be possible in the Eurozone under the common monetary authority, the European Central Bank.

7.5 Conclusions

The results of the cross-correlation analysis provide evidence of relatively high similarity of business cycles (particularly in the case of growth cycles) among the Eurozone member countries in comparison to the lower similarity among the candidate countries. Hungary and Slovenia (a new Eurozone member state) reach the best results in terms of business cycles synchronicity with Germany and the Eurozone. Accordingly they would currently face the lowest risk of the candidate countries analysed when joining the Eurozone. On the other hand a very low and non-significant association with the business cycle of the Eurozone was found in the cases of the Czech Republic and Slovakia. Indeed the Czech Republic demonstrates a negative correlation with some EMU member countries in the case of GDP cycles. In addition to the mentioned results there was no profiling European cycle identified in the analysis.

As for the concordance index, a relatively low level of concordance was indicated in the case of the Czech business cycle with respect to the Eurozone. The results imply that for more than half of the period under analysis the Czech economy has been experiencing a different phase of the cycle than Germany and the other member states. From the prospect of OCA theory the actual adoption of the euro in the Czech Republic would be more costly than beneficial (in 2004, the end of the input time series). Similar results can be found in Artis et al. (2004), who measured the concordance index of the business cycles approximated by the industrial production index from 1993–2002. A low level of business cycle similarity between the Czech Republic and the Eurozone, in contrast to the indicated similarity in Hungary, Poland, Estonia and the current member state of Slovenia has been found in the study. However, it should be mentioned that the IP index is a more volatile variable than GDP. In addition to that, a longer part of the input time series was influenced by the initial and intensive transformation process in the previously centrally planned economies.

Apart from business cycle similarity, evaluation of the results shows evidence of the influence of different data stylizing methods on the final identified cycle and measured correlations. The resultant correlation coefficients are absolutely higher in the case of growth cycles (using detrending techniques). In addition to this different approach to business cycle identification the appropriate detrending technique option is also a significant determinant of measured similarity. Such filters often need a relatively long input time series, which could be a problem in the case of CEE countries.

Low identified similarity in business cycles of candidate countries might not necessarily imply that such countries are not suitable for joining the Eurozone. Unlike the current Eurozone members, most of the candidate countries went through a process of wide national economic transformation, including a more recent convergence process towards the EMU economies. From that point of view it seems to be a useful research impetus to augment the analysis of actual business cycles similarities with a dynamic analysis to find out whether the candidate economies converge towards the Eurozone members. A survey in economic convergence is a necessary condition for the verification of the OCA characteristics endogeneity hypothesis in the sense of works by Frankel and Rose (1998) or Fidrmuc (2001). The OCA endogeneity hypothesis predicts the fulfilment of the OCA criteria by the candidate countries ex post – after joining the Eurozone – because of more intensive economic relations between members after monetary union enlargement.

Appendix 7.1

Table A7.1 Cross-correlation of IP cycles, 1993–2004

	CR	HU	POL	SVK	SLO	AT	GER	FRA	ESP	POR	IRL	EUR	USA
CR													
HU	0.082												
POL	0.359	0.141											
SVK	0.328	0.079	0.492										
SLO	−0.019	−0.085	0.056	0.081									
AT	0.170	0.059	0.262	0.253	0.245								
GER	0.114	−0.049	0.026	0.108	0.209	0.080							
FRA	0.005	0.162	0.126	0.137	0.083	0.279	0.109						
ESP	0.058	0.079	0.155	0.013	0.056	0.146	0.200	0.204					
POR	0.024	0.046	0.069	0.004	−0.050	0.092	−0.015	0.035	0.211				
IRL	0.050	0.021	−0.196	−0.253	−0.015	−0.101	0.288	−0.059	0.195	−0.091			
EUR	0.210	0.181	0.227	0.194	0.135	0.286	0.584	0.582	0.531	0.176	0.323		
USA	0.078	0.068	−0.009	−0.101	0.106	0.011	0.172	−0.037	0.179	−0.013	0.087	0.162	
RUS	0.007	0.137	0.070	0.050	−0.082	−0.069	0.065	−0.069	0.055	0.093	−0.014	0.022	−0.022

Source: IMF, author's calculations.

Table A7.2 Cross-correlation of IP cycles, 1993–2004 (stylized with HP filter)

CR	CR												
HU	0.208	HU											
POL	0.387	0.461	POL										
SVK	0.345	0.128	0.326	SVK									
SLO	0.291	0.297	0.222	0.238	SLO								
AT	0.228	0.479	0.351	0.249	0.430	AT							
GER	0.365	0.570	0.375	0.296	0.530	0.580	GER						
FRA	0.331	0.564	0.402	0.238	0.462	0.624	0.642	FRA					
ESP	0.231	0.489	0.353	0.149	0.365	0.485	0.555	0.652	ESP				
POR	0.005	−0.198	−0.136	0.165	−0.181	−0.049	−0.172	−0.187	−0.118	POR			
IRL	0.172	0.222	0.010	0.137	0.124	0.168	0.303	0.192	0.229	0.152	IRL		
EUR	0.427	0.656	0.460	0.376	0.516	0.689	0.851	0.846	0.739	−0.072	0.410	EUR	
USA	0.167	0.563	0.417	0.032	0.276	0.517	0.596	0.498	0.552	−0.250	0.132	0.636	USA
RUS	−0.008	0.026	0.167	0.079	−0.143	0.020	0.005	0.051	−0.087	0.068	−0.037	0.027	0.124

Source: IMF, author's calculations.

Table A7.3 Cross-correlation of IP cycles, 1993–2004 (stylized with BK filter)

	CR	HU	POL	SVK	SLO	AT	GER	FRA	ESP	POR	IRL	EUR	USA
CR													
HU	−0.107												
POL	0.510	0.316											
SVK	0.782	−0.016	0.331										
SLO	0.511	0.557	0.412	0.715									
AT	−0.130	0.983	0.246	−0.089	0.491								
GER	0.137	0.945	0.435	0.180	0.652	0.934							
FRA	0.080	0.893	0.285	−0.041	0.466	0.930	0.881						
ESP	−0.024	0.755	0.393	−0.299	0.109	0.796	0.728	0.807					
POR	−0.014	−0.084	−0.602	0.278	0.021	−0.044	−0.119	−0.012	−0.307				
IRL	−0.061	0.849	−0.008	−0.002	0.361	0.859	0.825	0.853	0.682	0.242			
EUR	0.161	0.951	0.452	0.156	0.610	0.941	0.979	0.935	0.783	−0.077	0.860		
USA	−0.198	0.675	0.499	−0.380	−0.009	0.673	0.637	0.567	0.891	−0.505	0.496	0.647	
RUS	0.074	0.319	0.435	0.011	0.391	0.278	0.284	0.394	0.058	−0.355	0.065	0.326	0.012

Source: IMF, author's calculations.

Notes

1. Similar and synchronized business cycles are considered synonymous in the chapter.
2. The basic precondition of the analysis is the maximal comparability of the researched time series. The availability of sufficiently long seasonally adjusted economic time series of CEECs from the same source was a problem. The seasonally adjusted quarterly GDP data were not surprisingly available in the cases of Poland and Slovakia from the same source (Eurostat) whereas IP was available for all the researched countries in sufficiently long time series from the IMF.
3. See Hodrick and Prescott (1980).
4. See Baxter and King (1999); BK filter application is influenced by the truncation period, which is 3 years. Accordingly application of the filter is limited by the reduction of the initial time series for 3 years at its end and beginning.
5. The resulting correlation coefficients characterize linear association between two (or more) economic time series in the range of (−1, 1). Positive correlation indicates that the researched time series vary in the same direction whereas negative correlation describes the opposite direction of variation. Low correlation coefficient values may not mean weak association. There could still be high non-linear association between variables. The precondition of sufficiently long time series is important; so is an indication of spurious correlation resulting from an existing dominant trend in the series. Both are instrumental for correct measurement among other things.
6. All cross-correlation results for all countries using three techniques of time series modification and detrending are shown in Appendix 7.1.
7. Many authors consider band-pass filters, including the Baxter-King modification, as the current dominant filtering technique, and as superior to the Hodrick-Prescott filtering technique. See Baxter and King (1999), Artis (2003).
8. For instance the concordance index measure is involved in Artis (2003) complementing the official report of HM Treasury on the UK's preparedness to adopt the euro.

References

Artis, M. (2003). 'Analysis of European and UK Business Cycles and Shocks', HM Treasury, 2003; www.hm-treasury.gov.uk.

Artis, M., M. Marcellino and T. Proietti (2004). 'Characterising the Business Cycles for Accession Countries', CEPR-EABCN Conference on Business Cycle and Acceding Countries, Vienna.

Baxter, M. and R.G. King (1999). 'Measuring Business Cycles: Approximate Band-Pass Filters for Economic Time Series', *Review of Economics and Statistics*, 81(4): 575–93.

Burns, A.F. and W.C. Mitchell (1946). 'Measuring Business Cycles', Vol. 2 of Studies in Business Cycles, New York: NBER.

Canova, F. (1999). 'Does Detrending Matter for the Determination of the Reference Cycle and the Selection of Turning Points?' *Economic Journal*, 109(452): 126–50.

Fidrmuc, J. (2001). 'The Endogeneity of Optimum Currency Area Criteria, Intraindustry Trade and EMU Enlargement', BOFIT Discussion Paper, No. 8.
Frankel, J.A. and A.K. Rose (1998) 'The Endogeneity of the Optimum Currency Area Criteria', *Economic Journal*, 108(449): 1009–25.
Harding, D. and A. Pagan (2002). 'Dissecting the Cycle: a Methodological Investigation', *Journal of Monetary Economics*, 49: 365–81.
Harding, D. and A. Pagan (2006). 'Synchronisation of Cycles', *Journal of Econometrics*, 132(1): 59–79.
Hodrick, R. and E.C. Prescott (1980). 'Post-War U.S. Business Cycles', Working Paper, Carnegie Mellon University, Pittsburgh PA.
Ingram, J.C. (1962). 'Regional Payments Mechanisms: the Case of Puerto Rico', Chapel Hill, NC: University of North Carolina Press.
Kenen, P. (1969). 'The Theory of Optimum Currency Areas: an Eclectic View', in R. Mundel and A. Swoboda (eds), *Monetary Problems in International Economy*, Chicago: University of Chicago Press.
Lucas, R.E. (1977). 'Understanding Business Cycles', in K. Brunner and A.H. Meltzer (eds), *Stabilisation Domestic and International Economy*, Carnegie-Rochester Conference Series on Public Policy 5, Amsterdam: Elsevier, pp. 7–29.
McKinnon, R. (1963). 'The Theory of Optimum Currency Area', *American Economic Review*, 4 (September): 717–29.
Mongelli, P.F. (2002). 'New Views on the Optimum Currency Area Theory: What is EMU Telling Us?' ECB Working Paper No. 138, April.
Mundell, R.A. (1961). 'A Theory of Optimum Currency Areas', *American Economic Review*, 51(4): 657–65.

8

Monetary Policy before Euro Adoption: Challenges for New EU Members

Jan Filáček, Roman Horváth and Michal Skořepa

8.1 Introduction

Several European countries currently face, or will face in the near future, the question of whether and within what time frame their economies will be capable of fulfilling the conditions for entering the euro area. In general, these conditions can be understood as attaining those parameters in various fields of economic life that will ensure successful operation of the economy in the environment of the single monetary policy of the European Central Bank (ECB). More specifically, we can comprehend the conditions for entry into the euro area within the meaning of the convergence criteria officially incorporated into the EU treaty at the Maastricht summit in 1992.

The requirement to fulfil the 'Maastricht criteria' before entering the euro area implies a number of challenges for domestic economic policy-makers in relation to the state of the economy (see Angeloni et al., 2005; Buiter and Grafe, 2002; Coricelli, 2002; de Grauwe and Schnabl, 2005; Hochreiter and Tavlas, 2004; or Dabrowski and Rostowski, 2006). This chapter focuses on the challenges ensuing from the Maastricht criteria for the monetary policies of the relevant countries' national central banks. The inflation criterion, the exchange rate criterion and the long-term nominal interest rate criterion are of primary concern to the central banks. Fulfilment of the criterion for long-term nominal interest rates, in particular, is closely linked with fulfilment of the inflation criterion and with market confidence in the country's entry into the euro area; for the sake of simplicity we will therefore consider this criterion as fulfilled.[1] Consequently, we will concentrate on the inflation and exchange rate criteria.

The particular value of this chapter compared to other studies discussing the preparations for euro area entry is its comprehensive approach, encompassing all the main issues relevant to the national central bank, including, for example, the transparency and credibility of monetary policy strategies. Our pragmatic focus on the interpretation of the criteria, and, conversely, the fact that we refrain from analysing the economic meaningfulness of their wording in the treaty, should, in our opinion, also be considered a step in the right direction. Pushing through changes in the wording of the treaty itself (and its protocols) is something that we consider politically very difficult and improbable. As a result, we regard any analysis of a potential change of the wording of the treaty as of limited use.

One of the main problems for domestic central banks is the degree of ambiguity which exists in the formulations of the inflation and exchange rate criteria in the treaty. Given this indeterminacy, the manner in which the individual Maastricht criteria are interpreted by the ECB and the European Commission in their convergence reports is gaining in importance. At the level of the practical implementation of monetary policy, the question, then, is which monetary policy regime is a priori appropriate from the point of view of the fulfilment of the criteria and from the point of view of the needs of the economy.

The questions to which this chapter seeks answers, are, or will be, relevant to the EU member states with a derogation from adopting the euro and which have not yet entered the ERM II mechanism (currently the Czech Republic, Hungary and Poland), and also to those countries which will find themselves standing at the gates of the euro area in the future after joining the European Union (for example, Bulgaria, Croatia, Montenegro, Romania and Turkey). All these countries will, for simplicity, be termed euro-candidates (even if some of them are not EU members yet and thus their prospects of euro adoption are still distant). Notwithstanding all the evident differences between these countries, there are some prevailing tendencies in their current monetary policy strategies which should be borne in mind, such as their clear preference for inflation targeting (this applies to all euro-candidates mentioned except Bulgaria). We can also see, at least in the countries where the question of ERM II entry is already relevant (the Czech Republic, Hungary and Poland), a prevailing intention to spend the minimum necessary time in the ERM II system. In order to simplify some of our considerations, in this chapter we will assume that this intention applies generally, that is, we will assume that the euro-candidates intend to enter the ERM II only for around 2–3 years in order to meet the requirements of the exchange rate criterion. Given that assumption, the period of membership in the ERM II more or less coincides with the period of fulfilment of the criterion. In the following text we will call this period, for simplicity's sake, the period of fulfilment of the criteria.

The chapter is structured as follows: Section 8.2 looks in detail at the interpretation of the exchange rate and inflation criteria, drawing on the experience of countries which have already adopted the euro and on the convergence reports of the ECB and the European Commission. Section 8.3 builds on these interpretations, analysing the monetary policy regime options in the run-up to euro area entry. Section 8.4 concludes. The Appendix discusses the relevant experience of selected countries in fulfilling the inflation and exchange rate criteria.

8.2 The exchange rate criterion and the inflation criterion

In order to discuss monetary policy options in the period of fulfilment of the criteria, we must first identify the requirements and restrictions ensuing from these criteria for monetary policy. In other words, we must identify the probable manner in which the euro-candidate will be evaluated against these criteria by the Commission and the ECB in their convergence reports. This problem may seem trivial at first sight: it is sufficient to read the wording of the criteria in the treaty. In fact this is only the first step, as the wordings of both criteria in the treaty (and in the relevant protocol to the treaty) contain some ambiguous passages.

The Commission and the ECB are thus forced to choose and describe in their convergence reports interpretations which eliminate these ambiguities. A detailed reading of these interpretations, however, reveals that some vagueness remains even here. Our last chance to get a more precise idea of the application of the criteria is to rely on the principle of equal treatment and, in the light thereof, to examine the experience of countries which have already undergone the evaluation process. Where a given country with a particular value of a given parameter has (un)successfully undergone the review process, the Commission and the ECB have thereby revealed an interpretation of the relevant criterion under which that value is (un)acceptable, and it can be hoped that both institutions will retain this revealed interpretation in the future. The interpretation of the criteria described explicitly in the convergence reports will be called the 'written interpretation', while the interpretation derived from the experience of the countries that have already been evaluated will be called the 'revealed interpretation'.

It should be borne in mind, of course, that at the time when a given euro-candidate asks for an assessment of how it fulfils the Maastricht criteria, the situation in this euro-candidate's economy as well as the whole international macroeconomic and political environment may differ from circumstances that prevail when other euro-candidates ask for assessment. These differences may then be reflected in slight differences in the revealed interpretation. Therefore, when taking lessons from past Commission and ECB convergence reports in terms of revealed interpretation of the criteria, we should be careful to avoid excessive generalization. In order to refrain from speculations, however, we will assume that both the Commission and the ECB will strictly follow the principle of equal treatment.

8.2.1 The wording and written and revealed interpretation of the exchange rate criterion

The third indent of Article 121(1) of the Maastricht Treaty stipulates a requirement to participate in the exchange rate mechanism for at least two years and that during this period the exchange rate should fluctuate within the normal fluctuation band and its central parity should not be devalued (without the need to spend an additional two years in the ERM II the parity may only be revalued). The exact wording of Article 121(1) of the treaty is as follows:

> . . . the observance of the normal fluctuation margins provided for by the exchange-rate mechanism of the European Monetary System, for at least two years, without devaluing against the currency of any other Member State.

Article 3 of Protocol No. 21 to the treaty further specifies with respect to the convergence criteria that the exchange rate should fluctuate within the set band without severe tensions and that the parity may not be devalued on the initiative of the member state striving to enter the EMU. The exact wording of Article 3 of Protocol No. 21 to the Treaty is as follows:

> . . . the criterion on participation in the exchange rate mechanism of the European Monetary System referred to in the third indent of Article 121 (1) of this Treaty shall mean that a Member State has respected the normal fluctuation margins provided for by the exchange rate mechanism of the European Monetary System without severe tensions for at least the last two years before the examination. In particular, the

Member State shall not have devalued its currency's bilateral central rate against any other Member State's currency on its own initiative for the same period.

The wording of the criterion in Article 121 of the treaty, despite being clarified in the protocol, remains ambiguous and has become the subject of much debate (see for example Égert et al., 2005). A question mark hangs over the actual margins of the fluctuation band within which movement of the exchange rate is considered acceptable by the European institutions. Also not entirely clear is the tolerated intensity of the tensions which accompany the maintenance of the exchange rate within this band, and the period of time for which the exchange rate must participate in the ERM II system.

Some clarification as regards the question of which band is in fact tolerated can be found in the formulations that have appeared in past convergence reports produced by the Commission and the ECB. Of these two, the reports prepared by the Commission can be considered more important, for it is the Commission that will prepare, on the basis of the reports and the member state's application to enter the EMU, the recommendation for the EU Council on whether to grant the application or not.

The Commission's convergence reports reveal that a deviation of the exchange rate in excess of the normal ERM fluctuation band of ±2.25 per cent is not automatically evaluated as failure to satisfy the exchange rate criterion. When evaluating an exchange rate deviation outside the ±2.25 per cent band, the Commission takes into consideration the duration of the deviation, its amplitude and above all its direction, that is, whether it is on the weak or strong side of the band. A deviation towards a stronger exchange rate beyond the 2.25 per cent limit is not, according to the Commission, inconsistent with fulfilment of the exchange rate criterion (Convergence Report, 1998, p. 153). The ECB's approach in its convergence reports is similar.

Furthermore, we may attempt to trace the outlines of the revealed interpretation of this criterion by looking at the exchange rate developments which the present member countries underwent prior to entering the euro area and which were found to be in compliance with the treaty. Specifically, the exchange rate of the Irish pound in the review period fluctuated within the margins of −5 per cent to +10 per cent relative to the parity and the exchange rate of the Greek drachma fluctuated near the limit of +10 per cent. The experiences of Greece and Ireland are described in greater detail in the Appendix.

As regards the tolerated intensity of the tensions underlying the fluctuations of the exchange rate close to the central parity, the ECB concentrates on indicators such as the distance of the exchange rate from the central parity, the short-term interest rate differential and the size of foreign exchange interventions. It also takes into account whether there are any reasons for appreciation of the exchange rate (Convergence Report 2004, p. 11). It is not, however, clear from the ECB's and the Commission's statements, or from the experience of the founder members of the EMU, whether there is a maximum permissible size of foreign exchange interventions which is still compatible with the fulfilment of the exchange rate criterion and whether significant interventions in one direction only are permissible.

In any case, one can assume that, provided the exchange rate is maintained – by whatever means – within the narrow band of ±2.25 per cent during the ERM II, it would be very difficult for the Commission to talk of non-fulfilment of the exchange rate criterion. This assumption arises in particular in the case of the countries participating in the ERM II with a currency board (Estonia and Lithuania). Under this exchange rate regime, the size of the interventions is, by definition, beyond the decision of the central bank and may take on significant values.

Another uncertainty connected with the interpretation of the exchange rate criterion concerns the period of stay in the ERM II. Figure 8.1 sums up the experience of the countries that have participated in the past, or are currently participating, in the ERM/ERM II mechanisms, showing the timing of the evaluation of the exchange rate criterion and their euro area entry.

What brings uncertainty into this seemingly unambiguous aspect of the exchange rate criterion are the experiences of Finland and Italy which spent more than two years in the then ERM before adopting the euro. Nevertheless, the Commission and the ECB evaluated the fulfilment of the Maastricht criteria by these countries before they had participated for two years in the ERM II, and the same goes for the EU Council's final decision on the fulfilment of the convergence criteria by these countries. In these two cases, therefore, the revealed interpretation of the criterion was inconsistent with the wording of the criterion, introducing a new ambiguity into it. It may be, however, that the then more liberal approach of the European institutions was due in part to an endeavour not to complicate the early phase of existence of the euro area and that this tolerance will not be repeated in the case of the expansion of the euro area.

On the basis of all the information mentioned above, we can identify the following 'pragmatic' interpretation of the exchange rate criterion, which on the one hand will provide clear scope for exchange rate

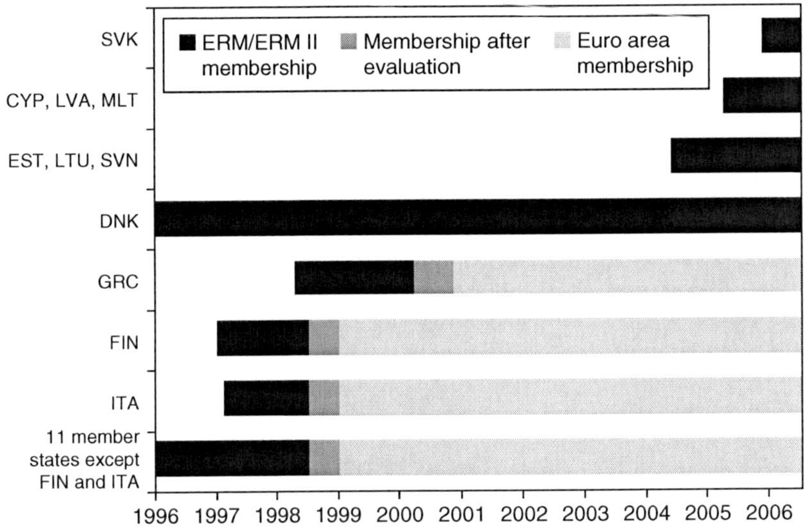

Figure 8.1 Length of ERM/ERM II membership and the timing of the evaluation of the criteria

fluctuations, and on the other should ensure, with an acceptable degree of probability, approval of the fulfilment of the criterion by the Council:

> Participation in the ERM II exchange rate mechanism for a period of two years within a fluctuation band of −2.25 per cent to +10 per cent. A short-term deviation outside this band (even in the depreciation direction, see the experience of Ireland) may be tolerated; in the case of a marked strengthening, the parity may be revalued bilaterally. Significant interventions are acceptable at least where they lead to the exchange rate being maintained within a band of ±2.25 per cent.

Let us add that maintaining the exchange rate in any band narrower than the standard ±15 per cent ERM II band is exclusively up to the given country: under the rules of the ERM II system any interventional assistance by the ECB can be expected mainly when the limit of ±15 per cent is in jeopardy.

8.2.2 The wording and written and revealed interpretation of the inflation criterion

The first indent of Article 121(1) of the Maastricht Treaty stipulates price stability as a further condition for adoption of the single currency. This condition is fulfilled if inflation in the candidate country does not exceed that in the three best performing countries by more than 1.5 percentage points. The exact wording of the treaty is as follows:

> the achievement of a high degree of price stability; this will be apparent from a rate of inflation which is close to that of, at most, the three best performing Member States in terms of price stability.

The subsequent protocol to the treaty, first paragraph, specifies the calculation method. Inflation is measured by means of the HICP and as a twelve-month moving average:

> the criterion on price stability referred to in the first indent of Article 121 (1) of this Treaty shall mean that a Member State has a price performance that is sustainable and an average rate of inflation, observed over a period of one year before the examination, that does not exceed by more than 1½ percentage points that of, at most, the three best performing Member States in terms of price stability. Inflation shall be measured by means of the consumer price index on a comparable basis, taking into account differences in national definitions.

Just as in the case of the exchange rate criterion, the wording of the inflation criterion, despite being clarified in the protocol, is ambiguous.[2] The vagueness relates above all to the term 'best performance', which constitutes the key for selecting the three countries whose inflation rates are to enter the calculation of the reference value. Also vague, however, is the meaning of the term 'sustainable'.

No matter how vague the words 'best performance' may be, in the older convergence reports the Commission and the ECB agreed on a plain and unambiguous written interpretation, that is, that 'best performance' means the lowest inflation. In the convergence reports for 2004 a country with negative inflation (Lithuania) appeared for the first time, and both institutions thus faced the question of whether to apply their interpretation to countries with negative inflation. The Commission took a rather strict and still unambiguous stand on this issue: 'best performance', according to the Commission, is the lowest non-negative inflation.

By comparison, the ECB adopted a rather more benevolent position:

> The price developments in Lithuania over the ERM II period, which resulted in a 12-month average rate of –0.2% due to the accumulation of specific factors, have been judged to be an outlier. This figure

> has consequently been excluded from the calculation of the reference value as it might otherwise have given rise to a distortion in the reference value and reduced the usefulness of the reference value as an economically meaningful benchmark
>
> (Statistical Database of the ECB)

It is, therefore, the ECB's written interpretation in particular that leaves some degree of ambiguity as regards the inflation criterion. This interpretation has so far explicitly been used only once. Thus, it is impossible to get a clear idea about the revealed interpretation. At least, we can perhaps infer that the ECB intends to use the outlier concept only very cautiously. What leads us to this hypothesis is the fact that in 2004 one of the countries included in the calculation of the reference value of the criterion in the ECB's convergence report was Finland, with an inflation rate of only 0.4 per cent. Moreover, the extraordinarily low inflation in Finland during 2004 was largely due to a clearly exceptional, administrative measure: a sharp decrease in the excise duty on alcohol (Bank of Finland, 2005). The reluctance of the ECB to use the concept of outlier transpires also from the spring 2006 convergence report where the reference value is calculated from three 'best performers' of which at least two – Finland and Sweden – are again countries with exceptionally low inflation rates (not exceeding 1 per cent).

Although it cannot entirely be ruled out that in the future countries with low positive inflation might also be exempted from the calculation of inflation in the reference countries, on the basis of the above-mentioned considerations it is possible to designate as a pragmatic interpretation of the inflation criterion the one which appeared in the Commission's convergence report for 2004, that is, the interpretation in which the reference countries are the three EU member states with the lowest non-negative inflation.

This interpretation, however, in no way clarifies the use of the term 'sustainable'. Sustainability was raised – at least indirectly – as an issue in the 2006 convergence reports for Lithuania and Slovenia where the assessment included a look at whether inflation had been above or below the reference values in the previous months, whether it was likely to grow or fall and whether it was likely to be above or below the reference values in the months ahead. For both member states, however, these sustainability considerations were pointing in the same direction as the single-month comparison of the reference value versus actual value. Therefore, it is not obvious how much such considerations would influence the overall assessment in other cases. Even if Lithuanian inflation

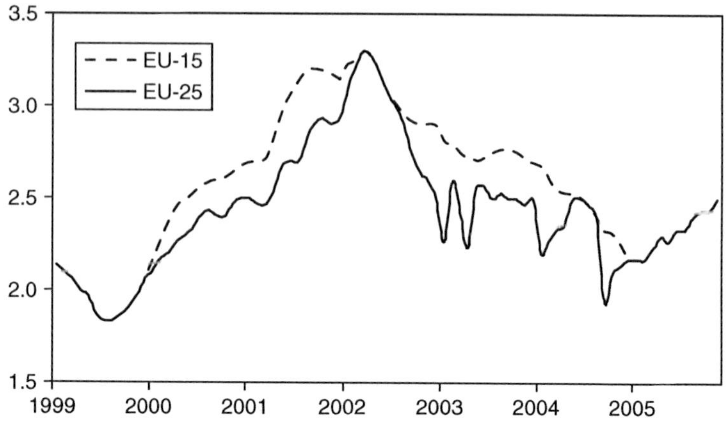

Figure 8.2 Development of the inflation criterion

were below the reference value and the assessment were still negative, it would still be unclear to what extent the negative verdict would be based on the simple forecast of growing inflation or on the forecast of the difference between future inflation and future reference values (these two types of forecast may obviously point in different directions). So far there is a lack of clear signals for a 'pragmatic' interpretation of the term 'sustainable'.

As an aside, we may note that the convergence report of 2006 produced by the Commission confirmed that this institution intends to apply the criterion as it is written: while the reference value was only 0.1 of a percentage point below Lithuanian inflation at the moment of assessment (moreover, alternative ways of rounding the figures might squeeze this difference even further), the Commission made no effort to suggest that this difference was negligible in either statistical or economic terms.

The past development of the reference value of the inflation criterion according to the above-mentioned interpretation is shown in Figure 8.2. The variability of this value over time is quite evident in the figure. At the same time one can see that the reference value computed on the basis of the EU-25 (regardless of when the EU-25 actually came into existence) has often fallen to a lower level than has been the value computed for the EU-15 (the maximum difference between the reference value based on EU-15 and EU-25 recorded so far has been 0.5 of a percentage point in early 2003). This increases the risk that not even relatively low inflation

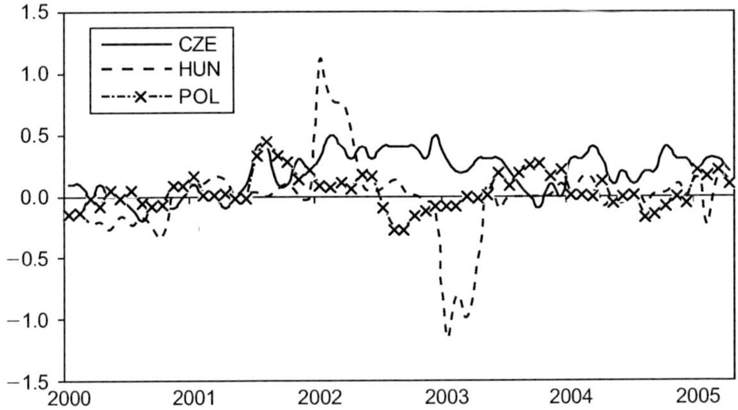

Figure 8.3 Difference between the CPI and HICP in selected countries targeting CPI inflation (Czech Rep., Hungary, and Poland)

Note: Positive values – in percentage points – indicate higher CPI inflation than HICP inflation.

can guarantee with certainty the fulfilment of the inflation criterion in accordance with the above-mentioned pragmatic interpretation.

As regards euro-candidates whose monetary policy operates under a regime of inflation targeting with inflation targets set in terms of their national consumer price indexes (CPI), these countries should, of course, also take into consideration any methodological, and therefore also quantitative, differences between this CPI and the harmonized index of consumer prices (HICP), with which the criterion operates. As shown in Figure 8.3, this difference may be, at least temporarily, relatively large.

8.3 Monetary policy regime options in ERM II

This section discusses the main issues related to monetary policy strategy for euro-candidates. It first investigates the attributes of an optimum monetary policy regime and then discusses the complexity of the choice of exchange rate regime and ERM II central parity.

8.3.1 Five important aspects of the optimum regime

The choice of optimum monetary policy regime is complicated by the fact that the concept of 'optimum regime' may have a different content depending on what weight we attach to its individual aspects. When trying to structure decision-making on the optimum monetary policy regime during the period of fulfilment of the criteria, we need to take the following five basic aspects into consideration:

(i) The probability of fulfilment of the Maastricht criteria
(ii) Internal consistency
(iii) Economic appropriateness
(iv) Transparency
(v) Continuity with the previous regime

Re (i), almost all the countries that aspire, or will aspire in the future, to enter the euro area are experiencing marked long-term appreciation of their equilibrium real exchange rates (Égert et al., 2006). This real appreciation can take place either through an inflation differential or through the nominal exchange rate appreciation, or through a combination of the two. Apparently, there is a trade-off between the fulfilment of the two criteria. The manoeuvring space for safe parallel fulfilment of both criteria is of course larger, the smaller is the equilibrium appreciation. Assuming that the period of fulfilment of the convergence criteria is too long for the national central bank to be able, or willing, artificially to maintain the economy out of equilibrium throughout this period using monetary policy instruments, monetary policymakers indeed face a difficult task: to distribute the overall equilibrium appreciation between the above-mentioned two channels in such a way that both the exchange rate and the inflation criteria are fulfilled, or in such a way that these criteria are fulfilled with the same probability.

Re (ii), some aspects relating to ERM II membership, or to fulfilment of the Maastricht criteria, are not necessarily mutually consistent if the country retains its existing monetary policy regime. From the point of view of successful fulfilment of the exchange rate criterion it is very difficult to retain, for example, an unmanaged float. From the point of view of fulfilling the inflation criterion it is, on the other hand, dangerous to completely fix the exchange rate in a context of real equilibrium appreciation. Another example of inconsistent monetary policy is targeting a rate of inflation that is clearly higher than the probable inflation criterion.

Re (iii), even if monetary policy strategy is internally consistent during the period of fulfilment of the criteria, it might not necessarily be appropriate for the economy at that particular moment in time. For example, trying to keep inflation too low may result in an excessively restrictive monetary policy and a loss in the form of reduced economic growth. The opposite situation, that is, an overheating of the economy, may occur if the exchange rate is fixed at too depreciated a level.

Re (iv), if the central bank is transparent to the public, it is usually also more credible and attains its aims more easily (Blinder, 1998). Transparency and the ensuing effectiveness is doubly important for a central bank that is obliged to attain several objectives at the same time and can only be successful if it fulfils all of them. On the other hand, the pursuit of transparency has its limits, as it may lead to a reduction in flexibility (Mishkin, 2004). In spite of this, during this period the central bank should be as open as possible as regards its objectives and should not attempt to conceal any facts from the public.

Re (v), a change of monetary policy regime entails considerable costs, especially if the previous regime has been in place for a long time and economic agents have adapted their behaviour to it. For this reason, central banks usually resort to a change of regime only in situations where there is no other way out (see, for example, Masson and Ruge-Murcia, 2005).

While some euro-candidates operate under a fixed exchange rate (for example, Bulgaria and Montenegro), the majority are inflation targeters (for example, the Czech Republic, Hungary, Poland, Romania, Sweden and Turkey), mostly with managed floating. It is within the latter group that ERM II entry and the need to fulfil the Maastricht criteria confront the central bank with the dilemma of whether or not to modify its regime. If a country has a favourable experience with inflation targeting and if it has succeeded in making its inflation target credible, the costs of changing the regime are understandably higher. A credible inflation target may better anchor low inflation expectations and thus foster fulfilment of the inflation criterion. Regarding the former group, countries with a fixed exchange rate would find it difficult to explain the abandonment of their previous nominal anchor in the form of a fixed exchange rate, no matter how this might facilitate their fulfilment of the inflation criterion. This is also what the experience of the countries which have already entered the mechanism would suggest (Estonia, Lithuania and Latvia retained their currency boards, while Malta switched from an exchange rate fixed to a currency basket to a rate fixed to the euro).

For most of the euro-candidates there is no regime that would satisfy all the above-mentioned desirable aspects to the full. If, for example, we gave priority to the aspect of fulfilment of the criteria, this could only be done to the detriment of continuity with a previous regime, internal consistency and/or economic sustainability. For the majority of the euro-candidates, therefore, the choice of monetary policy regime for the period of fulfilment of the criteria represents a challenge to find a suitable compromise.

8.3.2 Exchange rate regime and loss of autonomy

In the case of exchange rate regimes, the practice of the last two decades, as well as the consensus in the academic literature (see Fischer, 2001), typically favours 'corner solutions', that is, it recommends adopting either a very fixed exchange rate commitment (preferably without any inflation or other targets) or, on the contrary, a very loose exchange rate commitment (and, possibly, other targets). While a fixed exchange rate is in conformity with the 'pragmatic' interpretation of the exchange rate criterion as mentioned in Section 8.2, a flexible exchange rate regime may be at variance with it. From the point of view of fulfilment of the exchange rate criterion, the nearest solution to the 'corner' is the widest possible fluctuation band compatible with the pragmatic definition of fulfilment of the exchange rate criterion. Fulfilment of the exchange rate criterion in the 'pragmatic' interpretation, as mentioned in Section 8.2, may be achieved by exchange rate regimes ranging from a completely fixed rate to a rate fluctuating within the maximum fluctuation band of −2.25 per cent to approximately +10 per cent. In this regard, we discuss only these two generic solutions, that is, a completely fixed exchange rate and an exchange rate fluctuating within the maximum fluctuation band compatible with fulfilment of the exchange rate criterion.

For both these options there is an implicit possibility of a change of central parity; given the wording of the exchange rate criterion, however, only a revaluation comes into consideration. This possibility will be explicitly mentioned only in those cases where it will have to be allowed for in advance. In all the options it is also possible to consider sub-options differing in whether the fluctuation band would be officially declared or whether it would be targeted only implicitly (see Crespo-Cuaresma et al., 2005 for empirical investigation on some euro-candidates). Refraining from any active endeavour to fulfil the exchange rate criterion, that is, the alternative of not targeting any exchange rate band except for that given directly by ERM II membership, can also, of course, be considered one of the generic alternatives; in such a case, however, the risk of the actual development of the exchange rate leading to non-fulfilment of the criterion increases.

An unpleasant fact which the central bank of a euro-candidate must take into consideration is the loss of monetary policy autonomy.[3] Although formally the loss of domestic monetary policy autonomy does not occur until accession to the euro area, in reality the central bank loses part of its autonomy much earlier. The reason for this is that as the credible date of the country's assumed entry into the euro area approaches, its long-term interest rates become increasingly determined by expectations of the future development of short-term euro rates rather than by domestic rates. Where a fixed exchange rate is chosen for the period of fulfilment of the criteria, the central bank must maintain interest rates at the same level as euro rates (in the case of credible entry into the euro area the risk premium will equal zero), and will thus, for example, begin to lose its influence on annual rates a year before the expected fixing of the exchange rate. In the case of the wide fluctuation band the loss of autonomy is less apparent (the risk premium is non-zero even in the case of credible entry into the euro area). The movement of interest rates, however, is significantly curbed by the evolution of the exchange rate. Given that exchange rate appreciation expectations are typical of a large proportion of the euro-candidates, domestic interest rates should be roughly at the same level as those of the ECB (with a low, positive, risk premium), or lower than those of the ECB (with a zero risk premium).

8.3.3 Fixing of the exchange rate versus utilization of the maximum bandwidth

In this sub-section we address the question of choosing the optimum exchange rate bandwidth and central parity so as to minimize the risks ensuing from the requirement to fulfil the Maastricht criteria and make maximum use of the merits of each of the options discussed.

As noted above, the exchange rate criterion permits revaluation of the central parity. If the exchange rate, owing to adverse circumstances or a speculative attack, shows a strong tendency towards appreciation, it is, in principle, possible in both regimes discussed – the fixed exchange rate and the wide fluctuation band – to take advantage of this asymmetry and revalue the parity. However, the possibility that the pressure concerned is only transitory can never be ruled out; this might lead to a later requirement to devalue the parity back to its original level and thus to breach one of the requirements of the exchange rate criterion. It will therefore be important to make use of the opportunity for revaluation only after careful consideration and, where appropriate, after making use of the options available for defending the original parity.

In many countries the fixed exchange rate regime has not proved successful, frequently ending in speculative attacks (Fisher, 2001). Nevertheless, this experience is not necessarily shared by the euro-candidates. A fixed exchange rate based on a fixed point in the form of a permanent fixing of the exchange rate on euro area entry (so-called 'exit') at a pre-determined moment in time may be much more robust to speculative pressures.[4] A fixed exchange rate within the ERM II is the approach that so far predominates among the new EU member states, which is probably due to the fact that these countries operated in the fixed exchange rate regime before their ERM II entry.

It is true that in the case of a fixed exchange rate – provided that the selected assumptions of equilibrium exchange rate and price development apply – the stability of the nominal exchange rate implies some inflationary pressure and hence also the threat of failure to satisfy the inflation criterion. This danger, however, can be consciously reduced. The parity can be fixed, for example, at a slightly overvalued level which will roughly correspond to the equilibrium exchange rate at the horizon of the permanent fixing against the euro. The issues of the optimum parity setting will be discussed in greater detail in sub-section 8.3.4 below. The contradiction between the fixed exchange rate and fulfilment of the inflation criterion, however, is not unambiguous. Firstly, in a small open economy, as is characteristic of the majority of the euro-candidates, any fluctuation in the exchange rate passes through significantly to the price level (Coricelli et al., 2006). A fixed exchange rate, then, may eliminate the risk of inflation fluctuations resulting from excessive exchange rate movements.

The second generic exchange rate regime option for the period of fulfilment of the criteria is maximum utilization of the fluctuation band, that is, within the margins of approximately −2.25 per cent to +10 per cent. The main theoretical advantage of the wide fluctuation band should be the ability to absorb shocks through the exchange rate. However, this has received little empirical support for euro-candidates. For example, Borghijs and Kuijs (2004) have studied the ability of Central European currencies to respond to shocks and have found that currencies in Central Europe have tended to generate shocks rather than to absorb them. As regards the approximately two-year period of fulfilment of the criteria, it is, therefore, not possible to say with certainty whether maximum utilization of exchange rate flexibility will foster a stabilization of the economy or, on the contrary, will damage it. Another advantage of the wide fluctuation band is that it preserves some degree of domestic monetary policy autonomy during the period of fulfilment of the criteria.

8.3.4 Setting the parity

Regardless of the choice of exchange rate regime, during the period of fulfilment of the criteria each euro-candidate will be faced with the question of setting a suitable parity against the euro (see de Grauwe and Schnabl, 2005). The experience of the countries that are fulfilling or have already fulfilled the criteria speaks in favour of fixing the parity at the current market value. The only exceptions have been Slovenia, which fixed at a rate other than the current market value due to its earlier than planned entry into the ERM II, and Cyprus, which set its parity at the level of an earlier parity (the current exchange rate was more appreciated). However, the relevance of these countries for many of the future members of the ERM II is reduced by the fact that neither of them had a floating exchange rate, hence they de facto continued to fix their exchange rate at the previous level.

Considerations of setting the parity at a rate other than the current exchange rate are supported by the asymmetry of the exchange rate criterion, which affords more space for appreciation than for depreciation. It would, therefore, be logical to set the parity at a more depreciated level than the current exchange rate and thus make the criterion more symmetrical around the current exchange rate. The potential misinterpretation of this step by the markets, however, argues against such procedure.

Another issue that enters into the debate on the setting of the initial ERM II parity is that of the long-term equilibrium exchange rate. It is reasonable to assume, especially under the fixed exchange rate regime, that the irrevocable conversion rate of the domestic currency to the euro will be identical to the ERM II parity and so this parity should be set near to the equilibrium exchange rate at the time of expected entry to the euro area. This strategy is supportive for fulfilment of inflation criterion, as the real equilibrium appreciation will take place mainly via the exchange rate. For most of the euro-candidates this would imply setting the parity at a stronger level. It is not, however, entirely clear whether the benefits of such a step (lower inflation over a longer period, that is, an endeavour to maximize aspect (i) from sub-section 8.3.1) will prevail over the potential costs (an excessively strong exchange rate over a short period and increased market volatility, that is, a deterioration of aspect (iii)).

The question is whether the expected parity value (equal to the estimated equilibrium exchange rate as of the ERM II entry date) should be signalled by the central bank in advance, and, if so, how far in advance. On the one hand, early publication would quash speculation and steer the exchange rate in the right direction from the central bank's point of view. On the other hand, however, such a signal represents a commitment which in time may prove to be hasty. It is also necessary to take into consideration that the parity is set by the joint decision of the

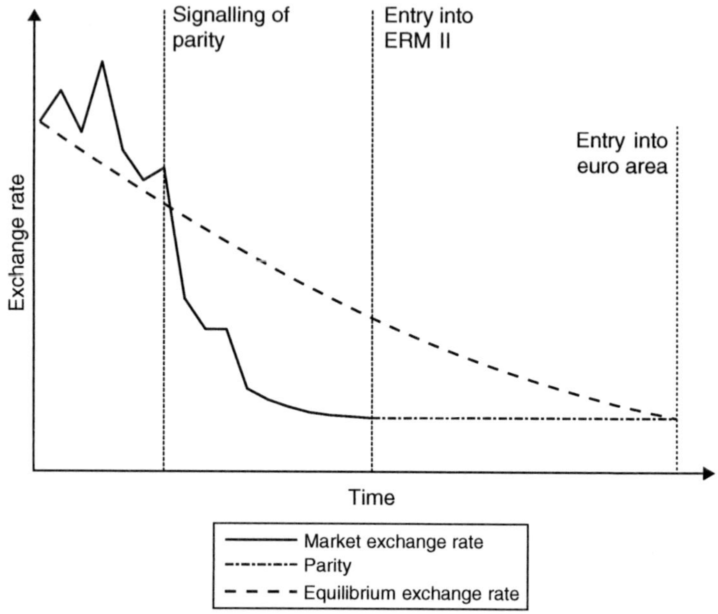

Figure 8.4 Exchange rate development under the fixed exchange rate regime

EU member states and the authorities of the EU and so any signalling of the parity may be seen as anticipating the result of this joint decision. This interpretation can be avoided by the central bank declaring in advance that the parity will be set roughly at the equilibrium value of the exchange rate as of the ERM II entry date and by the central bank estimating this equilibrium value within a given range. A similar scenario is proposed by Buiter and Grafe (2002). Figure 8.4 illustrates this hypothetical exchange rate scenario with early signalling of the parity.

This strategy requires a fairly accurate idea of the value of the equilibrium real exchange rate at a horizon of around three years. Estimates of the equilibrium value of the exchange rate are associated with considerable uncertainty (see Égert et al., 2006) and central banks tend to have only a general idea of the band within which the exchange range is more or less in equilibrium (and this band may be quite wide). A faster appreciation would, moreover, obviously have a negative impact on economic activity. The strategy of an overvalued parity also increases the risk of speculation on a devaluation of the exchange rate and hence the risk of a subsequent actual devaluation (depending on the effectiveness

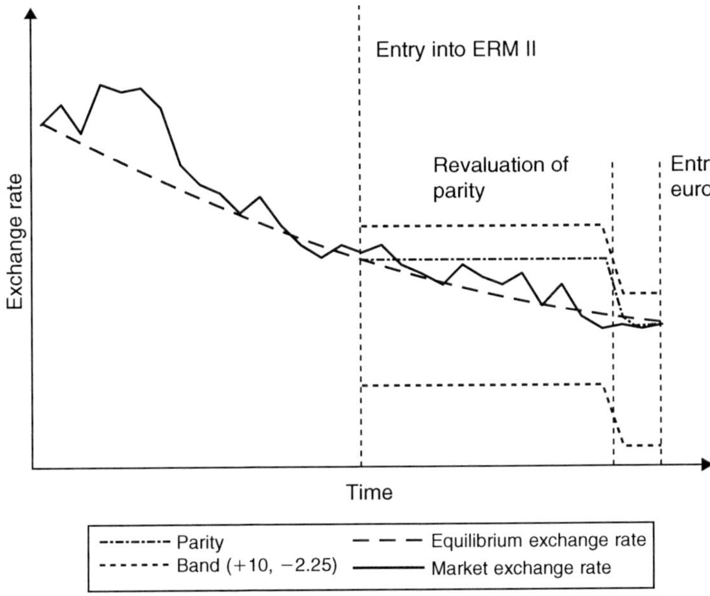

Figure 8.5 Illustration of exchange rate development under the wide fluctuation band regime

of foreign exchange interventions), leading to the commencement of a new compulsory two-year stay in the ERM II.

If the wide fluctuation band is opted for, the solution might be to set the ERM II parity near to the equilibrium exchange rate as of the ERM II entry date, from which the current market exchange rate should not differ too much. Assuming that the annual pace of real equilibrium appreciation is lower than 5 per cent and that the exchange rate does not deviate markedly from its equilibrium path, the exchange rate would stay within the wide fluctuation band during the roughly two-year period of fulfilment of the criteria and there would likely be no need for any major interventions or early revaluation of the parity.

In such a situation it may be desirable to revalue the parity shortly – perhaps several months – before euro area entry (based on an assessment of the current market rate and on the authorities' idea of the development of the equilibrium), as in the case of Ireland and Greece. This would allay concerns that the currency will be fixed at the initial parity level (as these concerns would probably lead to depreciation of the exchange rate back towards this parity). The exchange rate development under the wide fluctuation band regime is shown schematically in Figure 8.5.

8.4 Conclusions

The aim of this chapter is to investigate the monetary policy options of an euro area accession country during the period of fulfilment of the Maastricht exchange rate and inflation criteria. We first analyse the 'rules of the game' (that is, how the two criteria are implemented by the Commission and the ECB) and then we identify possible monetary policy strategies within these rules.

We point out that some degree of ambiguity is contained not only in the wording of both criteria in the Maastricht Treaty and the protocols to it, but also in the interpretation of both criteria as recorded in the past convergence reports of the Commission and the ECB. Hence there is a need to search for the probable interpretation with the help of the experience of the countries that have already, successfully or unsuccessfully, undergone the evaluation. Even at the end of this search, however, some ambiguities still persist with respect to both criteria, hence the efforts of the euro-candidates to satisfy these criteria are, to some extent like shooting at a target which is only vaguely defined.

We then give some thought to the question of whether and how a candidate can steer a course through the probable interpretations of the two criteria (with all their ambiguities). The considerations of the national central bank of a euro-candidate country in the period of fulfilment of the criteria are not concentrated solely on fulfilment of the criteria; the central bank must also keep in mind other aspects such as the internal consistency and economic appropriateness of its monetary policy, transparency, and continuity with the previous monetary policy regime. A deeper analysis of these aspects reveals that for most of the euro-candidates there is no regime which would satisfy all the above-mentioned desirable aspects to the full and hence that for the majority of the euro-candidates the choice of monetary policy regime for the period of fulfilment of the criteria represents an attempt to find a suitable compromise.

In line with the prevailing current trend of favouring 'corner' solutions in the exchange rate regimes, we have focused our attention on two specific exchange rate regime options for a euro-candidate country: a completely fixed exchange rate and an exchange rate fluctuating within the widest fluctuation band compatible with fulfilment of the exchange rate criterion. The choice between these two regimes depends on many factors which are typically country-specific, such as expected equilibrium real appreciation, the previous monetary policy regime and its credibility or the ability and willingness of the government to coordinate fiscal policy. We therefore investigate the advantages and disadvantages of both exchange rate regime options and make proposals for the specific implementation of the chosen regime until the setting of the central parity. It is, of course, up to the policymakers in the relevant countries to set all these considerations into the specific context of their economy and to identify the approach that will maximize the chances of successful adoption of the euro.

Appendix 8.1: The experience of selected countries

The Appendix considers the experience of Ireland and Greece as regards fulfilment of the exchange rate and inflation criterion and also looks at the experience of Hungary as regards concurrent targeting of the exchange rate and inflation.

The Irish and the Greek experiences are interesting primarily from the point of view of the interpretation of the exchange rate criterion, as the development of the currencies of these countries in the period reviewed by the convergence report was rather volatile and deviated markedly from the central parity. As a result, it provides a precedent for the interpretation of the vague wording of the exchange rate criterion in terms of allowed deviation of currency from central parity. We discuss the fulfilment of the inflation criterion as something of a side issue, as this criterion is interpreted by the Commission and the ECB in clearer terms than is the exchange rate criterion. In the case of the inflation criterion the question is rather whether it is too 'strict' for economies undergoing real convergence and whether the rate of inflation implied by this criterion is sustainable (Buiter and Grafe, 2002). Both Ireland and Greece recorded a lower rate of inflation in the reference period than before and after this period. The rate of inflation in the reference period was influenced by appreciation of currency and, in the case of Greece, also by cuts in indirect taxes. The Commission's estimate in the convergence report for 2000 states that the cuts in indirect taxes in Greece led to inflation being 0.7–1.0 percentage point lower in the reference period (under the assumption of full pass-through of the tax changes to consumer prices).

The Hungarian experience is also noteworthy, as with its dual targeting Hungary is de facto shadowing the ERM II regime in that it is maintaining its exchange rate within a fluctuation band of ±15 per cent around the set parity while declaring an inflation targeting regime. The Hungarian experience also shows the importance of monetary and fiscal policy consistency.

A8.1.1 Ireland

The Commission's 1998 convergence report found that Ireland had fulfilled the exchange rate criterion, as the currency had not experienced severe tensions nor had its central rate been devalued during the period under review, that is, between March 1996 and February 1998. In March 1998, the Commission proposed to the Council that Ireland had fulfilled all the preconditions for adopting the euro. On 3 May 1998, the Council decided that Ireland, along with another ten countries, had fulfilled the necessary conditions for adopting the euro. Ireland adopted the euro on 1 January 1999.

Ireland's experience during the ERM is interesting primarily from the point of view of the interpretation of the exchange rate criterion, as the development of the Irish currency during the period reviewed in the convergence report was generally volatile, as Figure A8.1 shows. The figure illustrates the percentage deviation of the currency from the central parity. It is clear that the Irish pound remained within the narrow margin of ±2.25 per cent only from around April 1996 to October 1996, that is, for only for 7 of the 24 months under review. At the start of the reference period the currency was even below the depreciation level of −2.25 per cent, staying there for at least a month (to be precise for 32 trading days, that is, 6 per cent of all the trading days during the review period).[5] The maximum deviation of the pound from its parity was −4.24 per cent

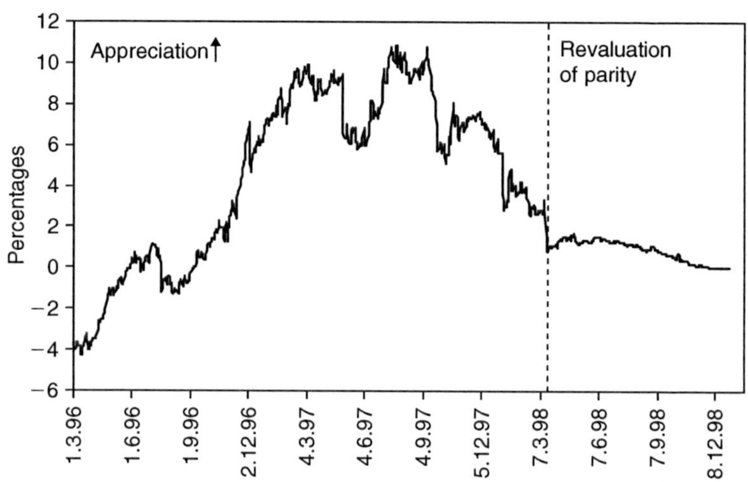

Figure A8.1 Deviation of the Irish pound vis-à-vis the median currency, March 1996–December 1998

(calculated against the 'median' exchange rate, as this approach was used by the Commission when evaluating exchange rate stability[6]). Ireland's experience, in line with the principle of equal treatment, leads to a legitimate assumption that a transitory breach (lasting a month and a half at least) of the depreciation level of −2.25 per cent is tolerated.[7] In such a situation, however, much will also probably depend on how the Commission evaluates the reasons which led to this short-term swing of the currency in the depreciation direction and on the ability of the country to defend such a swing.

However, from around October 1996 until the end of the period under review, the Irish currency fluctuated above the appreciation level of +2.25 per cent (the currency appreciated significantly from April to November 1996). The maximum deviation from the central parity was 10.91 per cent. This appreciation was due in particular to optimism connected with the buoyant growth of the Irish economy and also to a strong appreciation of the UK pound. In the course of 1997 the exchange rate began to move slowly back towards the parity. On 16 March 1998 (after the close of the Commission's two-year review period in February 1998), the parity was revalued by 3 per cent, taking the exchange rate very near to the central parity. The Central Bank of Ireland justified this step by stating that without the revaluation the currency, given its fixing to the previous central parity, would have had to depreciate too much, which, in turn, would have jeopardized price stability. The revaluation had been expected by the market. The Annual Report of the Central Bank of Ireland for 1998 also states that the interventions conducted in the foreign exchange market in 1997 reduced the official external reserves by £1098 million, whereas there were no direct interventions in 1998. On 31 December 1998, ECOFIN announced the conversion rate of the Irish pound at £0.79 to the euro.

A8.1.2 Greece

Greece did not fulfil the convergence criteria in 1998 as it had not participated in the ERM, and so, unlike the other 11 EU countries, it did not adopt the euro on 1 January 1999. Greece entered the ERM on 16 March 1998 and then moved smoothly into the ERM II when that came into being on 1 January 1999. This means that when assessing exchange rate stability the Commission in 1998 took into consideration the development of the drachma vis-à-vis the median ERM currency, and from 1999 onwards the relevant indicator became the development of the drachma in relation to its parity against the euro.

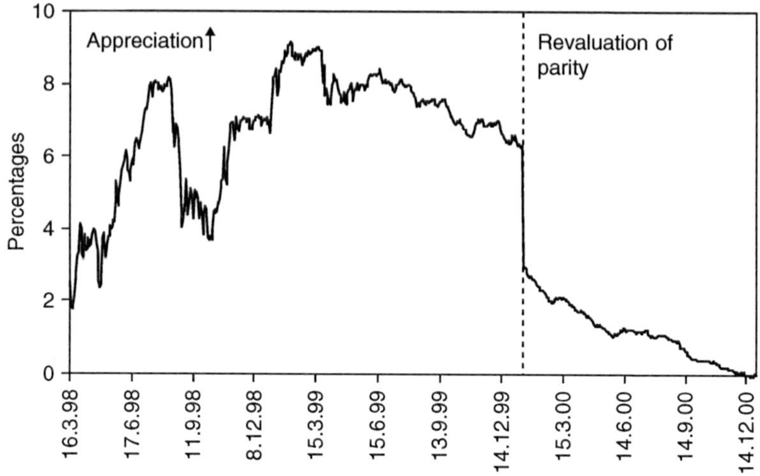

Figure A8.2 Deviation of the Greek drachma vis-à-vis the median currency (1998) and the euro (1999–2000)

Greece entered the ERM with its central parity markedly depreciated against the market exchange rate in the period before entry (the parity was set at 357 GRD/ECU, that is, 12.3 per cent more appreciated than the market exchange rate). The setting of the central parity was evaluated by both the Bank of Greece and the financial markets as sustainable and consistent with the overall euro adoption strategy. The devaluation of the parity was a result of the so-called 'hard drachma' policy practised by the Bank of Greece in the mid-1990s, aimed at bringing down the rate of inflation.[8] This policy resulted in appreciation of the real exchange rate, so the setting of a 'depreciated' parity was interpreted as a return towards equilibrium. Entry into the ERM was accompanied by a declaration by the government of its intention to consolidate public finances.

Following a jump depreciation connected with the devaluation of the parity, the drachma began gradually to appreciate, thanks to a high interest rate differential and market optimism regarding the future development of the Greek economy. This appreciation was briefly interrupted by the Russian crisis at the end of the summer of 1998 (see Figure A8.2). The large appreciation of the drachma significantly aided the fulfilment of the inflation criterion.

The Commission's convergence report for 2000 (p. 26) states that: 'The drachma had been relatively stable against the ERM currencies in the review period but had at times experienced tensions which were counteracted by increases in domestic interest rates and by foreign exchange intervention.' Such measures were particularly necessary during the crisis in Russia and Asia. The drachma was 5.7 per cent above its parity on average in 1998. The maximum and minimum distances from the parity were +8.2 per cent and +2.4 per cent (see Figure A8.2).

Greece entered the new ERM II on 1 January 1999 with a central parity of 353.109 GRD/EUR. This parity had been moderately revalued relative to the ERM parity (357 GRD/ECU), although this was merely the result of a recalculation of the parity via the final conversion rates. The revaluation was therefore a 'technical' rather than an 'economic' one. The average deviation from the ERM II parity during the review period was 6.76 per cent. The maximum and the minimum deviations during the ERM II were +9.16 per cent and +1.78 per cent respectively. After the decision to set the conversion rate at the central parity, the exchange rate gradually converged towards the central parity. The drachma was therefore more appreciated than the central parity throughout its participation in the ERM II (as in the ERM).

The drachma's membership in the ERM II was characterized by depreciation, coupled with a reduction of the interest rate differential, and gradual convergence towards the parity. This convergence was hastened by a 3.6 per cent revaluation of the parity on 17 January 2000. Thanks to this, the drachma did not have to depreciate so much in order to attain the parity.

Annual HICP inflation fell to approximately 2 per cent during the reference period and increased to 3–4 per cent after adoption of the euro. Cuts in indirect taxes implemented in 1998–1999 were another factor that aided fulfilment of the inflation criterion.

On 9 March 2000, Greece submitted an official request for the preparation of a convergence report and a subsequent assessment of the convergence criteria by the Council. On 19 June 2000, the Council decided that Greece had fulfilled all the necessary conditions for the adoption of the euro and set the conversion rate of the drachma at the existing central parity and also set the date of adoption of the euro. Greece adopted the euro on 1 January 2001.

A8.1.3 Hungary

In May 2001, Hungary abandoned its crawling peg and widened the fluctuation band of the forint from ±2.25 per cent to ±15 per cent. At the same time, the Hungarian central bank introduced inflation targeting and set inflation targets for 2001 and 2002. This put the Hungarian

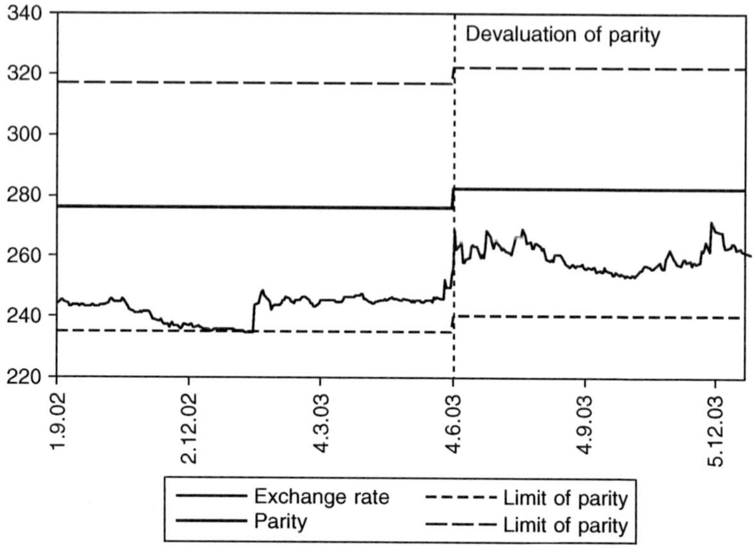

Figure A8.3 HUF/EUR exchange rate, September 2002–December 2003

National Bank in a situation where it was targeting two variables simultaneously – the exchange rate and inflation. This regime of shadowing the ERM II and simultaneously targeting inflation was meant to be temporary, aimed at bringing inflation down to the Maastricht criterion level and achieving rapid adoption of the euro. The fluctuation band of ±15 per cent was seen as sufficiently wide to avoid conflicts between the inflation and exchange rate targets. This evaluation, however, was based on an assumption of restrained fiscal policy supporting disinflation. The approaching elections in April 2002, however, brought a large fiscal expansion, and in order to attain the inflation target tighter monetary conditions became necessary. The central bank responded by raising rates by 1 percentage point during the summer of 2002. As a result of the higher rates the Hungarian forint gradually appreciated, reaching the edge of the fluctuation band towards the end of 2002 (see Figure A8.3).

Meanwhile, at the end of 2002, the EU accession treaties were signed and the Hungarian government communicated its willingness to a marked decrease in the public finance deficit from 2003 onwards. On the strength of this development, the market believed the government's announcements in favour of the fastest possible adoption of the euro

(Barabas, 2003). These factors fostered a short-term decrease of the risk premium and consequently also a further appreciation of the forint (by less than 1 per cent towards the stronger margin of the band). However, the government, fearing a loss of competitiveness of Hungarian exporters on account of the strong forint, insisted that the exchange rate regime and the existing fluctuation band must not be abandoned (a change of exchange rate regime requires agreement between the government and the Hungarian National Bank). The Hungarian National Bank thus found itself in a situation where it evidently would not be able to fulfil one of the targets it had set itself (either the exchange rate target or the inflation target).

This economic policy inconsistency triggered a speculative attack on the strong boundary of the fluctuation band of the forint in January 2003. The Hungarian National Bank withstood the attack by means of a large interest rate cut (by 2 percentage points) and interventions in the foreign exchange market (over the two days of the speculative attack – 15–16 January 2003 – it purchased a total of EUR 5.3 billion) and thus de facto gave priority to the exchange rate target over the inflation target. As a result, the disinflation process of the Hungarian economy slowed, and the markets interpreted this step as meaning that the authorities valued exchange rate stability more than rapid incorporation into the euro area (the level of inflation at that time meant that the inflation criterion would not be fulfilled). The subsequent stability of the exchange rate observable in Figure A8.3 was due to intervention activity by the Hungarian National Bank. The bank was present in the foreign exchange market until May 2003 (although it did not publish the volume of its interventions).

On 4 June 2003, the central parity of the forint was devalued by 2.26 per cent. This step was again due to government concerns about an excessively strong forint. It was argued that any overshooting of the exchange rate would jeopardize export competitiveness. The markets, however, viewed this step as a change in the central bank's priorities towards a weaker forint and a weaker future central parity in the ERM II.[9] A rapid depreciation of the forint – by almost 10 per cent – followed. The central bank responded by gradually increasing rates by 3 percentage points. The bank justified this increase by the fact that the forint had depreciated too far (to the limit of 270 HUF/EUR), whereas it preferred to maintain the exchange rate within the band of 250–260 HUF/EUR. For the market this was a signal that the central parity was again not to anchor exchange rate expectations. Given such uncertainty (exacerbated by the low credibility of both fiscal and monetary policy), it is no surprise that the forint was very volatile for several months thereafter. There has been no repeat of such dramatic exchange rate changes since then.

Notes

1. Besides the three criteria mentioned, the treaty formulates another two criteria in the fiscal policy area. These criteria within the euro adoption processes in the new EU member states are discussed, for example, by Coricelli (2004).
2. Proposals have been made for a change of wording of the criterion directly in the treaty (Buiter, 2004; Buiter and Grafe, 2002, among others). For example, it has been proposed to select the three reference countries only from among the euro area countries; to base the reference value of the criterion not on the average of the three countries with the best inflation results, but instead on the average for the entire euro area; to concentrate only on inflation of traded goods and so on. In this chapter, however, we concentrate exclusively on the issue of the interpretation within the limits of the present wording of the treaty.
3. Crespo-Cuaresma and Wojcik (2006) measure monetary policy autonomy in selected EU new member states and find that although greater exchange rate flexibility is associated with greater monetary policy autonomy, none of the countries analysed has a fully autonomous monetary policy, even with a floating exchange rate.
4. Nevertheless, it is vital to note that a breach of the fixed exchange rate commitment would not necessarily mean failure to satisfy the exchange rate criterion.
5. A similar situation arose with the Finnish mark and Italian lira. Both currencies were fluctuating well below the depreciation band of −2.25 per cent during 1996; nevertheless, the two currencies did not enter the ERM until October and November 1996 respectively, by which time they were fluctuating within the narrow band of ±2.25 per cent.
6. The deviation from the parity was calculated as follows. A separate central parity against the ECU was set for the exchange rate of each country in the ERM; from this it was possible to calculate the percentage deviation of each exchange rate from this parity. The median currency was then selected as the currency for which the percentage deviation from its parity was the median of all the deviations of the individual exchange rates from their parities. Then, the percentage deviation was calculated for each currency by deducting this median deviation from the percentage deviation of the exchange rate from its parity against the ECU. This calculation was 'necessary' due to the non-existence of the euro at that time.
7. France had a similar experience, as the franc deviated to −2.35 per cent from its parity on two days of the reference period.
8. More information on the monetary policy of the Bank of Greece during the pre-accession period can be found in Mourmouras and Arghyrou (2000) and Garganas (1998).
9. The then intention was to enter the ERM II in 2004 and to adopt the euro as late as 2008, which is why the market considerations as regards the parity for the ERM II were relevant.

References

Angeloni, I., M. Flad and F.P. Mongelli (2005). 'Economic and Monetary Integration of the New Member States: Helping to Chart the Route', ECB Occasional Paper, No. 36.

Bank of Finland (2005). 'Bank of Finland Bulletin', 1/2005.

Barabas, G. (ed.) (2003). 'Coping with the Speculative Attack against Forint's Band', Magyar Nemzeti Bank Background Studies, No. 2/2003.

Blinder, A. (1998). *Central Banking in Theory and Practice*, Cambridge, MA: MIT Press.

Borghijs, A. and L. Kuijs (2004). 'Exchange Rates in Central Europe: Blessing or Curse?' IMF Working Paper, No. 2.

Buiter, W. (2004). 'To Purgatory and Beyond: When and How Should the Accession Countries from Central and Eastern Europe become Full Members of the EMU?' CEPR Discussion Paper No. 4342.

Buiter, W. and C. Grafe (2002). 'Anchor, Float or Abandon Ship: Exchange Rate Regimes for the Accession Countries', *Banca Nazionale del Lavoro Quarterly Review*, 55: 111–42.

Convergence Reports, various issues (1999–2008), October, March, ECB, Frankfurt.

Coricelli, F. (2002). 'Exchange Rate Policy during Transition to the European Monetary Union: the Option of Euroization', *Economics of Transition*, 10(2): 405–17.

Coricelli, F. (2004). 'Fiscal Policy in Enlarged Europe', *Revue de l'OFCE*, special issue: 191–209.

Coricelli, F., B. Jazbec and I. Masten (2006). 'Exchange Rate Pass-Through in EMU Acceding Countries: Empirical Analysis and Policy Implications', *Journal of Banking and Finance*, 30(5): 1375–91.

Crespo-Cuaresma, J. and C. Wojcik (2006). 'Measuring Monetary Independence: Evidence from a Group of New EU Member Countries', *Journal of Comparative Economics*, 34: 24–43.

Crespo-Cuaresma, J., B. Égert and R. MacDonald (2005). 'Non-Linear Exchange Rate Dynamics in Target Zones: a Bumpy Road towards a Honeymoon', William Davidson Institute Working Paper, No. 771.

Dabrowski, M. and J. Rostowski (eds) (2006). *The Eastern Enlargement of the Eurozone*, Dodrecht: Springer.

De Grauwe, P. and G. Schnabl (2005). 'Nominal versus Real Convergence – EMU Entry Scenarios for the New Member States', *Kyklos*, 58(4): 537–55.

Égert, B., R. Kierzenkowski and T. Reininger (2005). 'Asymmetric Fluctuation Bands in the ERM and ERM II: Lessons and Challenges for New EU Member States of Central and Eastern Europe', *Eastern European Economics*, 43(1): 81–144.

Égert, B., L. Halpern and R. MacDonald (2006). 'Equilibrium Exchange Rates in Transition Economies: Taking Stock of the Issues', *Journal of Economic Surveys*, 20(2): 257–324.

Fischer, S. (2001). 'Exchange Rate Regimes: is the Bipolar View Correct?', *Journal of Economic Perspectives*, 15: 3–24.

Garganas, N. (1998). 'Greece and EMU: Prospects and Challenges', *Economic Bulletin No. 12*, Bank of Greece, December: 7–20.

Hochreiter, E. and G. Tavlas (2004). 'On the Road Again: an Essay on the Optimal Path to EMU for the New Member States', *Journal of Policy Modeling*, 26(7): 793–816.

Masson, P. and F. Ruge-Murcia (2005). 'Explaining the Transition between Exchange Rate Regimes', *Scandinavian Journal of Economics*, 107(2): 261–78.

Mishkin, F. (2004). 'Can Central Bank Transparency Go Too Far?', NBER Working Paper No. 10829.

Mourmouras, I.A. and M.G. Arghyrou (2000). *Monetary Policy at the European Periphery: Greek Experience and Lessons for EU Candidates*, Berlin: Springer.

9

Fiscal Performance and Economic Growth in the Old and New Member States of the EU

István Benczes

9.1 Introduction

Joining the Eurozone requires candidates to fulfil the strict Maastricht convergence criteria. In the 1990s, old member states of the European Union implemented serious fiscal consolidations in order to qualify for EMU membership. Nevertheless, not just the 1990s but also the 1980s witnessed some major attempts to consolidate the general government, thereby putting an end to the further acceleration of unsustainable debt ratios.

The experience of EU countries with fiscal consolidations implemented over the past twenty to twenty-five years enables us to make comprehensive assessments on the role and effectiveness of fiscal policy and also on the real and alleged macroeconomic consequences of adjustment. The scrutiny of these effects is not without reason, however. First, according to the standard (Keynesian) textbook approach, fiscal adjustment has two main consequences: it can reduce indebtedness and it can trigger a deterioration in economic activity through direct and indirect effects. Yet, the great abundance of empirical evidence in the last 25 years does not lend unequivocal support to this general conviction. Instead, EU countries often experienced a further increase in their debt ratios in times of consolidation, and more surprisingly, fiscal retrenchment was not necessarily followed by a drop in economic output. Second, the new member states of the EU are obliged to adopt the single currency as soon as they are capable of meeting the convergence criteria, inclusive of the 3 and 60 per cent (in GDP) limits on fiscal deficit and debt, respectively. However, these countries are still lagging behind the level of wealth of the old member states. The challenge for countries in Central and Eastern Europe is therefore to introduce the euro without compromising their growth potential. The argument in this chapter, accordingly is that there is in fact no trade-off between catching up and fiscal discipline – just the opposite, it is the relatively low level of redistribution and the lack of (a permanent) deficit financing that can prove to be conducive to growth in both new and old member states. Importantly, the chapter remains on a relatively abstract level while analysing the economic performance of old and new member states; the intention is not to provide a full-fledged analysis on all the related fields such as institutional or structural reforms. The focus is exclusively on the relationship between fiscal aggregates and economic growth.

Section 9.2 concentrates on the experience of old member states. Using the sample of EU-14 countries between 1980 and 2005, first the so-called level (or size) effect will be addressed by reflecting upon the relationship between the size of the state and economic growth. Next the composition effect will be investigated, by revealing whether expenditure or revenue-based adjustments are more likely to prevent a further build-up of debt and to maintain a relatively good level of economic growth. Section 9.3 turns to the new member states, and – based on the generalizable experiences of old members – tries to provide some hints on their fiscal and economic output on the road towards the single currency. Unfortunately, due to space limitations, the chapter does not investigate the fiscal profile of the early years of transformation, only the post-accession years will be assessed in some length. Section 9.4 concludes.

9.2 Fiscal performance and economic growth in old member states

Keynesian anti-cyclical policy used fiscal policy as the fundamental device in short-term economic stabilization. Nevertheless, contrary to the original aims of the Keynesian recipe – managing aggregate demand across cycles – fiscal policy followed a highly asymmetric nature in Europe after World War II. Governments eagerly applied fiscal spending in the years of economic slowdown, but forgot to accumulate surpluses in periods of boom (European Commission, 2000). It is worth emphasizing, however, that it was not always the case that governments could produce deficit year by year, independently of the business cycles. Before the 1960s, practically no written formula was needed in order to attain a balanced budget position in the medium run (Buchanan, 1997). It is a relatively recent phenomenon that a government can finance its spending by producing deficits in both 'good' and 'bad' times.[1]

9.2.1 The size effect

Western European countries witnessed a substantial increase in the size of the public sector following World War II. While the size of the state increased in absolute terms, the increase was more robust in the field of welfare spending as compared to public investment or government consumption. The dynamic increase of the size of the European welfare states, however, did not immediately cause concern for sustainability. In fact, economists of the time strongly propagated the idea of a state with extensive intervention in the market economy, since the latter was believed to function ineffectively on many occasions. Moreover, during the 1950s, 1960s and 1970s these countries were not yet deeply integrated into the world economy. Europe was still far away from being a single market; movement of labour and capital was not prevalent. Except for trade in goods, European countries were generally closed economies, and policymakers enjoyed relative autonomy in making decisions.

The general tendency in modern democratic regimes is that as they move along the development ladder, they tend to spend more on public activities. According to the Wagner law, the catching up process, the modernization and urbanization of countries, triggers an increase in overall government spending. With the increase of national income in European nations in the last five decades, total government spending has accelerated as well, reaching a level that is close to or even beyond half of their GDPs.[2]

Nevertheless, in the last 25 years or so the expansion of the public sector has come to an end in most EU countries. Following oil crises and stagflation, a couple of countries decided to implement large-scale reforms in their general government. Potentially unsustainable debt ratios in some countries – such as Ireland and the Netherlands – made it necessary to induce changes in the course of fiscal policy from the early 1980s. The attempts of the 1980s were followed by another wave of adjustment efforts between 1992 and 1997. The second wave was triggered by the agreement of European nations on the necessity to coordinate their economic and monetary policies under a new framework, the Economic and Monetary Union.

Thus, during the late 1970s and the 1980s, total government expenditure averaged 46.8 per cent of GDP, while the start of the Maastricht process (1992) witnessed a remarkably high ratio of 51.2 per cent in the EU/EC. The ratio had declined to 49.3 per cent by 1997 and to 45.8 per cent by 2000, which was followed by some bouncing back in the new millennium – although 50 per cent has never been reached again.[3]

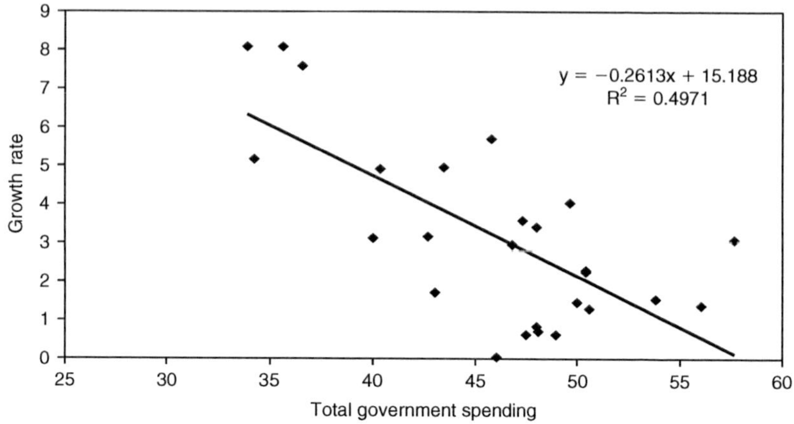

Figure 9.1 Relationship between total government spending and economic growth in the EU-26

Notes: numbers are as per cent of the GDP. The correlation between total spending and economic growth is –0.7. Data as of 2007.

Source: Based on EC (2007).

There is a big debate in the literature on the relationship between size (proxied by total spending to GDP) and macroeconomic (and socio-economic) performance. The general view is that countries that have been willing to undertake a sizeable reform in their public budget (measured in a significant reduction in their total spending) did not perform worse than those which were not prepared to take the same measures. In fact, most of the empirical studies on the size of the public sector and economic growth have found some negative correlation between the two. In a large cross-country sample of 90 countries, Barro and Sala-i-Martin (1995) identified a very strong negative effect of increased total spending on economic activity. Using a historical data set of OECD countries (between 1960 and 2000) Tanzi and Schuknecht (2003) found a strong negative correlation between total spending and growth rates. Our EU-26 sample (excluding Luxembourg) strengthened the previous findings, too – see Figure 9.1. Although there are some studies that could not reject the null hypothesis of no relationship between general government expenditure and economic output (Lee, 1995 for instance), no empirical work has yet documented a positive correlation between these macroeconomic variables.

Some authors managed to differentiate between countries on the basis of the political willingness and readiness of policymakers to implement reforms. Tanzi and Schuknecht (2003) grouped countries into 'ambitious'

Table 9.1 Total government expenditure as percentage of GDP, EU-14

	1980	Maximum (year)	2005	Change
Austria	50.0	56.5 (1993)	50.1	6.4
Belgium	56.5	63.7 (1983)	49.9	**13.8**
Denmark	53.6	61.7 (1993)	55.8	5.9
Finland	40.6	64.1 (1993)	51.0	**13.1**
France	46.6	55.4 (1996)	54.5	0.9
Germany	47.6*	50.3 (1996)	47.1	3.2
Greece	32.6	52.1 (2000)	49.8	2.3
Ireland	50.4	54.3 (1982)	35.2	**19.1**
Italy	41.7	57.7 (1993)	49.5	8.2
Netherlands	56.0	59.8 (1983)	48.1	**11.7**
Portugal	35.3	49.1 (2005)	49.1	0.0
Spain	34.2	49.4 (1993)	40.1	9.3
Sweden	64.6	72.9 (1993)	57.4	**15.5**
UK	45.7	49.1 (1981)	44.5	4.6
Mean	46.8	56.8	48.7	8.1

Notes: Change means the difference between the maximum value and the data of 2005. *: average between 1974 and 1985. Bold: changes higher than 10 per cent.
Source: Data set of OECD (2006).

and 'timid' reformers. According to their findings, the macroeconomic consequences of downsizing the state sector proved to be significantly better in the medium and long term in the group of ambitious reformers. Moreover, ambitious reformers did not suffer in terms of poorer socio-economic performance (Tanzi and Schuknecht, 2005).[4]

Table 9.1 provides comparative data on the size of the general government in old EU member states. The data support the claim that some countries indeed embarked on a drastic reduction of the size of the state, while others are still hesitating to do so (albeit some minor changes did happen in almost every country during 1996–97, the time when the first members of the Eurozone were selected).

Table 9.1 shows that Portugal, France, Germany and Greece have not managed to reduce the size of the state in the last few decades. At the other extreme, Belgium, Finland, Ireland, the Netherlands and Sweden successfully downgraded the level of state involvement, thereby providing – in principle, at least – more room for the working of market incentives.

Certainly, it is almost impossible to quantify the optimal size of the state.[5] And there is a trade-off regarding the level of public spending. On the one hand, lower public spending is associated with higher growth. On the other hand, in principle, a larger public sector is expected to

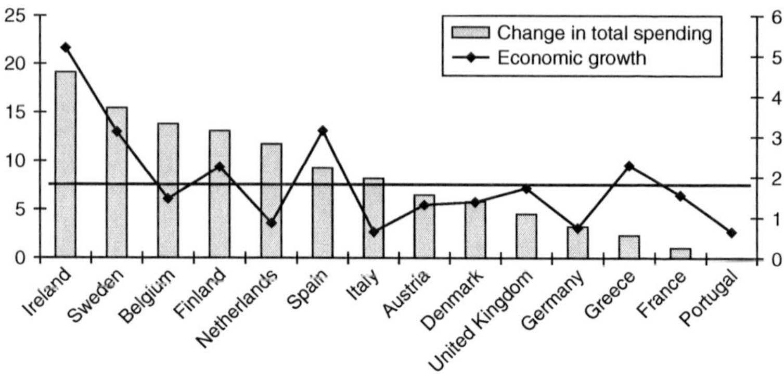

Figure 9.2 Change in total spending and economic growth, EU-14
Notes: Change in total spending has been reproduced from Table 9.1. Economic growth is an average of data between 2001 and 2005. The horizontal line indicates the average EU-14 growth rate.
Sources: Based on OECD (2006) and EC (2006).

provide a more egalitarian redistribution of income. Socio-economic studies have empirically proven that relatively homogeneous societies tend to redistribute more, since preferences on fairness are highly ranked. This is partly the reason why European nations tend to favour higher redistribution rates, while the US – with its more fragmented and heterogeneous society – refrains from advocating a larger state (Alesina and Giavazzi, 2006).

The ultimate question, however, is whether the reduction in size promoted positive effects, as is assumed in the literature. Figure 9.2 shows convincingly that countries which were ready to reduce their total spending have also been able to perform better with respect to economic output. In fact, countries that have proved to be unwilling to reduce the size of the general government are the sick men of Europe today.

Reducing the size of the state enabled countries to moderate the level of their debt-to-GDP ratio as well – sometimes significantly. Ireland for instance managed to achieve a decline of 81.8 per cent (in GDP) between 1987 (111.7 per cent) and 2005 (29.9 per cent). Sweden, Finland, Denmark, Spain, the Netherlands and Belgium also achieved a minimum of 10 per cent (in GDP) decline in the debt ratio. Portugal, Germany and France, on the other hand, did not manage to reduce their indebtedness. While on average, EU countries have managed to reduce their debt ratios by 20.6 per cent in the last two and a half decades, these three countries have faced an upward trend in their indebtedness. Data are provided in the Appendix.

9.2.2 The composition effect

By elaborating on size effects, it has been shown that in principle reducing the size of the state can bolster economic activity. However, a drop in the size of the public sector can be achieved only if the government is willing to cut public expenditure, which has never been a risk-free political undertaking. Reducing politically sensitive budget items, such as the public sector wage bill or household transfers, can provoke serious political tensions and social unrest. It is not surprising, therefore, that governments are inclined towards the easier option in times of fiscal adjustment, that is, towards tax increases.

In a provocative paper, Alesina and Perotti (1995) claim that fiscal adjustment can bring success in terms of a declining debt-to-GDP ratio only if governments are brave enough to initiate a spending cut. The authors argue that in cases of successful consolidations, four-fifths of the deficit reduction took place on the expenditures side. In another study, Perotti et al. (1998) have shown that fiscal adjustments would fail if the bulk of the consolidation was placed on the revenue side. Accordingly, what matters in delivering positive macroeconomic effects triggered by a fiscal adjustment (in terms of a reduced debt-to-GDP ratio or an accelerated economic growth after adjustment) is the quality (or composition) of adjustment.

In fact, the old EU member states put considerable efforts into the consolidation of their general governments during the 1990s. However, as was convincingly documented by von Hagen et al. (2001), most of these countries seemed to avoid the politically more challenging expenditure-cutting scenario and came across with an increase on the taxation side. Albeit the deficits were moderated to the Maastricht criterion of 3 per cent, the higher tax burden and the unwillingness of governments to downsize the public sector made it impossible for several countries – such as Germany, France, Portugal or Greece – to achieve a durable consolidation and increased economic growth (EC, 2005).[6]

Accordingly, the chapter now takes a more detailed look at the disaggregation of the general budget. The sample of the old member states provides an easy ground for testing whether these countries indeed turned to the revenue side or not. The macroeconomic consequences of adjustment will also be briefly addressed. In order to distinguish episodes of large fiscal adjustment between 1980 and 2005, the following definition for 'large' fiscal consolidation will be adopted: *a fiscal adjustment is said to be large if the cyclically adjusted primary balance improves by at least 1.5 percentage points of the GDP from year t-1 to year t.*

Unfortunately, setting arbitrary limits is not without problems because the results can be sensitive to the chosen concept. Nevertheless, our definition is in harmony with the literature (see especially Alesina et al., 1998; or McDermott and Westcott, 1996). By focusing on a cyclically adjusted balance, the effects of business cycles can be filtered out (for example, in times of upswings, the general balance improves automatically) and only the discretionary part of fiscal impetus can be touched upon.[7] Restricting the focus on the primary balance is important because interest payments do not play a part in the actual decisions of the policymakers.

For 14 EU countries over the period of 1980 and 2005, in principle, there can be 364 observations (25 years times 14 countries), out of which 61 qualified as large. The results are reported in Table 9.2, which also displays the time-distribution of large fiscal adjustments. The bulk of adjustment episodes were implemented during the 1980s. Countries were also active during the 1990s, although fiscal consolidations were largely concentrated between 1993 and 1997. In the new millennium, 2005 witnessed some resurgence of fiscal severity.

Having set up a data pool of large fiscal adjustments, fiscal episodes can be grouped into expenditure-based, revenue-based and mixed adjustments. It is rarely the case that a government initiates fiscal consolidation by applying exclusively either expenditure cutting or a revenue increase. Nevertheless, based on the magnitude of changes on the two sides of the general government, a borderline can be drawn. Accordingly, a fiscal adjustment has been characterized as *expenditure-based* in our sample of EU-14 if the drop in total public spending (from year t–1 to t) exceeded the increase in public revenues (from year t–1 to t) by a minimum of 30 per cent. A fiscal adjustment was defined as *revenue-based* if the increase in total revenues (from year t–1 to t) exceeded the decline in public expenditure (from year t–1 to t) by a minimum of 30 per cent. A fiscal adjustment was characterized as *mixed* if the change in one parameter (from year t–1 to t) was not higher than 30 per cent as compared to the change in the other variable (from year t–1 to t). Changes are interpreted in GDP. The total number of observations (61) followed the distribution given in Table 9.3.[8]

In close harmony with general expectations, governments in old member states proved reluctant to make significant cuts in expenditures over the 25 years under investigation. Expenditure-based consolidations account for only one-third of the total, which undeniably supports the intuition. On the other hand, an increase in revenues was a more frequently chosen strategy by European governments – more than half of

Table 9.2 Large fiscal adjustments

	1980–89	1990–99	2000–05
Austria	**2.4(1984)**	**1.8(1996)** 1.7(1997)	2.4(2001)
Belgium	5.0(1982) **4.0(1984)** **1.6(1985)**	**2.1(1993)**	
Denmark	**3.8(1983)** **2.5(1984)** 1.9(1986)	1.8(1999)	1.6(2005)
Finland	2.1(1981) 1.9(1984) **2.5(1988)**	**1.5(1998)**	3.0(2000)
France	**1.9(1996)**		
Germany	2.1(1989)		
Greece	**1.6(1982)** **2.5(1986)** 2.5(1987)	**4.0(1991)** 5.2(1994) 2.0(1996)	**1.8(2005)**
Ireland	**2.6(1982)** **3.1(1983)** **1.7(1987)** **2.7(1988)** 1.5(1989)		**1.6(2003)**
Italy	**3.4(1982)** 1.8(1983)	**1.7(1991)** **2.3(1992)** 1.8(1993) 2.0(1997)	
Netherlands	**1.5 (1982)**	3.2(1991) 3.2(1993) 2.0(1996)	1.5(2005)
Portugal	**2.5(1982)** **3.9(1983)** 1.8(1986) 1.6(1988)	3.2(1992)	2.3(2002)
Spain		2.0(1992) **2.0(1996)**	
Sweden	3.0(1981) **1.6(1983)** **2.0(1986)** 2.7(1987)	**4.5(1996)**	1.6(2005)
UK	2.7(1980)	**1.5(1996)** **1.8(1997)** **2.0(1998)**	

Notes: Data display the size of adjustment in the cyclically adjusted primary balance that proved to be equal to or higher than 1.5 per cent of GDP. Year of adjustment in brackets. Data in bold remark adjustments where the balance did not deteriorate in year t+1.
Source: Based on OECD (2006) and EC (2007).

Table 9.3 Categorization of fiscal consolidations

Type of adjustment	Number of observations	Share of the total
Expenditure-based consolidation	22	37
Revenue-based consolidation	32	53
Mixed consolidation	6	10
Total	60	100

Notes. The number of total observations in the table is one less (60) than the total sample (61) because it was not possible to put Greece 1987 into any of these categories, due to considerable contradictions in the data.
Source: Based on OECD (2006) and EC (2007).

the fiscal adjustments were implemented by generating an additional burden for taxpayers. Presumably due to the strict definitions, the share of mixed strategies remained relatively low – only every tenth adjustment qualified for this category. The basic question is now whether the different strategies induced different macroeconomic consequences.

Two main consequences have been studied: the change in the debt-to-GDP ratio and the change in economic output. Regarding the first, the standard textbook approach is that adjustment will reduce indebtedness. As far as economic growth is concerned, the situation is not that clear. It is hardly questioned nowadays that the long-term growth effects of stabilization are positive. However, the short- (and medium-) term consequences are still considered to be negative, thereby providing a trade-off between the short-term costs and the long-term benefits of fiscal consolidation.

In analysing the effect of adjustment on the dynamics of indebtedness, only those episodes will be taken into account where the debt-to-GDP ratio declined by at least 5 percentage points of the GDP three years after the consolidation. (We can call these adjustments *successful*.) Surprisingly, only a total of 21 episodes succeeded in reducing the debt ratio by 5 points, that is, the majority (39) of attempts failed to overcome the dynamism of indebtedness in EU countries. More interestingly, however, two out of three debt-reducing adjustments came from the group of expenditure-based consolidations. An increase in revenues, therefore, is hardly the way to reverse the acceleration of debt-to-GDP ratio. In fact, concentrating on revenue-side adjustments only, the picture is even more sombre: only 4 out of 32 cases (12.5 per cent) provided a debt-reduction. The distribution of episodes can be seen in Table 9.4 in more detail.

Table 9.4 The composition of adjustment and main macroeconomic consequences, number of episodes

	Change in indebtedness		Change in economic growth	
	Successful episodes	Failed episodes	Growth-supporting episodes	Growth-limiting episodes
Expenditure-based adjustment	14	8	12	10
Revenue-based adjustment	4	28	10	22
Mixed adjustment	3	3	3	3
Total	21	39	25	35

Notes: The total number of observations is 60.

While breaking down the dynamism of indebtedness is an important element in restoring the sustainability of public finances in countries with a relatively high debt-to-GDP ratio, the effect of fiscal adjustment on economic growth is possibly an even more decisive political factor. Generally speaking, politicians try to avoid adjustments because the assumed short-term costs can easily outweigh the long-term benefits of fiscal consolidation. Our sample of old EU member states, however, does not fully support this general conviction. In fact, even a large adjustment can trigger a relatively quick recovery in economic activity, thereby compensating for the inevitable short-run losses. Based on the measured economic activity before and after the fiscal corrections, the total sample of 60 observations was grouped into two: growth-supporting and growth-limiting consolidations. The borderline between the two groups was based on the following definition: *a large fiscal adjustment was characterized as growth-supporting if the difference between the average real GDP growth rate of the particular country and the EU-15 average during and after the adjustment (that is, in years t, t+1 and t+2) exceeded the difference between the average real GDP growth rate of the particular country and the EU-15 average before the adjustment (that is, in years t−2 and t−1).*

The findings are somewhat surprising. Twenty-five of the total of 60 episodes proved to be growth-supporting. A quick look at Table 9.4 shows that a growth-supporting fiscal consolidation can be based either on spending cuts or revenue increases. Nevertheless, scaling down public spending is more likely to achieve intensified economic activity than a tax increase. The fact that fiscal adjustment can provide an acceleration in economic growth even in the short run is not that new, however.

Giavazzi and Pagano (1990) were the first to identify such a perverse effect of fiscal policy by scrutinising the Irish (1987–89) and Danish (1983–84) consolidations. Several subsequent papers have found some evidence for expansionary effects triggered by fiscal retrenchment, a phenomenon also known as 'non-Keynesian effects'.[9]

Analysing the data on a country-by-country basis shows which countries proved to be more willing to implement expenditure-based consolidations. Ireland stands out from the group. Austria, Belgium, Denmark, Finland, the Netherlands and the UK used both strategies alternately over the last 25 years. Those attempts that proved successful were almost always those which touched upon the spending side as well. Greece, Italy or Portugal generally preferred revenue-based adjustments, although Greece also pursued mixed strategies in the 1990s. Only on relatively few occasions did European countries manage to achieve both a reduction in the debt ratio and an acceleration of economic growth. These episodes were the following: Denmark (1983, 1984), Finland (1988), Ireland (1987, 1988, 1989), the Netherlands (1993, 1996), Sweden (1996) and the UK (1997, 1998).

Nevertheless, several theoretical and empirical studies pointed out that in considering the success of fiscal consolidation it also matters which item of public spending is reduced by the government. In their seminal paper, Alesina and Perotti (1995) showed that successful adjustments were those where half the cuts in expenditure were attained by reducing two politically sensitive items: public sector wage expenditure and household transfers. Furthermore, Schuknecht and Tanzi (2005) have shown that the cutback of public expenditures in countries which proved to be ambitious and successful in their fiscal consolidation did not fall on education or public investment expenditure; instead, the reduction was implemented on household transfers, subsidies and interest spending. These findings were supported by Hauptmeier et al. (2006), who documented that ambitious reformers – as opposed to timid ones – are willing to reduce spending on household transfers, subsidies and government consumption and leave education spending mostly untouched.[10]

Tanzi and Schuknecht (2005) also claimed that in the case of ambitious reforms, the assumed negative side effects on the distribution of income (that is, a deterioration in fairness) are relatively small. Moreover, these deteriorations can be overcome in absolute terms by more robust economic growth and a better targeted redistribution of public spending.

In a panel assessment on EU countries, Afonso and Alegre (2008) found a negative association between public consumption and social security contributions on the one hand and economic growth on the other. Investigating the effect of government size and fiscal volatility on

Table 9.5 Disaggregating the expenditure side

	Expenditure-side consolidations	**Revenue-side consolidations**	**Total**
Total government spending	−4.9(2.9)	+1.5(2.3)	−1.0(4.0)
Final government consumption	−2.9(2.7)	0 (2.6)	−1.3(3.0)
Compensation of public sector employees	−2.7(3.2)	+0.26(3.6)	−1.06(3.8)
Social transfer in kind	−3.1(2.9)	−0.4(5.1)	−1.6(4.4)
Social transfers other than social transfers in kind	−3.6(3.1)	+1.3(3.0)	−0.9(3.9)
Public capital formation	−11.0(11.6)	−4.5(8.6)	−7.3(10.4)
Government interest payments	−4.3(9.1)	+8.9(12.4)	+3.8(12.9)

Notes: The data are averages and were calculated as percentage change between (t−1) and (t). A negative sign refers to a decline. Standard deviation in parentheses.
Sources: Based on OECD (2006) and EC (2006).

economic growth on two samples (OECD and EU countries), Afonso and Furceri (2008) have come to the conclusion that government consumption (both size and volatility), social contributions (size and volatility), indirect taxes (size and volatility), subsidies (size) and government investment (volatility) have a robust and statistically significant negative effect on economic growth.

Table 9.5 underlines the above-mentioned trends. Our EU-14 sample – divided into an expenditure and a revenue-based adjustment group – displays robust differences between countries. Generally speaking, each item reflects a significant decline in the case of expenditure-side adjustments. On the other hand, in most of the cases, revenue-side adjustments failed to achieve substantial cutbacks in spending items – in fact, these items increased most of the time. The only item that experienced a relatively strong decline was public capital formation.

A standard question in economic literature has been whether public investment generates economic growth. Easterly and Rebelo (1993), among others, have shown empirically that the accumulation of public investment is conducive to growth only if it is able to facilitate private investment as well. That is, spending on public capital should enhance the crowding-in of private initiatives. Lucas (1988) added to this that public investment should be directed at education in order to facilitate economic growth in the long run – a claim that was backed by Afonso and Alegre (2008).

Yet our sample is rather discouraging in this sense. Both revenue and expenditure-side consolidations insisted on scaling down public investment dramatically in order to eliminate deficit. The so-called growth supporting expenditure-side consolidations reduced public investment spending more (by 13.2 per cent) than growth-decelerating adjustments (10.1 per cent). However, the small number of observations makes any conclusion rather ambiguous. What is certain, however, is that the most successful countries – such as Ireland (1987–89), Finland (1996), Sweden (1996) and the UK (1997–98) – did not hesitate to cut social transfers and public sector salaries substantially in times of fiscal consolidation.

Concluding this discussion of the EU-14, it is worth underlining what Afonso et al. (2005) found in their study. According to the authors, government spending is growth-supporting if and only if it is limited to and directed at investments that are able to contribute to the formation of human capital and research and development capacities. It should include basic education, health, infrastructure, security and so on. Spending can also stimulate growth if it serves the creation and maintenance of the proper institutional environment in the economy. Expenditure with an exclusively redistributive character on the other side may considerably limit growth potential by reducing incentives for private agents to work and invest.

9.3 Fiscal performance of CEE countries on the road towards the euro

The stylized facts from the old member states have demonstrated that the standard textbook approach to the macroeconomic consequences of fiscal consolidation cannot be supported by evidence. In fact, the EU-14 sample supported a rather different view: a breakdown of the dynamic increase of the debt-to-GDP ratio is rare in times of fiscal consolidation; it can happen only in case of an expenditure-based adjustment. Moreover, the idea of a necessary deterioration of economic activity due to a reduced deficit could not be unequivocally supported either. While debt accumulation is not a real problem in most of the CEE countries (the exceptions are Hungary and Poland), the supposedly adverse effects of fiscal discipline (that is, the reduction of deficit) on economic growth can bring about serious concerns in countries where the average national income (in PPP) is still far away from that of the EU-15 – 54 per cent (CEE10) or 60 per cent (CEE8) by 2007 – see Figure 9.3. By any comparison, the CEE countries need to perform well above the annual growth rate of the old member states in order to close the development gap. The basic question, however, is whether the adoption of the euro and the consequent narrowing of room for fiscal manoeuvre erodes the growth potential or not. In order to answer this question, the macroeconomic performance of CEE10 will be considered below.

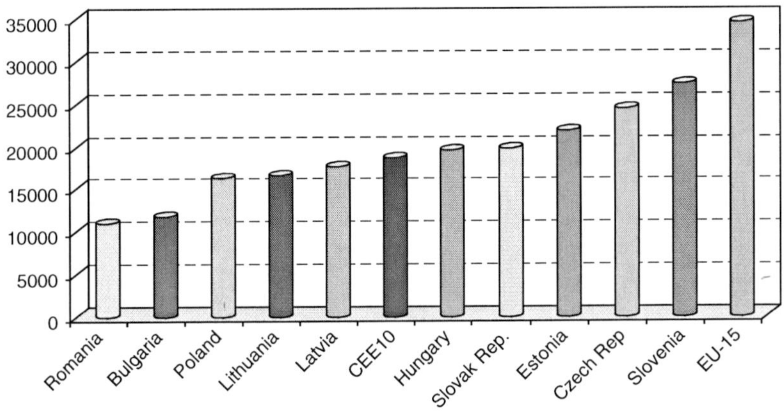

Figure 9.3 GDP per capita (PPP) in CEE countries
Source: Based on the data set of EC (2007).

Before the transformation, planned economies tried to acquire full control of their economies. With the monopoly of state ownership and the bureaucratic coordination mechanism, socialist countries maintained an undeniably high redistribution rate. By 1981 for instance, Czechoslovakia and Poland had a ratio of 53 per cent of GDP, while Hungary peaked at 63 per cent (Kornai, 1992). Transformation meant that nations reshaped the role of the state: the state tried to withdraw from the economy and leave the allocation of resources largely to market forces.

Nowadays it is a commonly held that the early and quick adoption of stabilization policies and structural reforms contributed significantly to the recovery of economic activity in most of the CEE countries (Fischer and Sahay, 2000). Delay and postponement of structural reforms were responsible for negative or low growth rates in Eastern Europe (especially in the states of the former Soviet Union) rather than initial conditions (Berg et al., 1999).[11]

Focusing on the post-EU membership years, it is interesting to note that following the early years of transformation, most of the new member states initiated some additional downsizing of the public sector during the years of the new millennium and joined the EU with a total spending ratio of 39 per cent of GDP (on an unweighted average).[12] Regarding the level (or size) effect on growth, the results are staggering. Based on data in 2007, the correlation between the two variables are extremely strong and have a negative sign (−0.83). Figure 9.4 displays the data on an individual country basis as well.

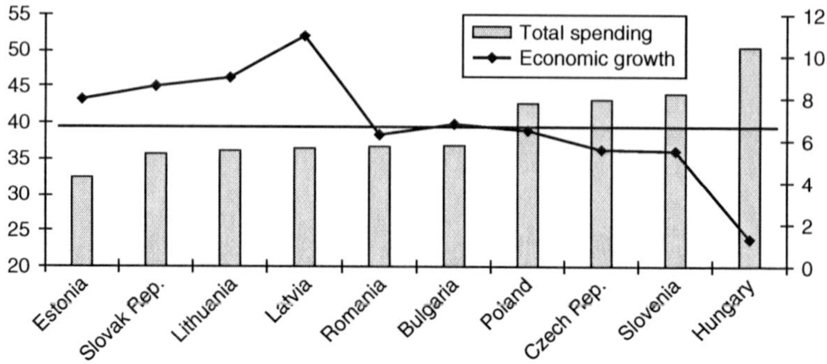

Figure 9.4 Total public spending and economic growth in the CEE10
Notes: Data as of October 2007. The solid horizontal line indicates the average growth rate.
Source: Based on a data set of EC (2007).

CEE countries experienced robust economic growth in the years of the new millennium: the average growth rate between 2002 and 2007 was 6.3 per cent. The high growth ratio was accompanied by a relatively low average deficit ratio of 2.4, which would imply a solid qualification for EMU membership. Nevertheless, performance varies significantly amongst countries in the region. Table 9.6 is an explicit attempt at categorizing CEE countries according to their growth performance. Three different groups can be established: the advanced transformation economies (Slovenia, Poland, the Czech Republic and Hungary) have achieved an average growth rate between 2002 and 2006 of 4 to 5 per cent. They clearly have the largest states, fiscal balance is in the worst situation and the debt-to-GDP ratio is outstandingly high as compared to other countries. In the second group, comprising Slovakia, Romania and Bulgaria, growth rates range between 5 and 7 per cent, while the size of redistribution is below 40 per cent. The best performing countries are the Baltic states, which comprise the third group in our categorization. The average growth rate has been above 8 per cent annually. The state in these small countries has restricted itself substantially to core activities; fiscal balance has been well below the Maastricht reference criteria, while debt is more or less negligible.[13] Generally speaking, the larger the state, the worse are fiscal performance (that is, deficit and debt) and economic activity.

In a relatively early empirical work – concentrating exclusively on the 1990s – Purfield (2003) found that larger fiscal consolidations achieved a more successful and durable cure for fiscal imbalances in CEE countries – especially if governments were willing to reduce public expenditure.

Table 9.6 Grouping CEE countries: economic growth and fiscal aggregates

	Economic growth	Total expenditure	Fiscal balance	Primary balance*	Debt**
Slovenia	4.1	46.4	−2.0	0.3	25.6
Poland	4.1	43.7	−5.0	−2.0	46.8
Czech Rep.	4.4	45.5	−4.6	−2.8	30.2
Hungary	4.5	50.2	−7.9	−3.8	66.1
Slovak Rep.	5.5	39.6	−3.9	−1.0	30.8
Bulgaria	6.3	39.3	1.5	3.0	19.3
Romania	6.9	34.9	−1.7	−0.1	12.5
Lithuania	8.6	33.8	−1.2	−0.3	17.7
Estonia	9.3	34.2	1.9	2.0	2.8
Latvia	9.6	35.8	−1.1	−0.4	10.2
CEE10	6.3	40.3	−2.4	−0.5	26.2

Notes: Ranking by the economic growth rates. Numbers are per cent of GDP. The data are averages between 2002 and 2006. *: in cyclically adjusted terms, **: as of October 2007.
Source: EC (2007).

Yet, evidence for growth acceleration in times of adjustment was rather weak and no negative impact of fiscal consolidation on economic growth was identified either. However, the positive short-term growth effects of fiscal consolidation may not be restricted to advanced market economies, as was documented subsequently by Rzonca and Cizkowicz (2005) or Segure-Ubiergo et al. (2006). By using a panel estimation, Rzonca and Cizkowicz (2005) were able to demonstrate the existence of non-Keynesian effects in the group of CEE countries, albeit the exact channels that delivered the surprising outcomes could not be recognized. However, the authors emphasized that the export sector received a substantial boost in times of fiscal adjustment, especially if the consolidation was implemented by the scaling back of wages.

As far as the latest tendencies are concerned, Hungary's economic and fiscal performance has deteriorated dramatically in the last few years. Economic growth decelerated to 1.3 per cent in 2007 as a consequence of a severe consolidation effort that started in the second half of 2006. The adjustment was inevitable: from 2001 onwards alternating governments shaped their spending decisions without being sensitive to financial constraints. Hungary's public finances became unsustainable. Albeit Hungary's fiscal deficit is expected to decline to the Maastricht level by 2009, forecasts on economic growth are still disappointing. Hungary has implemented a mainly revenue-based adjustment; the size and the structure of the state have been mostly untouched. The vicious circle of low employment, a too generous welfare redistribution and the extremely high level of marginal taxation and overall tax burdens makes it impossible to break out of the current low equilibrium trap.

This short data analysis on CEE10 supported our earlier claims made in the context of the old member states; that is, too large spending ratios are less conducive to growth. Amongst the CEE10 those countries proved to be successful which did not hesitate to embark on fiscal retrenchment in the last couple of years. In fact, setting fiscal discipline against economic growth seems to be superficial. No country in the CEE should postpone the adoption of the single currency on the basis of growth sacrifices. The experience does not validate such a claim.

9.4 Conclusions

By reviewing the literature and conducting empirical research on both old and new EU member states, this chapter has attempted to provide a falsification of some generally shared views, namely that (i) fiscal adjustment always ends in a breakdown of the dynamism of indebtedness and a drop in economic activity, and that (ii) new member states may find it counterproductive to switch to the euro, because of the assumed costs paid in terms of decelerated economic growth.

The bulk of empirical evidence in the last 25 years has failed to support these general claims unequivocally. Instead, it has been shown in this chapter that EU countries often experienced a further increase in their debt ratios in times of consolidation, and more surprisingly, that fiscal retrenchment was not necessarily followed by a drop in economic output. The borderline, however, was whether governments were committed enough to reduce politically sensitive spending items. Based on the experience of old member states and taking a quick look at the main macroeconomic trends of Central and Eastern European countries, the chapter also argued that it is possible to introduce the euro without compromising the growth potential of the new member states. The most robust growth rates have been achieved by those countries in CEE which are running a relatively small public sector and are refraining from deficit-financing. The lesson is clear: fiscal spending should be targeted at fields where employment, investment, technological upgrades and a solid institutional environment can be facilitated. As has been pointed out in the context of old EU member states, governments should be committed to the downsizing of household transfers, subsidies and government consumption, otherwise no return to the path of sustainable long-run economic growth can be expected. In fact, CEE countries are no different at all from old member states in this respect.

Appendix 9.1

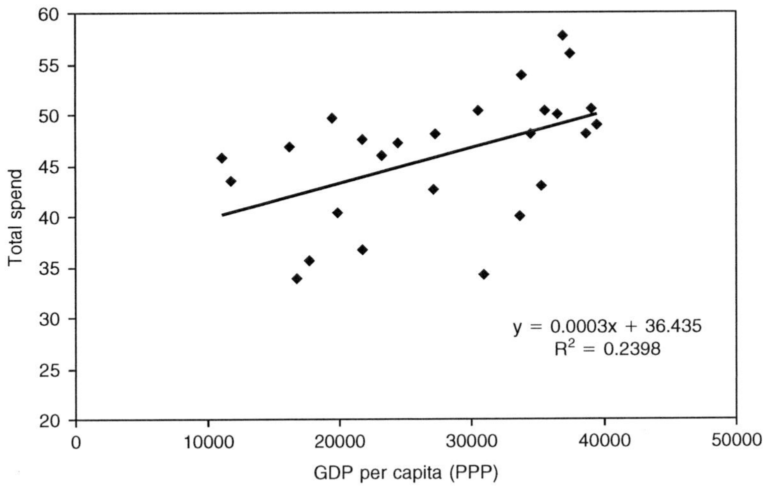

Figure A9.1 Relationship between the level of national income and total government spending

Notes: Correlation is +0.49. The relationship remains as strong if the logarithms of GDPs are used instead: +0.45.

Sources: Based on the data set of OECD (2006) and EC (2006).

Table A9.1 Gross domestic debt as percentage of GDP

	1980	Maximum (year)	2005	Change
Austria	36.1	71.6(2002)	65.3	6.3
Belgium	77.2	144.3(1993)	99.7	**44.6**
Denmark	45.9	88.9(1993)	47.7	**41.2**
Finland	13.8	66.6(1996)	54.7	**11.9**
France	30.1	74.2(2005)	74.2	0.0
Germany	31.2	71.6(2005)	71.6	0.0
Greece	22.8	114.0(2000)	108.3	5.7
Ireland	69.0	111.7(1987)	29.9	**81.8**
Italy	59.4	134.9(1998)	120.8	**14.1**
Netherlands	59.0	97.7(1993)	66.1	**31.6**
Portugal	30.6	78.0(2005)	78.0	0.0
Spain	16.4	77.1(1996)	55.2	**21.9**
Sweden	47.3	83.5(1994)	61.4	**22.1**
UK	56.0	53.8(1998)	46.3	7.5
Mean	42.5	90.6	69.9	20.6

Notes: Change means the difference between the maximum value and data in 2004. Bold: higher than 10 per cent change.

Source: Based on the data set of OECD (2006).

Notes

1. The political economy literature on permanent deficit has proliferated in the last two decades. See especially Grilli et al. (1991), Hallerberg and Hagen (1999) and Persson et al. (2000).
2. Using the sample of EU-26 (Luxembourg has been omitted), Appendix 9.1 shows that every $10,000 increase in GDP (on PPP) triggers a 3 percentage point increase in total spending (measured in GDP).
3. Importantly, individual countries varied substantially regarding the size of their public sector. At one extreme, there was Sweden with a ratio of 73 per cent (1993), while at the other extreme, Ireland produced a 32 per cent ratio (2000). Data have been taken from OECD (2006).
4. In Tanzi and Schuknecht (2003, 2005), a country was defined as an ambitious reformer if a minimum of 5 per cent (in GDP) decline in total spending between the maximum value of total spending and data in 2004 occurred.
5. Nevertheless, major international financial institutions are generally of the opinion that most governments – especially in Europe – have 'outgrown' their optimal size and entered a phase where spending crowds out private activity (see, for instance, Afonso et al., 2005).
6. Admittedly, the 1993 Treaty on the EU did not oblige national governments to initiate expenditure-based adjustments in their general budget. The Maastricht Treaty left the choice of option entirely up to national governments.
7. Specifically, OECD measures have been applied in our analysis, which estimates the cyclical effects on the structural budget by applying a production function approach.
8. The results were contrasted with the findings under a different measure, namely current expenditure and revenue. However, there was no significant change when such a different measure was applied.
9. For a critical assessment of the literature see Benczes (2006) for instance.
10. In Hauptmeier et al. (2006), ambitious reformers were those countries which initiated a minimum of 5 per cent recovery in primary spending (measured in GDP) in the seven years after the reform.
11. Regarding the relationship between fiscal policy and economic growth, the picture was rather ambiguous during the first few years of the transformation. By reviewing the empirical literature, Havrylyshyn (2001) for instance came to the conclusion that while inflation was a limiting factor to growth, previous works had not yet been able to disentangle the separate effects of fiscal imbalances and inflation on economic growth.
12. The spread around the mean is quite substantial, however. At the one extreme is Hungary with 50.3 per cent, while Estonia maintains a relatively small public sector, comparable in size to that of the US or Japan (32.4).
13. In fact, the real concern in the Baltic states is not fiscal performance but the overheating of their economies, which is reflected mostly in the accelerated inflation rate and the dramatically high annual deficit of the current account.

References

Afonso, António and González Alegre (2008). 'Economic Growth and Budgetary Components. A Panel Assessment for the EU', ECB Working Paper Series No. 848.

Afonso, António and Davide Furceri (2008). 'Government Size, Composition, and Economic Growth', ECB Working Paper Series No. 849.

Afonso, António, Werner Ebert, Ludger Schuknecht and Michael Thöne (2005). 'Quality of Public Finances and Growth', ECB Working Paper Series No. 438.

Alesina, A. and F. Giavazzi (2006). *The Future of Europe*, Cambridge, MA: MIT Press.

Alesina, A. and R. Perotti (1995). 'Fiscal Expansions and Adjustment in OECD Countries', *Economic Policy*, 10(21): 207–48.

Alesina, A., R. Perotti and J. Tavares (1998). 'The Political Economy of Fiscal Adjustments', *Brookings Papers on Economic Activity 1*, Washington DC: The Brookings Institution, pp. 197–266.

Barro, Robert and Xavier Sala-i-Martin (1995). *Economic Growth*, Cambridge, MA: MIT Press.

Benczes, István (2006). 'The Importance of Institutions in Expansionary Fiscal Consolidations: a Critical Assessment of Non-Keynesian Effects', TIGER Working Paper Series No. 88, May, Warsaw.

Berg, Andrew, Eduardo Borensztein, Ratna Sahay and Jeromin Zettelmeyer (1999). 'The Evolution of Output in Transition Economies', IMF Working Paper No. 99/73, May.

Buchanan, James M. (1997). 'The Balanced Budget Amendment: Clarifying the Arguments', *Public Choice*, 90(1–4): 117–38.

Easterly, William and Steven Rebelo (1993). 'Fiscal Policy and Economic Growth: an Empirical Investigation', *Journal of Monetary Economics*, 32(3): 417–58.

European Commission (2007). 'European Economy', autumn, Brussels.

European Commission (2006). 'European Economy – Statistical Annex', spring, Brussels.

European Commission (2005). 'Public Finances in EMU – 2005', Brussels.

European Commission (2000). 'Public Finances in EMU – 2000. European Economy', No. 3, Brussels.

Fischer, Stanley and Ratna Sahay (2000). 'The Transition Economies after Ten Years', IMF Working Paper No. 00/30, February.

Giavazzi, Franceso and Marco Pagano (1990). 'Can Severe Fiscal Contractions be Expansionary?' in O. Blanchard and S. Fischer (eds), *NBER Macroeconomics Annual*, Cambridge, MA: MIT Press.

Grilli, Vittorio, Daniel Masciandro and Guido Tabellini (1991). 'Political and Monetary Institutions and Public Finance Policies in the Industrial Democracies', *Economic Policy*, 13(2): 341–92.

Hallerberg, Michael and Jürgen von Hagen (1999). 'Electoral Institutions, Cabinet Negotiations and Budget Deficits in the European Union', in J. Poterba and J. von Hagen (eds), *Fiscal Institutions and Fiscal Performance*, Chicago: University of Chicago Press.

Hauptmeier, Sebastian, Martin Heipertz and Ludger Schuknecht (2006). 'Expenditure Reform in Industrialised Countries', ECB Working Paper Series No. 634.

Havrylyshyn, Oleh (2001). 'Recovery and Growth in Transition: a Decade of Evidence', *IMF Staff Papers*, 48(4): 4 pages.
Kornai, János (1992). *The Socialist System*, Oxford: Oxford University Press.
Lee, J-W. (1995). 'Capital Goods Imports and Long-Run Growth', *Journal of Development Economics*, 48: 91–110.
Lucas, R. (1988). 'On the Machanics of Economic Development', *Journal of Monetary Economics*, 22(1): 3–42.
McDermott, Christopher and Robert Westcott (1996). 'An Empirical Analysis of Fiscal Adjustments', *IMF Staff Papers*, 43(4): 725–53.
OECD (2006). *Economic Outlook*, No. 77, Paris: OECD.
Perotti, Robert, R. Strauch and Jürgen von Hagen (1998). *Sustainability of Public Finances*, Cambridge: Cambridge University Press.
Persson, Torsten, Gérard Roland and Guido Tabellini (2000). 'Comparative Politics and Public Finance', *Journal of Political Economy*, 108(6): 1121–41.
Purfield, Catriona (2003). 'Fiscal Adjustment in Transition Countries: Evidence from the 1990s', IMF Working Paper No. 36, February.
Rzonca, Andrzej and Piotr Cizkowicz (2005). 'Non-Keynesian Effects of Fiscal Contraction in New Member States', ECB Working Paper Series No. 519, September.
Segure-Ubiergo, Alex, Alejandro Simone and Sanjeev Gupta (2006). 'New Evidence on Fiscal Adjustment and Growth in Transition Economies', IMF Working Paper No. 06/244, October.
Tanzi, Vito and Ludger Schukneckt (2005). 'Reforming Public Expenditure in Industrialised Countries: are there Trade-offs?', ECB Working Paper Series No. 435.
Tanzi, Vito and Ludger Schukneckt (2003). 'Public Finances and Economic Growth in European Countries', in *Fostering Economic Growth*, proceedings of the 31st economics conference of the Oestereichsche National Bank on Fostering Economic Growth in Europe, 12–13 June, Vienna: OeNB, pp. 178–96.
Von Hagen, J., A. Hughes Hallett and R. Strauch (2001). 'Budgetary Consolidation in EMU', European Economy Papers No. 148, European Commission, Brussels, March.

Part III

Various Aspects of EU Economies: China and the World Economy, FDIs, Company Taxation, the ECB and the 'New' Member States

10
Company Taxation in the European Union: Current Developments and Implications for the Coordination Debate[1]

Margit Schratzenstaller

10.1 Introduction

International tax competition has become one of the most debated research areas within the field of public finance. Although opinions about its effects differ widely among scientists as well as policymakers, the existence of the phenomenon of tax competition as such is hardly disputed any longer. Recent empirical research corroborates the theoretical expectation that countries do indeed react to changes of the tax rate of other countries – particularly adjacent ones – by adapting their own tax rates to maintain or improve 'competitiveness' and/or to attract tax base in the form of mobile firms, investment, and profits.[2]

Within the 2004 and 2007 rounds of eastern enlargement 12 new member countries with generally rather attractive company tax rates joined the European Union. Accordingly, in the last few years, particularly Germany and France, which belong to the group of European 'high-tax countries', have been trying to push the coordination of company taxation in the European Union, an issue which has been on the European Commission's agenda for several decades now. The more progress is becoming visible concerning the work on the concrete design of a coordinated European company tax regime, however, the more explicit and even fierce opposition is voiced by those countries that fear for their fiscal autonomy should any binding coordination measure in the field of taxation be introduced.

This chapter reviews the most important recent trends in company taxation in European member states and the challenges they imply for European company tax policy. Against this background, the status quo and perspectives of company tax coordination in Europe are discussed.

10.1.1 Long-term developments in European company taxation

There are clear empirical indications for a gradual alignment of European company tax systems (for details see Schratzenstaller, 2007a). The most obvious convergence indicators are tax rates; but other important elements of company tax systems are also converging across member countries.

Table 10.1 shows the decreasing trend of nominal company tax rates which can be observed in practically all EU member states.[3] Between 1997 and 2007, the average nominal company tax rate fell by 9 percentage points (from 37.2 per cent to 28.3 per cent) across the old EU-15 and by 11.4 percentage points (from 30.3 per cent to 18.9 per cent) across the new EU-12. For the enlarged EU-27, between 1997 and 2007 the average statutory corporate tax rate went down by 8.9 percentage points, from 34.2 per cent to 25.2 per cent.

Up to now, no convergence of the level of company taxation between the old and the new member countries has taken place; at least not considering average company tax rates: the difference between the EU-15 and the EU-12 average widened from 6.9 percentage points to 9.4 percentage points in the last decade. However, several dispersion measures (standard deviation, variation coefficient, spread between highest and lowest tax rate) point at a downward convergence within old and new member states.

Statutory corporate tax rates are only one side of the coin, however, insofar as they do not reflect the overall effective tax burden on firm profits.[4] The effective tax burden is determined by statutory tax rates as well as by the rules by which to calculate the tax base. A number of different tax burden measures have been developed in the theoretical and empirical literature since the beginning of the 1980s.[5] Table 10.2 contains the development of several measures that capture the effective corporate tax burden for the EU-15 since the middle of the 1990s.

Among the most commonly used tax burden indicators are so-called forward-looking microeconomic effective tax rates for model investment projects, which are based on the current tax code and therefore capture the current or the future tax burden. While effective average tax rates (EATR) reflect the tax burden on model investment projects earning a positive rate of return, effective marginal tax rates (EMTR) refer to model investment projects yielding a zero rate of return. Both measures point to a decreasing corporate tax burden in the countries of the EU-15 between 1995 and 2005 (Table 10.2): EATR and EMTR, which are available for 13 old EU countries, decreased in the majority of old member states.

Table 10.1 Statutory corporate tax rates in the EU-27, 1997–2007 (%, including surcharges and local business taxes)

	1997	2000	2001	2002	2003	2004	2005	2006	2007	1997–2007
Belgium	40.2	40.2	40.2	40.2	34.0	34.0	34.0	34.0	34.0	–6.2
Denmark	34.0	32.0	30.0	30.0	30.0	30.0	28.0	28.0	22.0	–12.0
Finland	28.0	29.0	29.0	29.0	29.0	29.0	26.0	26.0	26.0	–2.0
Germany	57.5	51.6	38.4	38.4	39.6	38.3	38.3	38.3	38.4	–19.1
Greece	40.0	40.0	37.5	35.0	35.0	35.0	32.0	29.0	25.0	–15.0
Spain	35.0	35.0	35.0	35.0	35.0	35.0	35.0	35.0	32.5	–2.5
France	36.7	36.7	35.3	34.3	34.3	34.3	33.8	33.3	33.3	–3.4
Ireland	36.0	24.0	20.0	16.0	12.5	12.5	12.5	12.5	12.5	–23.5
Italy	53.2	41.3	40.3	40.3	38.3	37.3	37.3	37.3	37.3	–15.9
Luxembourg	30.3	37.5	37.5	30.4	30.4	30.4	30.4	29.6	29.6	–0.7
Netherlands	35.0	35.0	35.0	34.5	34.5	34.5	31.5	29.6	25.5	–9.5
Austria	34.0	34.0	34.0	34.0	34.0	34.0	25.0	25.0	25.0	–9.0
Portugal	39.6	37.4	35.2	33.0	33.0	27.5	27.5	27.5	25.0	–14.6
Sweden	28.0	28.0	28.0	28.0	28.0	28.0	28.0	28.0	28.0	0.0
United Kingdom	31.0	30.0	30.0	30.0	30.0	30.0	30.0	30.0	30.0	–1.0
Average EU-15	37.2	35.4	33.7	32.5	31.8	31.3	30.0	29.5	28.3	–9.0
Standard variation	8.1	6.4	5.3	5.8	6.1	6.0	6.0	6.0	6.3	–1.8
Variation coefficient	0.2	0.2	0.2	0.2	0.2	0.2	0.2	0.2	0.2	0.0
Spread	29.5	27.6	20.3	24.3	27.1	25.8	25.8	25.8	25.9	–3.6
Czech Republic	25.0	31.0	31.0	31.0	31.0	28.0	26.0	24.0	24.0	–1.0
Estonia	26.0	26.0	26.0	26.0	26.0	26.0	24.0	23.0	22.0	–4.0
Latvia	25.0	25.0	25.0	22.0	19.0	15.0	15.0	15.0	15.0	–10.0
Lithuania	29.0	24.0	24.0	15.0	15.0	15.0	15.0	19.0	18.0	–11.0
Hungary[a]	18.0	18.0	18.0	18.0	18.0	16.0	16.0	16.0	16.0	–2.0
Slovenia	25.0	25.0	25.0	25.0	25.0	25.0	25.0	25.0	23.0	–2.0
Slovak Republic	40.0	29.0	29.0	25.0	25.0	19.0	19.0	19.0	19.0	–21.0
Poland	38.0	30.0	28.0	28.0	27.0	19.0	19.0	19.0	19.0	–19.0
Malta	35.0	35.0	35.0	35.0	35.0	35.0	35.0	35.0	35.0	0.0
Cyprus	25.0	29.0	28.0	28.0	15.0	15.0	10.0	10.0	10.0	–15.0
Bulgaria	40.0	35.0	30.0	20.0	23.5	19.5	15.0	15.0	10.0	–30.0
Romania	38.0	38.0	25.0	25.0	25.0	25.0	16.0	16.0	16.0	–22.0
Average EU-12	30.3	28.8	27.0	24.8	23.7	21.5	19.6	19.7	18.9	–11.4
Standard variation	7.1	5.4	4.1	5.3	5.8	6.1	6.5	6.2	6.5	–0.7
Variation coefficient	0.2	0.2	0.2	0.2	0.2	0.3	0.3	0.3	0.3	0.1
Spread	22.0	20.0	17.0	20.0	20.0	20.0	25.0	25.0	25.0	3.0
Average EU- 27	34.2	32.2	30.9	29.5	28.9	27.5	26.4	26.2	25.2	–8.9

Note: a. Additionally 2 per cent local business (on total turnover), since September 2006 solidarity surcharge of 4 per cent on modified pre-tax profit.
Source: KPMG.

Table 10.2 Effective corporate tax rates in the EU-15

	Statutory CIT rate			EATR			EMTR			CIT revenues/GDP		
	1995	2005	1995–2007	1995	2005	1995–2005	1995	2005	1995–2005	1995	2004	1995–2004
Belgium	40.2	34.0	−6.2	31	26	−5	27	22	−5	2.7	3.6	0.9
Denmark	34	28.0	−6.0	n.a.	n.a.	n.a.	n.a.	n.a.	n.a.	2.3	3.2	0.9
Finland	25	26.0	1.0	19	21	2	14	17	3	2.3	3.6	1.3
Germany	59	38.3	−20.7	41	32	−9	37	29	−8	1	1.6	0.6
Greece	35	32.0	−3.0	33	21	−12	30	12	−18	2	3.3	1.3
Spain	35	35.0	0.0	24	26	2	17	21	4	1.7	3.4	1.7
France	36.7	33.8	−2.9	19	21	2	21	20	−1	2.1	2.8	0.7
Ireland	38	12.5	−25.5	8	11	3	7	10	3	2.7	3.6	0.9
Italy	53.2	37.3	−15.9	36	26	−10	30	19	−11	3.5	2.8	−0.7
Luxembourg	40.3	30.4	−9.9	n.a.	n.a.	n.a.	n.a.	n.a.	n.a.	6.6	5.8	−0.8
Netherlands	35	31.5	−3.5	28	25	−3	24	21	−3	3	3.1	0.1
Austria	34	25.0	−9.0	24	22	−2	18	20	2	1.4	2.3	0.9
Portugal	39.6	27.5	−12.1	29	20	−9	24	15	−9	2.4	2.9	0.5
Sweden	28	28.0	0.0	21	21	0	16	16	0	2.8	3.2	0.4
United Kingdom	33	30.0	−3.0	26	24	−2	23	20	−3	2.8	2.9	0.1
Average EU- 15	37.7	30.0	−7.8	26.1	22.8	−3.3	22.2	18.6	−3.5	2.6	3.2	0.6

Source: KPMG; IFS; OECD.

On average, EATR fell by 3.3 percentage points, EMTR by 3.5 percentage points.

At first sight the finding that falling nominal and effective micro-economic tax rates have not yet led to a reduction of company tax revenues in most member states is counter-intuitive (OECD, 2006; European Commission, 2006): in general, company tax revenues in relation to overall tax revenues or to GDP have remained stable or have even increased. Corporate tax payments in relation to GDP (a so-called backward-looking measure of the effective corporate tax burden, as it is based on data from the past on actual tax payments) increased by 0.6 percentage points on average in the EU-15 between 1995 and 2004.

As the extent to which the firm sector is incorporated differs between individual countries, cross-country comparisons of the corporate tax revenue-to-GDP ratio are not meaningful. Moreover, it must be noted that this tax burden measure is subject to considerable fluctuations over time, as it is very cyclically-sensitive. Its interpretation must take into account, too, that a significant portion of corporate tax payments is not affected in the year of the accrual of the corresponding profits.

Most important in the context of this chapter, however, is to stress that it would be short-sighted to take the stability or the increase of the corporate tax revenue-to-GDP ratio that is observable in the majority of EU-15 countries considered here as evidence against the hypothesis of a long-term erosion of enterprise taxation. The seemingly paradoxical phenomenon of decreasing forward-looking effective corporate tax rates on the one hand and stable/increasing shares of corporate tax revenues in GDP on the other hand can be explained by various developments. The first explanatory factor is tax-cuts-cum-base-broadening: the vast majority of EU states (European Commission, 2005) combined tax rate reductions with measures to broaden the tax base. As often underlined in the literature, this compensation mechanism has played and still does play a significant role as a revenue-preserving measure (Devereux et al., 2004). While this is certainly the case for the majority of countries, it should not induce overly optimistic expectations with regard to the long-term future of enterprise taxation (as it obviously does for quite a few authors), because in the long run the options to expand the tax base are limited (Devereux, 2006). Second, there is accumulating evidence of a rising corporate tax base: due to an increase in the number of incorporated firms[6] (which is not least the result of an increasing non-neutrality of enterprise tax systems with regard to the legal form of firms, as most countries have decreased corporate tax rates for incorporated firms to a larger extent than income tax rates for non-incorporated firms; de Mooij and Nicodème, 2007) and of taxable profits.[7] Third, several small countries offering very low corporate tax rates (for example, Ireland and Cyprus) have obviously managed to attract sufficient tax base from abroad to offset revenue losses from tax rate cuts (Haufler, 2007).

Tables 10.1 and 10.2 also illustrate the persistent tax rate differentials between old and new member states: nominal as well as effective average tax rates are considerably higher in the EU-15 countries.

Differences can also be found with regard to other characteristics of European company tax systems. Although in most old member states company tax reforms enacted in the last 25 years followed the already mentioned principle of tax-cuts-cum-base-broadening, their tax bases are in general still narrower than those of the new EU states. The rules for the determination of taxable profits still differ widely within and across the two country groups; concerning depreciation schemes, the valuation of inventories, the valuation and amortization of intangibles, reserves for bad debts and contingent liabilities, carry-over of losses and the taxation of capital gains. Also, whereas there is a general trend towards the 'dualization' of profit and income taxation by lowering the tax burden on investment and capital income, and classical systems with shareholder relief have become the dominant method to alleviate the double taxation of distributed dividends in both country groups, the total tax burden on dividends (company taxes and personal income taxes) is considerably lower on average in the new member states. Because of lower company tax rates, but also because several countries completely exempt distributed dividends from personal income taxes at the shareholder level. Finally, other (local) business taxes in addition to corporate taxes are of even less importance in the new member countries than in the old ones.

10.2 Challenges for European company tax policy

The developments within European company tax systems outlined above are not assessed unambiguously in the theoretical and policy-oriented literature (see Schratzenstaller 2007b for an overview). Tax policy is an important location factor in international competition for firm headquarters and investment. The entrance of a large group of, on average, low-tax countries into the EU is expected to increase the downward pressure on company tax rates. Moreover, the need to abolish preferential tax regimes in the new member states in the medium term as well as current European Court of Justice (ECJ) judicature aiming at abolishing tax barriers to capital mobility in the internal market may well intensify competition via regular company tax rates.

This section presents the most pressing current challenges within company taxation in the EU. Hereby we focus on problems caused by and related to the increasingly international context in which firms as well as national governments are acting and deciding.[8]

10.2.1 Downward pressure on company tax rates

The data and developments presented in this part of the chapter demonstrate that corporate tax rates are exposed to downward pressure in the EU. Although a general decline of corporate tax receipts cannot yet be observed, the development of corporate tax rates during the past 25 years, which we have reviewed above, supports expectations that corporate taxation might lose further in importance in the future.

As we have seen, there is a broad consensus in the relevant literature that countries use taxes in general and company taxes in particular as one – and not the least important – policy instrument to compete for internationally mobile firms, investments and profits. Considerable empirical evidence has accumulated over the last few years showing that countries do indeed react to tax changes by their neighbours (see Winner 2005 for an overview). Based on theoretical as well as empirical reasoning, the majority of authors in the meantime acknowledge some positive relationship between the openness of countries and the mobility of firms and capital on the one hand and the intensity of enterprise taxation on the other. Or, to put it another way: the higher the international integration of markets and thus capital mobility, the more pressure corporate tax rates are exposed to. According to an empirical analysis by Bretschger and Hettich (2002), enterprise tax competition has increased since the mid-1980s as a result of the growing mobility of firms and investment. For a sample of 19 OECD countries, Garretsen and Peters (2007), for example, find a negative relationship between capital mobility and corporate tax rates. At the same time, their analysis shows that core countries – for example Japan – manage to maintain a higher corporate tax rate than peripheral ones. This result is in line with the theoretical predictions and empirical results derived (for Europe) by Baldwin and Krugman (2002) based on the so-called new economic geography, according to which as a result of agglomeration advantages core countries can afford a relatively high corporate tax rate. Also country size plays a role: larger countries can uphold a positive tax rate differential, as their tax base is less elastic with regard to variations of the corporate tax rate compared to small countries;

a theoretical expectation which is confirmed by recent empirical studies (see for example Ganghof and Genschel, 2007).

Essentially, an erosion of enterprise taxation could have two effects: a level effect and a structural effect. By level effect we mean that the increasing pressure on company tax rates might eventually lead to decreasing tax revenues. The effects of the growing pressure on capital taxation exerted by international tax competition are discussed controversially in the literature (Schratzenstaller, 2007a). The proponents of a fair, that is non-discriminatory and transparent, tax competition based on general tax rates and tax bases point out its efficiency-enhancing potential: they expect limits for the size of the public sector and the 'fiscal exploitation' of tax subjects by an ever-growing state (which is conceived as a 'Leviathan' pursuing its own, purely selfish goals) as well as incentives for the public sector to enhance the efficiency of its activities, that is to provide public services efficiently (in terms of structure and level as well as cost efficiency of public service provision).

The opposing strand in the literature, which views the state and the government as benevolent and altruistic, points out potential negative effects of (an overly fierce) tax competition causing a level effect. Critics fear that shrinking corporate tax revenues could endanger the financing of public expenditures if they are not compensated by an increase in other taxes or of public debt. They expect outcomes which are judged negatively from an equity point of view, if, for example, redistributional welfare provisions have to be dismantled due to budgetary constraints caused by tax competition (see also Sinn, 1997). The result of a tax-competition induced level effect could also be an inefficiently low level of public inputs for enterprises and consequently the worsening of overall investment conditions for firms. For the new member states, where public infrastructure and services often have deficits – particularly in comparison to the established EU countries – the catching up process thus might be retarded. The latter were able to attract foreign capital by offering low company tax rates in the past, thus compensating for deficits in other locational factors in the short run. However, a catching-up process which is to be sustainable in the long run will have to build upon the increase of productive public expenditures, such as investing in education or high quality public infrastructure (Bellak et al., 2008). Whereas this potential effect of an erosion of capital taxation due to tax competition has been convincingly demonstrated in the theoretical literature, beginning with the seminal contribution by Zodrow and Mieszkowski (1986), little work has been undertaken up to now to determine its empirical relevance.

The second strategy that governments could pursue to compensate decreasing corporate tax receipts is a change in the tax mix. If governments try to avoid the decline of overall tax receipts due to shrinking corporate tax revenues by exploiting other, less mobile, tax bases more intensely (particularly labour, but also consumption), a shift in the structure of overall tax revenues rather than their decline would be the result.[9] The past few years have brought about quite a few empirical contributions corroborating this theoretical hypothesis. Winner (2005), for example, shows for a sample of 23 OECD countries that tax competition shifts the tax burden from the mobile tax base, capital, to the immobile tax base, labour. According to Adam and Kammas (2007), working with a sample of 17 OECD countries, higher economic integration goes along with rising social security contributions (that is, taxes on labour) and a falling tax burden on capital. Using a sample of 20 OECD countries, Schwarz (2007) identifies a weak negative influence of capital mobility on the corporate tax–labour tax ratio. Haufler et al. (2006) show that an increasing portion of capital employed in multinational firms is associated with an intensification of the indicated structural shift in overall tax revenues. Interestingly, recent empirical results also indicate that the impact of capital mobility and tax competition on the tax mix is more pronounced in small countries than in large countries (Winner, 2005; Schwarz, 2007). Such a structural change in the composition of overall tax revenues away from capital taxes towards labour taxes can be expected – as an increasing number of empirical studies show[10] – to have negative effects on economic growth and particularly on employment. More generally, the distribution of income and wealth or an even development within the firm sector might be affected or distorted by (further) shifts of the tax burden away from mobile tax bases to immobile ones, such as small and medium-sized firms, immobile labour, or consumption.

10.2.2 Enterprise taxation and the location of FDI

The question of whether taxes do influence FDI decisions is disputed in the theoretical and empirical literature. Theoretical reasoning delivers controversial hypotheses (see Sorensen, 2007 for an overview). On the one hand, the existence of capital mobility represents an important precondition for the effective use of tax policy in locational competition – that is, in attracting FDI by offering lower corporate tax rates. On the other hand, the locations of production and profits need not coincide if there is sufficient scope for profit shifting, allowing firms to avoid high corporate tax rates so that they do not need to pay much attention to the level of corporate tax rates and to tax rate differentials when deciding on the location of their investment. Moreover, it is argued that taxes are only one instrument within a whole catalogue of locational factors, and that firms take into account the quality and quantity of public inputs as well as taxes as the 'price' charged for them.

Empirical analyses, however, yield generally unambiguous results, at least concerning the kind of principal relationship between FDI and enterprise taxation: while results differ widely with respect to the size of the impact of corporate tax rates and international corporate tax rate differentials on the location of FDI, the vast majority of empirical studies deliver evidence for the existence of such an impact. For example, the frequently cited paper by de Mooij and Ederveen (2003), who conduct a meta-analysis of a large number of empirical studies, shows that (taking the mean value of the studies included and considering significant estimates only) a 1 percentage decrease in the corporate tax rate in a country would increase FDI flows to that country by 4 per cent. Most of the studies cited in the critical overview by Becker et al. (2006) also show a positive and significant influence of corporate tax rate reductions on FDI.

Of particular interest are recent results indicating asymmetric effects of corporate tax rate variations. According to Bénassy-Quéré et al. (2005) who examine 11 OECD countries (9 EU countries, the US and Japan) a comparatively high corporate tax rate does discourage FDI inflows. Lower(ing) corporate tax rates, however, hardly seems a successful strategy for attracting additional FDI from abroad. This confirms earlier work by Head et al. (1999) who find that high corporate tax rates have a negative effect on Japanese investment in the US, but that Japanese investment hardly reacts to low corporate tax rates. Bénassy-Quéré et al. (2005) also show that the impact of corporate tax rates is mitigated by market potential and the quantity of public inputs offered for the enterprise sector.

Finally, it must be noted that the existing empirical studies use different (effective) corporate tax rates. The notion that locational decisions are not primarily determined by statutory corporate tax rates, but mainly by effective average tax rates (EATR), which was first strongly advocated by Devereux and Griffith (1998) and has been increasingly accepted in the literature in the past few years, is challenged by a recent study by Buettner and Ruf (2007) showing that the FDI location decisions of German multinational firms are influenced most by statutory CIT rates: which could, however, just indicate the relevance of profit-shifting activities pursued through foreign affiliates in low-tax countries. This issue is treated in the next sub-section.

10.2.3 Enterprise taxation and the location of profits

An issue that has been attracting significant attention in the European enterprise tax discussion only for the last few years is the relocation of profits to low-tax countries, that is profit shifting. Profit shifting – the transfer of profits within multinational enterprises from high-tax to low-tax locations by manipulating transfer prices or by shifting mobile intra-firm services (holding services, cross-border financing, royalty management, leasing, insurance and so on) to controlled foreign corporations is of particular concern for the European Commission. The minimization of an MNE's total tax liabilities effected by such transactions implies the reduction and redistribution of EU-wide total company tax revenues and undermines benefit taxation, as MNEs escape an adequate financial contribution to the public infrastructure they use.

Empirical findings for Europe concerning determinants and volume of profit shifting are still sparse; however the few existing empirical studies for the EU seem to confirm the results of earlier work concentrating on the US.[11] Huizinga and Laeven (2006), for example, show a significant sensitivity of profits to nominal corporate tax rates. Their analysis finds evidence that particularly in high-tax Germany the tax base is considerably eroded by profit shifting to other EU member states offering lower corporate tax rates, thus confirming the results by Mintz and Weichenrieder (2005). For the OECD countries Bartelsman and Beetsma (2003) estimate a loss of 65 per cent of additional potential tax receipts from a unilateral tax increase due to profit shifting.

Clausing (2007) derives a parabolic relationship between corporate tax rates and revenues for the OECD countries. The author interprets this finding as an indication for profit shifting, as the additional revenue potential of a rise in the corporate tax rate can be expected to be (over-) compensated by the transfer of profit to lower-tax countries, because an increasing corporate tax rate (differential) increases the incentive for multinational firms to relocate their profits in a way that minimizes the overall tax liability at the firm level. Clausing's results also indicate that the 'revenue maximizing' corporate tax rate is lower in smaller and more open economies.

10.2.4 Systematic aspects of European enterprise taxation

Besides profit shifting and so-called unfair tax competition (that is competition via preferential tax regimes), the largest concern of the European Commission with regard to enterprise taxation in the EU is its complexity and non-transparency, as multinational firms engaged in the EU have to deal with up to 27 different and – concerning the rules to determine the tax base – still rather diverse enterprise tax systems. As the brief presentation above of different corporate tax burden measures shows, the determination of the effective tax burden prevailing in individual countries is a task that cannot be solved easily. This bears the danger of misguided decisions taken by multinational investors. In addition, the diversity of national enterprise tax systems in the EU causes high compliance and administrative costs both for tax administrations and for MNEs.

Moreover, the European Commission criticizes tax-related obstacles to the mobility of firms and/or their investment in the European Common Market, that is so-called exit taxes or the absence of consolidation measures in almost all EU countries (Austria being one of the few notable exceptions, with its group taxation regime introduced in 2005) to offset losses incurred in one member state against profits realized in another.

10.3 The debate about company tax coordination in the EU: status quo and perspectives

It is against the backdrop of the arguments sketched in the preceding section that the European Commission has – over four decades now – launched a variety of initiatives intended to coordinate or harmonize company taxation.

Those economists whose arguments are based on a 'Leviathan' view of the state strongly oppose the introduction of supranational tax coordination/harmonization measures in the EU. They fear that these would restrict the autonomy of national governments, that is, that they would diminish national tax sovereignty and violate the subsidiarity principle, as national governments could no longer determine tax bases and tax rates according to their own needs and preferences. However, from a governance perspective the crucial question appears to be whether – contrary to this view – coordination/harmonization on the supranational level is a precondition *for* rather than a restriction *of* national tax sovereignty and subsidiarity (Ganghof and Genschel, 2006), and thus indispensable to regaining the scope for effective governance at the national level.

The discussion above of the effects of tax competition in the EU seems to provide a reasonably strong case for some harmonization of enterprise taxation in the EU. At the EU level, several approaches to the coordination of taxation – or modes of tax governance – have been and are discussed and pursued. One approach is an informal one. The most prominent example in this regard is the European Commission's fight against harmful tax competition via preferential (and discriminatory) tax provisions (European Commission, 1997), which is based on informal governance: the so-called code of conduct on business taxation is a legally non-binding governance instrument which can be considered as fairly successful in containing harmful tax competition among EU countries.

The alternative, formal governance approach aims at the introduction of binding harmonization measures codified in EU directives. However, up to now, all such formal initiatives of the European Commission taken since the beginning of the 1960s have failed.[12]

The scope, extent and speed of coordination/harmonization have differed markedly between direct and indirect taxes in the EU. Meanwhile, based on Articles 90 and 93 of the EU Treaty a far-reaching harmonization of indirect taxes (general as well as consumption taxes) has been achieved, which is a basic precondition for the realization of an internal market with free movement of goods and services without tax-induced distortions. In contrast, the EU does not have an explicit mandate to coordinate or harmonize direct taxes. According to Article 94 such measures can be justified only indirectly if otherwise the functioning of the common market is hampered. This has – in combination with the unanimity principle in decisions concerning tax matters – prevented the introduction of coordination or harmonization measures with a broader scope in the realm of company taxation in the past. During the last decades member states agreed only a few directives targeted at very specific problems (mostly connected with cross-border company relations), for instance the merger directive, the interest and royalty directive, or the parent-subsidiary directive. All of the more comprehensive initiatives proposed by the European Commission since the 1960s aiming at a general coordination of tax rates and the tax base have failed.

Member countries' reluctance to give up national tax sovereignty and the general conviction of the overall beneficial effects of 'fair' tax competition made the European Commission change its coordination strategy at the beginning of the 1990s: this followed the failure of its last comprehensive harmonization proposal, which was based on the so-called Ruding report and suggested minimum company tax rates combined with a uniform tax base. Since then, the Commission's priorities have been the elimination of unfair tax competition via discriminatory tax provisions and the harmonization of the company tax base.

To prevent profit shifting and for the sake of greater transparency and simplification of European company taxation, the European

Commission, inter alia, put forward the proposal to introduce a common consolidated corporate tax base (CCCTB) plus formula apportionment in 2001. Consolidated profits would be allocated according to an apportionment formula still to be defined, which could include turnover, the wage bill and/or fixed assets, to those countries in which an MNE is active (European Commission, 2001). Setting tax rates should, however, remain the prerogative of member states: the European Commission has no intention to harmonize company tax rates.

More recently, the European Commission has come forward with a series of initiatives aiming to promote compliance of national company tax systems with Community legislation and more coherent treatment of taxpayers subject to more than one tax system (European Commission, 2007), with Tax Commissioner Laszlo Kovacs explicitly stating, at the same time, that only the adoption of the CCCTB could enable a fully satisfactory solution to the problems of cross-border loss relief in Europe.

However, the European Commission's efforts to intensify and accelerate work on the CCCTB have been met with increasing resistance or at least fundamental scepticism by member states.[13] The European Commission's objective is the preparation of a formal proposal in 2008. In case of a veto by the sceptical member states, the Commission plans to refile the proposal under the 'enhanced cooperation' provision of the treaty allowing a minimum of eight countries supportive of the concept[14] to press ahead regardless and to put a CCCTB in place by 2010.

It is obvious that any solution involving only a small group of member countries is sub-optimal. The same holds for solutions which would not be mandatory but in which member states and/or firms could participate on a voluntary basis, as the European Commission also envisages in its most recent proposal. Not only would such half-hearted reforms add to the already existing complexity and non-transparency of European company taxation: they would also be unable effectively to tackle the profit shifting issue. The following deliberations focus on a more fundamental evaluation of the European Commission's plan to replace national rules to determine the company tax base by a CCCTB against the EU's economic and legal framework.

It seems beyond doubt that a coordinated solution on the EU level is indispensable to protect national tax revenues against erosion through profit shifting strategies by MNEs. Currently most member states try to counteract such tax-minimizing strategies via unilateral measures, many of which are, however, against Community law and therefore are increasingly endangered by ECJ judicature (Wissenschaftlicher Beirat beim Bundesministerium der Finanzen, 2007).

The alignment of the tax base is a first important step towards a coordinated solution within the EU, as it would enhance the transparency and simplicity of European company taxation and thus reduce compliance and administration costs. As Jacobs et al. (2007) show, however, a common tax base established, for instance, on International Accounting Standards/International Financial Reporting Standards (IAS/IFRS) will not reduce the existing differences in effective company tax rates, which implies increasing pressure on nominal tax rates as the only tax competition parameters to remain after harmonizing the tax base. Moreover, with persisting nominal tax rate differentials, incentives for cross-border profit shifting would continue to exist.

The move from separate accounting to the determination of a consolidated tax base based on uniform rules plus formula apportionment appears a more effective approach to the prevention of profit shifting. The implications of this coordination option for EU-wide company tax revenues and their distribution across member countries are the focus of several recent empirical studies. That these studies do not yield clear-cut results is due to methodological difficulties and differences, but underlines also the crucial importance especially of the design of the apportionment formula and the set of rules to determine the tax base. Devereux and Loretz (2006) show that almost all individual member states would realize higher company tax revenues and that EU-wide company tax revenues would increase considerably (by more than 8 per cent) if all companies were forced to participate in a profit consolidation and apportionment procedure. These results are in stark contrast to an analysis conducted by Fuest et al. (2006) according to which a common EU tax base with formula apportionment would significantly reduce the overall tax base. Moreover, according to this study smaller countries would lose more tax base than larger ones.

As this reform option means taxing company profits according to the source principle, however, cross-country tax rate differentials may distort location or other firm decisions, depending on the composition of the apportionment formula. A CCCTB plus formula apportionment may also provide incentives for member states to decrease their nominal tax rates to attract those economic activities or tax bases included in the apportionment formula. Therefore the introduction of a CCCTB plus formula apportionment without the alignment of tax rates might increase current economic distortions instead of reducing them.

The current debate among member states on the future of European company taxation leaves little doubt that unanimous political support for coordinated or harmonized company tax rates is highly unlikely.

From an economic point of view, however, a harmonization of European company taxation which goes beyond the adoption of common rules to determine the tax base can hardly be recommended without aligning company tax rates (Wissenschaftlicher Beirat beim Bundesministerium der Finanzen, 2007). However, also based on economic considerations, the introduction of a uniform minimum corporate tax rate in the enlarged EU cannot be considered a useful harmonization measure (Schratzenstaller, 2007b). If the minimum corporate tax rate was fixed at a relatively low level it would not represent an effective downward barrier for the old member states with their (on average) relatively high nominal tax rates. A relatively high minimum tax rate on the other hand would harm the new member countries in face of the prevailing economic divergences in the enlarged EU: most new members would be forced to increase their corporate tax rates, which would deprive them of the option to offer a tax rebate that compensates for other locational disadvantages, and which would thus divert FDI and tax base and as a consequence slow down the catching-up process to the established EU countries by deterring foreign and domestic investment.

It may be useful, therefore, to consider a coordination option that involves a CCCTB plus formula apportionment combined with the introduction of a two-tier minimum corporate tax rate – a higher one for the old member states and a lower one for the new ones – at least until the existing economic divergences between old and new member countries have been considerably reduced. Finally, it should be noted that isolated coordination/harmonization measures within corporate taxation will need to be complemented by coordination/harmonization measures in the overall systems of capital taxation, considering the existing diversity in the taxation of the non-incorporated business sector as well as of profits at the shareholder level (Brochner et al., 2007).

Notes

1. This chapter is an extended version of Schratzenstaller (2007c).
2. There is some new empirical evidence, too, for international fiscal competition via public spending (see, for example, Borck et al., 2007), which is a very relevant aspect particularly in the context of international competition for mobile firms and their investment. However, consideration of this would go beyond the scope of this chapter.
3. Exceptions are Sweden and Malta, where company tax rates remained constant in this period.

4. This is not to say that statutory corporate tax rates are of no importance: on the contrary, they are a psychological signal for potential investors and serve as a first orientation for the effective corporate tax burden, and they determine profit shifting from high-tax to low-tax countries.
5. For an extensive overview, see for example the contributions in Sorensen (2004).
6. For empirical evidence for Austria and Germany see Weichenrieder (2005).
7. For empirical evidence for the UK see Devereux et al. (2004); for a larger group of OECD countries see Sorensen (2007).
8. Thus structural problems (that is non-neutrality with regard to the capital structure or the legal form of firms) inherent in most national enterprise tax systems (for the enlarged EU, see Schratzenstaller, 2007b) will be neglected.
9. Other structural effects, for example the erosion of the so-called backstop function of corporate income tax for personal income tax and the ensuing erosion of the latter's revenue potential and/or progressivity (see, for example, Ganghof and Genschel, 2007) must – though certainly important – be neglected in this paper.
10. For an extensive overview of empirical studies, see Schratzenstaller (2007c).
11. See Hines (1999) for an overview of empirical analyses supporting the phenomenon of profit shifting from the US as a high-tax country to countries with lower corporate tax rates. Devereux (2006) provides a comprehensive overview of new empirical analyses focusing on profit shifting.
12. For an overview of the various initiatives taken by the European Commission to coordinate enterprise taxation in the EU, see Griffith and Klemm (2004) and Schratzenstaller (2007a). The latter also provides a detailed discussion of the alternative blueprints for enterprise tax coordination in the EU put forward by the European Commission in 2001.
13. According to press reports, explicit opponents are the United Kingdom and Ireland and several new member states, including Latvia, Lithuania, the Slovak Republic and Malta; the group of sceptics consists, inter alia, of Belgium, Cyprus, the Czech Republic, Denmark, Finland, Greece, Poland, Portugal, Slovenia and Sweden.
14. Explicitly supportive besides Germany are Austria, France and Italy.

References

Adam, A. and P. Kammas (2007). 'Tax Policies in a Globalized World: it is Politics After All?' *Public Choice*, 127: 321–41.

Baldwin, R.E. and P. Krugman (2002). 'Agglomeration, Integration and Tax Harmonization', NBER Working Paper, No. 9290.

Bartelsman, E.J. and R. Beetsma (2003). 'Why Pay More? Corporate Tax Avoidance through Transfer Pricing in OECD Countries', *Journal of Public Economics*, 87: 2225–52.

Becker, J., C. Fuest and Th. Hemmelgarn (2006). 'How Does FDI React to Corporate Taxation? A Replication Study with Aggregate Data', mimeo, University of Cologne.

Bellak, Ch., M. Leibrecht and A. Riedl (2008). 'Labour Costs and FDI Flows into Central and Eastern European Countries: a Survey of the Literature and Empirical Evidence', *Structural Change and Economic Dynamics*, 19: 17–37.

Bénassy-Quéré, A., L. Fontagné and A. Lahrèche-Rèvil (2005). 'How Does FDI React to Corporate Taxation?' *International Tax and Public Finance*, 12: 583–603.

Borck, R., M. Caliendo and V. Steiner (2007). 'Fiscal Competition and the Composition of Public Spending: Theory and Evidence', *FinanzArchiv/Public Finance Analysis*, 63: 264–77.

Bretschger, L. and F. Hettich (2002). 'Globalisation, Capital Mobility and Tax Competition: Theory and Evidence for OECD Countries', *European Journal of Political Economy*, 18: 695–716.

Brochner, J., J. Jensen, P. Svensson and P. B. Sorensen (2007). 'The Dilemmas of Tax Coordination in the Enlarged European Union', *CESifo Economic Studies*, 53: 561–95.

Buettner, T. and M. Ruf (2007). 'Tax Incentives and the Location of FDI: Evidence from a Panel of German Multinationals', *International Tax and Public Finance*, 14: 151–64.

Clausing, K. (2007). 'Corporate Tax Revenues in OECD Countries', *International Tax and Public Finance*, 14: 115–33.

de Mooij, R.A. and S. Ederveen (2003). 'Taxation and Foreign Direct Investment: a Synthesis of Empirical Research', *International Tax and Public Finance*, 10: 673–93.

de Mooij, R.A. and G. Nicodème (2007). 'Corporate Tax Policy and Incorporation in the EU', Solvay Business School Working Paper, No. WP-CEB 07-016.

Devereux, M.P. (2006). 'The Impact of Taxation on the Location of Capital, Firms and Profit: a Survey of Empirical Evidence', paper prepared for the European Tax Policy Forum Conference, The Impact of Corporation Taxes Across Borders, April, London.

Devereux, M.P. and R. Griffith (1998). 'Taxes and the Location of Production – Evidence from a Panel of US Multinationals', *Journal of Public Economics*, 68: 335–67.

Devereux, M.P. and S. Loretz (2006). 'The Effects of EU Formula Apportionment on Corporate Tax Revenues', Oxford University Centre for Business Taxation Working Paper, No. 07/06, Oxford.

Devereux, M.P., R. Griffith and A. Klemm (2004). 'Why Has the UK Corporation Tax Raised so Much Revenue?' *Fiscal Studies*, 25(4): 367–88.

European Commission (1997). 'Towards Tax Co-ordination in the European Union: a Package to Tackle Harmful Tax Competition', COM 97(495) final, Brussels.

European Commission (2001). 'Company Taxation in the Internal Market', COM 2001(582) final, Brussels.

European Commission (2005). 'Structures of the Taxation Systems in the European Union', 2005 Edition, Luxembourg.

European Commission (2006). 'Structures of the Taxation Systems in the European Union', 2006 Edition, Luxembourg.

European Commission (2007). 'Communication from the Commission to the European Parliament, the Council and the European Economic and Social Committee. Implementing the Community Programme for Improved Growth and Employment and the Enhanced Competitiveness of EU Business: Further

Progress during 2006 and Next Steps towards a Proposal on the Common Consolidated Corporate Tax Base (CCCTB)', COM(2007) 223 final, Brussels.

Fuest, C., Th. Hemmelgarn and F. Ramb (2006). 'How Would Formula Apportionment in the EU Affect the Distribution and the Size of the Corporate Tax Base? An Analysis Based on German Multinationals', Deutsche Bundesbank Discussion Paper, Series 1: Economic Studies, No. 20/2006, Frankfurt am Main.

Ganghof, S. and Ph. Genschel (2006). 'Tax Policy in an Enlarging EU: is there a Case for a Minimum Company Tax Rate?' MPIfG Discussion Paper, No. 06/1.

Ganghof, S. and Ph. Genschel (2007). 'Taxation and Democracy in the EU', MPIfG Discussion Paper, No. 07/02.

Garretsen, H. and J. Peters (2007). 'Capital Mobility, Agglomeration and Corporate Tax Rates: is the Race to the Bottom for Real?' *CESifo Economic Studies*, 53: 263–93.

Griffith, R. and A. Klemm (2004). 'What has Been the Tax Competition Experience of the Past 20 Years?' IFS Working Paper, No. W04/05.

Haufler, A. (2007). 'Sollen multinationale Unternehmen weniger Steuern bezahlen?' *Vierteljahrshefte zur Wirtschaftsforschung*, 76: 8–20.

Haufler, A., A. Klemm and G. Schjelderup (2006). 'Globalisation and the Mix of Wage and Profit Taxes', Münchener Wirtschaftswissenschaftliche Beiträge (VWL), No. 2006–7.

Head, C.K., C. Ries and D. Swenson (1999). 'Attracting Foreign Manufacturing: Investment Promotion and Agglomeration', *Regional Science and Urban Economics*, 29: 197–218.

Hines, J.R. (1999). 'Lessons from Behavioral Responses to International Taxation', *National Tax Journal*, 52: 312–17.

Huizinga, H.P. and L. Laeven (2006). 'International Profit Shifting within European Multinationals: a Multi-Country Perspective', paper prepared for the General Directorate Economic and Financial Affairs Workshop on Corporate Tax Competition and Coordination in Europe, 25 September, Brussels.

Jacobs, O.H., Ch. Spengel, Th. Stetter and C. Wendt (2007). 'EU Company Taxation in Case of a Common Tax Base', ZEW Discussion Paper, No. 05-37, Mannheim.

Mintz, J. and A. Weichenrieder (2005). 'Taxation and the Financial Structure of German Outbound FDI', CESifo Working Paper, No. 1612, Munich.

OECD (2006). *Revenue Statistics*, Paris: OECD.

Schratzenstaller, M. (2007a). 'Unternehmensbesteuerung in der Europäischen Union – Aktuelle Entwicklungen und Implikationen für die deutsche Steuerpolitik', *Vierteljahrshefte zur Wirtschaftsforschung*, 76: 21–38.

Schratzenstaller, M. (2007b). 'Company Tax Competition and Co-ordination in an Enlarged European Union', in J. McCombie and C. Rodriguez Gonzalez (eds), *The European Union: Current Problems and Prospects*, New York: Palgrave.

Schratzenstaller, M. (2007c). 'Company Tax Coordination in the EU – Status Quo and Perspectives', *Intereconomics*, 42: 116–20.

Schwarz, P. (2007). 'Does Capital Mobility Reduce the Corporate-Labor Tax Ratio?' *Public Choice*, 130: 363–80.

Sinn, H.W. (1997). 'The Selection Principle and Market Failure in Systems Competition', *Journal of Public Economics*, 66: 247–74.

Sorensen, P.B. (ed.) (2004). *Measuring the Tax Burden on Capital and Labor*, Cambridge, MA: MIT Press.

Sorensen, P.B. (2007). 'Can Capital Income Taxes Survive? And Should They?' *CESifo Economic Studies*, 53: 172–228.

Weichenrieder, A. (2005). '(Why) Do We Need Corporate Taxation?', in Oesterreichische Nationalbank (ed.), *Proceedings of OeNB Workshop No. 6 – Capital Taxation after EU Enlargement*, Vienna: Oesterreichische Nationalbank.

Winner, H. (2005). 'Has Tax Competition Emerged in OECD Countries? Evidence from Panel Data', *International Tax and Public Finance*, 12: 667–87.

Wissenschaftlicher Beirat beim Bundesministerium der Finanzen (2007). 'Einheitliche Bemessungsgrundlage der Körperschaftsteuer in der Europäischen Union', Bundesministerium der Finanzen, Berlin.

Zodrow, G.R. and P. Mieszkowski (1986). 'Pigou, Tiebout, Property Taxation, and the Underprovision of Local Public Goods', *Journal of Urban Economics*, 19: 356–70.

11
The Policy of the ECB and its Impact on the Economic Development of New EU Members

Milan Sojka

11.1 Introduction

During discussions in the Czech Republic of the possible positive and negative effects of joining the European Monetary Union, criticism frequently concentrates on the potential negative effects of giving up national monetary and exchange rate policies, and on the impact of ECB monetary policy on the small open economies of the new EU members in Central and Eastern Europe. Giving up national monetary and exchange rate policies and accepting the single EU monetary policy executed by the European Central Bank is frequently seen as a problem not only for the nominal convergence process but for real convergence as well.

The fear is that under present conditions, joining the EMU could have a negative effect on the process of real convergence, that barriers could be created as a result of the ECB's political preferences for curbing inflation within the framework of inflation targeting. Possible increases in interest rates could complicate access to financial resources for investment and decrease growth rates, with different impacts on the more and less developed members and regions of the EU.

Such fears are founded on analyses of the ECB statutes and are supported by the inflation targeting practised by the ECB, and by an asymmetry in monetary and fiscal policies at the EU level.

For post-communist and less developed EU member states, the monetary policy of the ECB in combination with the Maastricht criteria may result in slowing down the catching-up process. In this chapter, my aim is to evaluate those fears from the point of view of modern post-Keynesian monetary analysis based on the theory of a relative endogeneity of money supply, which is one of the most important contemporary alternatives to mainstream monetary theory.

In Section 11.2, the basic principles of the modern post-Keynesian monetary theory of production are briefly presented. In Section 11.3 the role of the ECB and its monetary policy are briefly assessed from the post-Keynesian point of view. Post-Keynesian criticisms of the 'new consensus' in monetary policy and monetary theory that forms the basis of inflation targeting are noted. In Section 11.4 I will try to explain the potential negative effects of ECB monetary policy on the macroeconomic development of the Czech economy and the economies of the new post-communist EU member states (or all the less developed EU members) after joining the Eurozone.

11.2 Post-Keynesian monetary theory

Post-Keynesian monetary theory (see for example, Arestis, 1992; Lavoie, 2003; Rousseas, 1986; Rochon and Rossi, 2003), which plays the role of anchor in this chapter, was born as a critical reaction to the monetarist counter-revolution at the beginning of the 1970s. Since the start of the twenty-first century it has developed into a full-fledged alternative to monetarist theory and new Keynesian monetary theory. In the post-Keynesian monetary theory of production the financial institutions play very important roles. Many post-Keynesian economists, following the heritage of John Maynard Keynes, consider money as an institution which has an important role as a tool to overcome uncertainty. It is for them a vehicle for transferring past and present economic values to the future (Davidson, 1978).

In this approach the role of credit is of utmost importance. Money is 'credit driven and demand determined' according to the post-Keynesians (Dow and Rodríguez-Fuentes, 1998, p. 7). By the assertion that money is demand determined, the post-Keynesians understand that the demand for money creates endogenously the supply of money when demand for credit due to investment expansion is increasing, and destroys money in recession when investment demand for credit is decreasing. The second assertion, according to which money is credit driven, describes the way in which money is created by credit multiplication processes in reaction to demand for credit based on investment activities. This leads to the theory of endogeneity of money supply according to which money is created and destroyed in reaction to changes in aggregate demand and particularly to the changes in demand for credit.

In its original simplified form, usually known as horizontalism (Kaldor, 1980, 1982; Weintraub, 1978; Moore, 1988, 2006, among others), commercial banks were viewed as price-setters and quantity takers. Thus, banks determine interest rates on the bases of marking up the central banks' discount rate and the demand for credit determines the quantity of money supplied. This resulted in the notion of a comparatively passive role for the banking sector and a very simplified role for the central bank, which uses the discount rate (understood as an exogenous policy variable) to (co-)determine bank interest rates. Under such conditions demand for money automatically creates a supply of money and a kind of 'perpetuum mobile' arises. The supply of money can be represented in the quantity of money and the interest rate space by a horizontal line given by an interest elasticity of demand for credits. However, the central bank is assumed to play the role of the lender of last resort and to practise an accommodative monetary policy (Kaldor, 1980).

In contemporary post-Keynesian economics this theory is usually considered as the first approximation to the endogeneity of money supply. It is still held by a minority of post-Keynesians. For example Basil Moore (2006) maintains the horizontalist view but he also incorporates in his explanation more realistic concepts of the behaviour of commercial banks when reacting to applications for credit (Moore, 2006, pp. 205ff.). According to the post-Keynesian monetary theory of production, monetarism leads to a very costly way of curbing inflation by denying the injection of adequate liquidity into the economy. Such a regime creates rising interest rates and its effectiveness is based on decreasing interest-elastic components of aggregate demand.

However, the post-Keynesian theory of the relative endogeneity of money supply does recognize that there are limits to the credit creation of money as a result of the behaviour of the monetary authority and of commercial banks. In this approach the monetary policy of the central bank is important even in the face of the endogeneity of money supply. In post-Keynesian monetary theory monetary policy includes not only 'traditional' tools (open market operations, reserve requirements, discount rate and so on) but also administrative regulatory (or qualitative) tools (bank regulation and supervision). According to many post-Keynesians, administrative or qualitative tools become increasingly more important for the stabilization of the banking sector than do traditional or quantitative tools. In mainstream economics textbooks 'financial regulation' is seen neither as an integral part of monetary policy nor as a 'positive factor which may encourage lending by providing confidence in the working of the financial system' (Dow and Rodríguez-Fuentes, 1998, p. 3).

Relationships between the central bank and commercial banks and between commercial banks and firms are taken into account, and the theory becomes more realistic as it does not ignore the behaviour of the banking sector. Commercial banks assess the risk connected with granting credit to different applicants on the basis of their creditworthiness, and set higher interest rates in cases of higher risk. When the risk exceeds an acceptable rate commercial banks are unwilling to grant credit at any interest rate. There is a ceiling on interest rates above which credit is not granted and credit rationing occurs (Stiglitz and Weiss, 1981; Wray, 1992; Wolfson, 1996). Under such conditions (especially where the central bank is fighting inflation by the usual restrictive monetary policy), the supply of credit becomes less and less elastic and its elasticity may potentially come close to zero (Minsky, 1982, p. 107).

Post-Keynesian theory states that money can be created in three ways. The first is based on the fact that production requires time and the purchase of inputs must be financed before outputs are sold. As a result of this money is created together with new credit. In a dynamic monetary economy of production (the concept used by many contemporary post-Keynesian economists for the capitalist market economy) credit arises in order to facilitate production and other activities of firms and to enable the purchase of long-run consumption goods by households. In such an economy money is created as the effect of credit flows (Eichner and Kregel, 1975). Under such conditions, institutions granting credit (especially banks) play a fundamental role and because of this we should thoroughly examine the way they behave. Though the granting of credit to facilitate production should be considered a standard case, credit may also be misallocated, as perhaps in the case of speculation created by a fundamental uncertainty. The misallocation of credit and the inability of firms to repay their debts underlie the formation of financial crises.

The second way in which money is created consists in financial operations and free market operations implemented by the monetary authorities. In this case an important asymmetry arises. Monetary authorities can generally increase the money supply on their own initiative.

The third way is represented in an open economy by flows of money in and out of the country. Generally a balance of payments surplus leads to money creation and a deficit to money destruction. In this context the rate of openness of the economy, the exchange rate regime and the behaviour of the monetary authorities should be taken into account (Dow, 1996, 1997).

Money is always created through interactions between economic agents (firms, households, commercial banks and the monetary authorities). The quantity of money in an economy is the result of the decision-making of economic agents. It is determined in an endogenous way, and measures taken by the monetary authorities may be negated by the behaviour of economic agents. As a result, the monetary authorities are unable to create or to destroy money in a direct way. They are able to do it only indirectly through increasing (or decreasing) interest rates, that is, in decreasing (or increasing) interest-elastic components of aggregate demand.

In post-Keynesian economics, entrepreneurs play a decisive role in these processes. Entrepreneurs must form their expectations of future developments of aggregate demand and its structure, and on the basis of this calculate the necessary money outlays for investments and purchases of factors of production. In this way they formulate their demand for credit. The central bank sets the discount rate and commercial banks set their interest rates taking into account estimated risks and value of collateral. Within this framework commercial banks are disposed to grant credit and the corresponding demand for credit creates an increase in the supply of money. Interest rates are the only tool available to regulate, indirectly via their impact on demand for credit, the quantity of money in the economy at the disposal of the monetary authorities. However no direct transmission mechanism exists in reality. The monetary authorities set the discount rate that affects the interest rates of commercial banks. Interest rates together with an evaluation of risk and the value of collateral determine demand for credit and the supply of money is determined by credit money creation or destruction processes (Artis and Lewis, 1981, 9; Chick, 1983).

According to the new Keynesian and post-Keynesian theories of credit rationing, commercial banks are disposed to grant credit to all creditworthy applicants. 'Banks consider the risk of inability to repay the credit of single applicants, and divide them into categories for which price (interest rates, payments connected with establishment of a credit line) and non-price conditions for granting credit are determined' (Wolfson, 1996, p. 457).

Commercial banks may ration credit not only by refusals and by increasing interest rates but also by increasing the value of required collateral (especially in relation to new applicants). Commercial banks are not automatically disposed to grant credit even in the case of very high interest rates because speculative demand for credit under asymmetric information may lead to moral hazard. Some applicants for credit may even be unwilling to repay credit from the outset (Stiglitz and Weiss, 1981).

The willingness of commercial banks to grant credits decreases in recessions and increases in expansions. It is closely connected with uncertainty. During recessions liquidity preference is high and the willingness of commercial banks to grant credit is affected by a more stringent estimation of creditworthiness and the credit supply curve is steeper than during expansions (Dow and Rodríguez-Fuentes, 1998, p. 11).

The indirect way in which the discount rate can affect the quantity of money makes monetary policy a very problematic tool for curbing inflationary pressures. Monetarist anti-inflationary policy aims at the direct decrease of the money supply. However in reality it operates through the restriction of demand for credit and the demand for money. It is inevitably costly as it increases interest rates and consequently decreases motivation to invest and macroeconomic performance (it decreases the rate of growth, increases unemployment and so on). As with a Keynesian approach, in which prices are relatively inflexible, the economy adjusts primarily through quantity adjustment processes, income effects are important, and the increase in interest rates must be significant in order to have any visible effects in curbing inflation.

According to post-Keynesians the major problem of anti-inflationary monetary policy is a mistaken diagnosis of the causes of inflation. Since the Second World War in the developed capitalist market economies inflationary pressures have usually been of the cost-push type, and are connected with the wage-price spiral. Demand-pull inflation is comparatively rare. Monetary policy is thus a very inadequate tool to fight inflation and its result is usually a very high cost in terms of production and jobs lost in the short and medium run. It may also have harmful effects on potential GDP growth. The present-day inflation targeting based on the new Keynesian consensus certainly provides a more sophisticated monetary policy framework. However, the basic mechanism of fighting inflation is only slightly different, as interest rates are also considered a major tool of monetary policy, and the anti-inflationary policy is accomplished directly through increasing discount rates. We may characterize inflation targeting as an 'aggregate demand fine-tuning' through monetary policy (Fontana and Palacio-Vera, 2006, p. 49).

11.3 The European Central Bank, its position and the role of its monetary policy from a post-Keynesian view

I now turn my attention to two basic areas of criticism in the recent post-Keynesian literature concerning the role of the ECB and its monetary policy. I will start with the problem of excessive independence of the ECB that is considered unacceptable. I will look at this through the statutes of the ECB, the Amsterdam Treaty and the Maastricht criteria. Then I will consider the theoretical foundations of inflation targeting in new

Keynesian monetary theory and present the critical assessment of it in contemporary post-Keynesian literature.

As mentioned above, the endogenous money supply theory has important effects on the position of the central bank and the formulation of monetary policy in a modern capitalist market economy. In this approach the velocity of money and the money multiplier are not stable and there is a causal link not between monetary base and bank money but vice versa. The central bank is thus unable to determine the quantity of money in circulation in a direct way. It is only able to influence it indirectly via manipulating interest rates.

According to post-Keynesians, the efficiency of monetary policy is limited and it is subject to asymmetric effects. Restrictive monetary policy is usually more efficient. Because of the emphasis on quantity adjustment processes, income effects, and taking into account the post-Keynesian theory of the interest rate that understands it primarily as the tool of redistribution, only relatively large changes in interest rates can have a significant impact.

The monetary authorities have a variety of tools at their disposal which can be used to decrease the liquidity of the banking sector. Such measures are employed only exceptionally. Usually the central banks accommodate growing demand for credit and provide the necessary reserves to the banking sector (on penalizing conditions if needed). The central bank should not give up its role as lender of last resort as to do so could endanger the solvency of the banking sector. Such a situation could easily produce a banking crisis and recession (as happened in the Czech Republic in 1997).

In post-Keynesian economics the central bank is unable to control directly the quantity of money in circulation. The quantity of money is determined by past decisions concerning credit. The endogenous nature of the money supply implies that no excess supply of money can arise in the economy as it is eliminated by repayment of debts. The central bank is able to influence the behaviour of commercial banks and conditions for granting credit to applicants by using traditional tools (discount rate, open market operations, creditor of the last resort) and other tools (called sometimes administrative or qualitative), such as bank regulation and supervision. As the efficiency of traditional tools decreases, the regulatory tools become more and more important in guaranteeing the stability of the banking sector and the developed capitalist market economy.

In this approach the central bank should not define currency stability as its main goal. The goal is unreachable, and the possible success of the bank in curbing inflation is dearly bought at the expense of a decrease in macroeconomic performance. The basic problem is that the tools that the central bank has at its disposal are only suitable against demand-pull inflation, where, as observed above, since the Second World War the more usual problem facing the capitalist market economies has been cost-push inflation. Monetary policy tools are the most costly way to fight inflation because of their negative impacts on real variables. We may call it 'political recession' (as an analogy with the political business cycle). In post-Keynesian economics as in the European form of new Keynesian economics (the theory of negotiated economy) the only efficient way of fighting cost-push inflation (or wage-push inflation) is via an incomes policy based on political consensus between trade unions, employers' associations and the government (tripartite or bipartite as in Sweden) institutional setting.

11.3.1 ECB statutes and the position of the bank in the EU

The monetarist experiment has failed but we can still distinguish the heritage of monetarism in mainstream monetary theory when considering the position of the central bank and the role of monetary policy. This is so despite the fact that the period when monetarism was the theoretical basis of monetary policy aiming at the direct regulation of monetary aggregates is definitely over. It lingers especially in the notion of an independent central bank as an institution that should take care of the stability of the purchasing power of money.

The existence of such an independent 'banking power', responsible in law only to itself, is highly problematic in a democratic society. We may speak about a considerable 'democratic deficit' in this connection. Looked at through a logic different from the monetarist logic it becomes completely untenable.

In post-Keynesian economics the role of the central bank consists in taking care of stability and assuring a sane development of the banking sector, and in providing adequate liquidity in cases of deflationary pressures According to post-Keynesian theory, monetary policy and all other regulatory tools should be coordinated with other measures of economic policy. The central bank should not have the status of an independent banking power. In this regard the independence of the Czech National Bank as defined in the Constitution of the Czech Republic loses its justification.

The statutes of the European System of Central Banks and of the European Central Bank were defined in the Treaty on European Union of 1992 and their accompanying protocol on the statute of the European System of Central Banks and of the European Central Bank.

According to Iain Begg and David Green (1998, pp. 123ff.) the initial source of inspiration for these were the statutes and the monetary policy framework of the Bundesbank, which are based on German ordoliberalism and influenced in an important measure by the German experience with hyperinflation during the 1920s. According to Begg and Green the major difference from the Bundesbank consists in the fact that the ECB and ESCB are more independent than the original Bundesbank because, unlike Germany, the EU lacks efficient fiscal policy tools. The mandate of the ECB is further influenced by monetarist theoretical concepts. Consequently, the ECB is too much concentrated on the stability of the purchasing power of money. This is also stressed by the formulation of the Maastricht criteria.

As David Howarth and Peter Loedel write in their book on the ECB:

> ...the Bundesbank both had a great deal of influence in the EMU discussions and became the model for the future ECB principally because of its impressive and long-standing record fighting inflation, and the role of the deutsche mark as the most credible EU currency and the ERM's anchor.
>
> (Howarth and Loedel, 2005, p. 18)

According to its statutes, the European Central Bank is completely independent of democratic political control (the democratic deficit of the ECB) and according to the Treaty on European Union all the EU member states were obliged to create legal frameworks for the independence of their own central banks.

In 1994, Charles Goodhart showed that the theoretical source of the independence of the central bank and of its concentration on inflation targets is the idea that there is no direct link between economic growth and inflation, and that the monetarist theory of the long-run Phillips curve formulated by Milton Friedman and Edmund Phelps and reinterpreted by the school of rational expectations is valid (Goodhart, 1994). It is highly probable that the low macroeconomic performance of the Eurozone at the turn of the century was in certain measure (among other factors, of which the most important is the lagging behind transformation to the knowledge-based society) caused by ECB monetary policy in combination with the Maastricht criteria.

Still more pronounced negative effects can be caused by this combination of the anti-inflationary orientation of ECB monetary policy (inflation targeting) and the Maastricht criteria for the real convergence of the small open economies of the new post-communist members of the EU. To clearly identify the anti-inflationary bias of the ECB I will turn now to post-Keynesian criticism of the 'new consensus' in monetary theory and policy based on the new Keynesian economics.

11.3.2 Inflation targeting and its theoretical new Keynesian underpinning from a post-Keynesian point of view

This 'new consensus' shows some (formal) similarities with the post-Keynesian theory of endogenous money supply. It appears to share some basic tenets of post-Keynesian horizontalism (for example, Moore, 1988; Kaldor, 1982). Short-term interest rates are understood as basic monetary policy tools and are determined exogenously. Because of the exogeneity of interest rates, money supply is endogenously created. This similarity does not mean, however, that we have to do with a kind of synthesis between post-Keynesian and new Keynesian economics.

As many post-Keynesian economists (Lavoie, 2004; Arestis and Sawyer, 2004; Palley, 2006) have clearly shown, the differences are important, and the monetary policy formulated under the 'new consensus' is very different to what we might expect to result from the post-Keynesian monetary theory of production.

According to Monvoisin and Rochon:

> This New Consensus, as it has been called, is interesting for it recognizes the exogeneity of the rate of interest – a key feature of post-Keynesian theory – while also recognizing the endogenous nature of the money supply. Yet it differs greatly from post-Keynesian monetary theory, given its acceptance of the natural rate of interest. Moreover, while it recognizes the endogenous nature of the money supply, they have no *theory* of money endogeneity.
>
> (Monvoisin and Rochon, 2006, p. 57)

According to post-Keynesians the 'new consensus' emerged as a more or less pragmatic solution to the unsuccessful attempts to determine directly the money supply on the basis of Friedman's monetary rule. It might thus be understood as a return to a more traditional form of monetary policy of the Keynesian type. However, it can still be interpreted as a compromise solution of the neoclassical synthesis kind, albeit a sophisticated one.

The new consensus can be described in a simplified form by three equations that may be used to show the principal differences from the post-Keynesian monetary theory of production (Arestis and Sawyer, 2004, p. 72).

$$y^g = a_0 + a_1 y^g_{-1} + a2(E_t y^g_{+1}) - a_3[i - E_t(\pi_{+1})] + s_1 \quad (11.1)$$

$$\pi = b_1 y^g + b_2 \pi_{-1} + b_3 E_t(\pi_{+1}) + s_2 (\text{with } b_2 + b_3 = 1) \quad (11.2)$$

$$i = r_0 + E_t(\pi_{+1}) + c_1 y^g_{-1} + c_2(\pi_{-1} - \pi^T) \quad (11.3)$$

where: y^g is the output gap, i is the nominal interest rate, π is the rate of inflation, π^T is the inflation rate target, r_0 is the 'equilibrium' real rate of interest which is consistent with a zero output gap, s_1 and s_2 represent stochastic shocks and E_t refers to expectations held at time t.

Equation (11.1) is the aggregate demand equation where the output gap is determined by the past and expected future output gap and the real interest rate.

Equation (11.2) is a form of Phillips curve where inflation is based on current output gap and past and future inflation.

Equation (11.3) is the monetary policy operating rule (a form of the Taylor rule) where the nominal interest rate is based on expected inflation, output gap, deviation of the rate of inflation from target rate of inflation and the equilibrium real rate of interest.

According to Arestis and Sawyer:

> The equilibrium of the economy in this approach has three important properties: the first is nominal neutrality, the assumption that the price level does not affect the long-run real equilibrium ... The second property is inflation neutrality, ensured by assuming dynamic homogeneity. This means that real equilibrium is not affected by the growth rates of nominal variables. The third property is the absence of path dependency in these models, whether relating to the experience of unemployment or in terms of investment added to the capital stock.
>
> (Arestis and Sawyer, 2004, p. 4)

There is only demand-pull inflation in the 'new consensus' model. The short-run non-neutrality of money is the effect of lagged adjustment of nominal and real variables, which is typical feature of new Keynesian microeconomic foundations (efficiency wages and so on). However, in the long-run, the quantity theory of money with its long-run neutrality of money holds. Inflation targeting in fact presupposes that even moderate rates of inflation are harmful, and that a low rate of inflation is important for good macroeconomic performance (according to new Keynesians such as John B. Taylor, Richard Clarida and others 1 or 2 per cent rate of inflation is accepted). The post-Keynesian theory of inflation based on wage or cost-push has no place in the model despite the fact that the bulk of inflationary pressures in the second half of the twentieth century originated in wage costs or oil price increases.

The introduction of the equilibrium real rate of interest shows some important Wicksellian roots of the 'new consensus'. Together with the requirements for independence of the central bank and the requirements for transparency and credibility (which are to be understood as a heritage of new classical macroeconomics), the 'new consensus' inflation targeting which is practised by ECB creates a stress on anti-inflationary policy at the expense of growth and employment.

According to Marc Lavoie the post-Keynesian alternative would require the introduction of path-dependence and hysteresis into the model. A post-Keynesian model should use an equation describing cost-push inflation. The target should be determined on the basis of a real growth rate and employment considerations. Otherwise zero or low-inflation targeting implies high real rates of interest, low real rates of growth and a persistent high rate of unemployment (Lavoie, 2004, pp. 30–1).

11.4 The effects of the role and monetary policy of the ECB for post-socialist and less developed EU member states from the post-Keynesian economics point of view

In post-Keynesian monetary economics money plays an important stabilizing role as the tool against uncertainty (Davidson, 1972, 1982). From the point of view of a small open economy (of which the Czech Republic is the typical case), joining the EMU and the introduction of the euro can be seen as part of a process of the reduction of uncertainty and economic stabilization. As such, speculative attacks on national currencies of the type the Czech Republic experienced in 1997 should become a thing of the past. The introduction of the euro should have many positive effects in decreasing the risks of unexpected exchange rate movements in national currencies. The growing integration of the new EU members, including the Czech Republic, important changes in international trade flows and the passage from trade with finished goods to the trade with components and semi-products should increase the savings in costs induced by the introduction of the euro. Those positive effects will, in the medium run, certainly outweigh short-run costs.

A majority of post-Keynesians would argue that the small open economies should not fear the loss of an autonomous monetary policy. The first argument concerns the comparatively low and decreasing efficiency of traditional monetary policy tools generally. In a small open economy with a liberalized capital account and high capital mobility it is impossible for interest rates to deviate significantly from the interest rates that predominate in the world economy (and especially in the Eurozone). In 1997 the Czech Republic fully realized this truth in connection with a speculative attack on the Czech crown. Since then the Czech National Bank should have been well aware of a quite narrow interval inside of which it is able to manipulate interest rates.

There are important doubts concerning an autonomous exchange rate policy in a small open economy integrated into a larger regional economy. The usual arguments of mainstream economics, based on the opportunity to increase the competitiveness of exports via devaluation or depreciation of the exchange rate, are not valid for trade in components in highly integrated economies. Such arguments were valid for traditional exports of final goods with a relatively high price elasticity of demand where the Marshall-Lerner condition was relevant. Exchange rate stability or the introduction of a common currency become of utmost importance under such conditions. But there is almost no independence granted to a small open economy in which it can develop its own monetary policy. Deviations of interest rate cannot be significant and the ability of the Czech National Bank to counteract the appreciation of the Czech crown versus the euro or the US dollar shows clearly that it is external factors that are decisive in determining the interest rates and exchange rates of small open economies.

Certainly we can say that in recent years the Czech National Bank has experienced lower interest rates than other EU member countries. However, we should take into account that in post-Keynesian economics we stress the role of income effects that may be significant only when there is a comparatively high difference between internal and external interest rates. A significant difference may bring about threats of speculative attacks on the national currency of a small open economy.

From the point of view of post-Keynesian economics the most problematic issue concerning the post-communist and less developed new member states of the EU is the independence of the ECB and its anti-inflationary policy, centred on inflation targeting, in combination with the Amsterdam Treaty and the Maastricht criteria. Joining the EMU under such conditions may result in a significant deceleration of real convergence processes as the monetary policy of the ECB with its extreme anti-inflationary orientation will cause economic growth to slow and create obstacles to the real convergence process.

As the Maastricht criteria determine limits on public expenditure deficits, it may become impossible to react to recessions using the traditional tools of Keynesian fiscal policy. In post-Keynesian economics fiscal policy should be the decisive tool of anti-cyclical and pro-growth economic policy. It is employed to accelerate the development of less developed EU member states and regions but is greatly limited by the Maastricht criteria.

In a paper written before the 2004 enlargement, Sergio Rossi proposed a change to the process of joining EMU for the associated countries and new members after enlargement. According to him new member states should not abandon their national currencies too early as this could delay their real convergence. He proposed a different path for the associated countries and the new less developed EU members based on a three-tier system which would, on the one hand, enable clearing in euros between associated countries and the EU and among all EU member states while, on the other, it would maintain national currencies in new member states, enabling them to follow a more independent monetary policy (Rossi, 2006). In fact it was an elaboration of Keynes's original plan for the reconstruction of international finances after the Second World War, based on the idea of the clearing union and bancor (Keynes, 1980), which also became the basis of reforms of international finances proposed by Paul Davidson (Davidson, 1992/3).

According to Rossi:

> The working of the proposed pan-European settlement system integrating associated countries monetarily would take stock of all these recent advances in the management of multilateral electronic funds transfer systems. In practice it would consist of adding a 'supranational' tier to the two-tier banking structure existing at present in each country, to allow for the ultimate settlement of international transactions in euros.
>
> (Rossi, 2006, p. 254)

Rossi proposed the creation of a pan-European clearing union called the European Settlement Agent (ESA). Euros were to be electronic interbank money to be used at a supranational level. Like the clearing union in Keynes's original plan, the ESA would enable the introduction of a system using the positive balances of 'creditor' countries to balance the deficits of 'debtor' countries. The implementation of this plan would create a two-speed EU towards EMU. New member states and relatively less developed members would continue to use their national currencies and would have some discretion in using monetary policy. Their route to joining EMU would be gradual and would depend on the pace of the convergence processes. In this connection Rossi accepts some of the arguments of the mainstream 'optimum currency area' literature. According to Rossi membership of the EMU and the introduction of the euro need as prerequisites a significant decrease in the gap in macroeconomic performance between the new member states and the EU average and the synchronization of the business cycle. Rossi's arguments and proposals are exceptional in post-Keynesian literature, and the acceptance of his plan is highly improbable.

Other post-Keynesian economists are more realistic in providing advice to monetary policymakers. They are even disposed to accept inflation targeting as a general approach of monetary policy (for example, Palley, 2006; Monvoisin and Rochon, 2006; Fontana and Palacio-Vera, 2006). However, post-Keynesian monetary theory would require some important amendments and changes in determination of the target. To avoid negative effects on macroeconomic performance (GDP, employment, unemployment) the determination of inflation target should be based on considerations of economic growth and a rate of unemployment. Cost-push inflation pressures should be taken into account. Thomas Palley proposed amending inflation targeting via a stabilizing tool based on the idea of asset-based reserve requirements that would serve as a fuse against speculative bubbles of a Minsky type. According to Palley all financial intermediaries would be required to hold reserve requirements against all assets. There might even be different requirements according to the quality of an asset, some may be even zero-rated (Palley, 2006, pp. 90 ff.)

To avoid the negative effects of ECB monetary policy on real convergence among post-communist and other less developed new EU members the inflation-targeting framework should be based on post-Keynesian monetary theory. The inflation target should be determined on broader considerations of macroeconomic performance, For less developed EU members a higher inflation target should be allowed in order not to hinder the real convergence of their economies to the EU average. According to post-Keynesian economics a robust institutional framework for an EU discretionary fiscal policy should also be constructed, and the EU budget should be reformed and increased to create a redistribution mechanism which could be used to counter recessionary pressures and backwardness in some member states or regions.

11.5 Conclusions

Post-Keynesian monetary theory leads to the conclusion that early EMU membership and the introduction of the euro under the ECB as presently constituted and the framework determined by the Amsterdam Treaty and the Maastricht criteria might be highly likely to have a negative impact on the real convergence of the new less developed members of the EU in Central and Eastern Europe. The most problematic area is the independence of the ECB in pursuing a monetary policy focused on anti-inflationary targets. Another problem consists in the 'new consensus' in monetary theory and policy underpinning the inflation targeting. The theoretical model used in the determination of an inflation target and in the corresponding manipulation of short-term interest rates stresses the danger of demand-pull inflation and as a result sets a very low target rate of inflation. This could have harmful effects for the EU as a whole but it might in particular hamper the processes of real convergence in the new member states.

Thus, an early introduction of the euro – which is otherwise very advisable – would require important changes in both the position and the monetary policy of the ECB. It should be re-designed according to the post-Keynesian proposals. Under such conditions the positive effects would outweigh the negative effects even in the short run.

References

Arestis, P. (1992). *The Post-Keynesian Approach to Economics*, Aldershot: Edward Elgar.

Arestis, P. and M. Sawyer (2004). 'Monetary Policy when Money is Endogenous: Going beyond the "New Consensus"', in M. Lavoie and M. Seccareccia (eds), *Central Banking in the Modern World: Alternative Perspectives*, Cheltenham, UK and Northampton, MA: Edward Elgar, pp. 70–87.

Artis, M.J. and M.K. Lewis (1981). *Monetary Control in the United Kingdom*, Oxford: Philip Allan.

Begg, I. and D. Green (1998). 'The Political Economy of the European Central Bank', in P. Arestis and M.C. Sawyer (eds), *The Political Economy of Central Banking*, Cheltenham, UK and Northampton, MA: Edward Elgar, pp. 122–35.

Chick, V. (1983). *Macroeconomics after Keynes: a Reconsideration of the General Theory*, Cambridge, MA: MIT Press.

Davidson, P. (1972). *Money and the Real World*, London: Macmillan.

Davidson, P. (1978). *Money and the Real World*, Second Edition, London: Macmillan.

Davidson, P. (1982). *International Money and the Real World*, London: Macmillan.

Davidson, P. (1992/3). 'Reforming the World Money', *Journal of Post-Keynesian Economics*, XV(2): 153–79.

Dow, S.C. (1996). 'Horizontalism: a Critique', *Cambridge Journal of Economics*, 20(4): 497–508.
Dow, S.C. (1997). 'Mainstream Economic Methodology', *Cambridge Journal of Economics*, 21(1): 73–93.
Dow, S.C. and C. Rodríguez-Fuentes (1998). 'The Political Economy of Monetary Policy', in P. Arestis and M.C. Sawyer (eds), *The Political Economy of Central Banking*, Cheltenham, UK and Northampton, MA: Edward Elgar, pp. 1–19.
Eichner, A.S. and J.A. Kregel (1975). 'An Essay on Post-Keynesian Theory: a New Paradigm in Economics', *Journal of Economic Literature*, 13(4): 1293–314.
Fontana, G. and A. Palacio-Vera (2006). 'Is there an Active Role for Monetary Policy in the Endogenous Money Approach?' in C. Gnos and L.-P. Rochon (eds), *Post-Keynesian Principles of Economic Policy*, Cheltenham, UK and Northampton, MA: Edward Elgar, pp. 49–77.
Goodhart, Ch. (1994). 'What should Central Banks do? What should be their Macroeconomic Objectives and Operations?' *Economic Journal*, CIV(427): 1424–36.
Howarth, D. and P. Loedel (2005). *The European Central Bank. The New European Leviathan?* Revised Second Edition, Basingstoke: Palgrave Macmillan.
Kaldor, N. (1980). *The Origins of Monetarism*, Cardiff: University College Cardiff Press.
Kaldor, N. (1982). *The Scourge of Monetarism*, London: Oxford University Press.
Keynes, J. M. (1980). *The Collected Writings of J. M. Keynes, vol. XXV Activities 1940–1944. Shaping the Post-War World: the Clearing Union*, London and Basingstoke: Macmillan.
Lavoie, M. (2003). *Foundations of Post-Keynesian Economic Analysis*, Cheltenham, UK and Northampton, MA: Edward Elgar.
Lavoie, M.(2004). 'The New Consensus on Monetary Policy Seen from a Post-Keynesian Perspective', in M. Lavoie and M. Seccareccia (eds), *Central Banking in the Modern World: Alternative Perspectives*, Cheltenham, UK and Northampton, MA: Edward Elgar, pp. 15–34.
Minsky, H.P. (1982). *Can 'It' Happen Again: Essays on Instability and Finance*, Armonk, NY: M.E. Sharpe.
Monvoisin, V. and L.-P. Rochon (2006). 'The Post-Keynesian Consensus, the New Consensus and Endogenous Money, in C. Gnos and L.-P. Rochon (eds), *Post-Keynesian Principles of Economic Policy*, Cheltenham, UK and Northampton, MA: Edward Elgar, pp. 57–77.
Moore, B.J. (1988). *Horizontalists and Verticalists: the Macroeconomics of Credit Money*, Cambridge: Cambridge University Press.
Moore, B. J. (2006). *Shaking the Invisible Hand. Complexity, Endogenous Money and Exogenous Interest Rates*, Basingstoke and New York: Palgrave Macmillan.
Palley, T.I. (2006). 'A Post-Keynesian Framework for Monetary Policy: Why Interest Rate Operating Procedures are not Enough', in C. Gnos and L.-P. Rochon (eds), *Post-Keynesian Principles of Economic Policy*, Cheltenham, UK and Northampton, MA: Edward Elgar, pp. 78–98.
Rochon, L.-P. and S. Rossi (2003). *Studies in Modern Theories of Money*, Cheltenham, UK and Northampton, MA: Edward Elgar.
Rossi, S. (2006). 'EMU and EU Enlargement: Lessons and Perspectives', in C. Gnos and L.-P. Rochon (eds), *Post-Keynesian Principles of Economic Policy*, Cheltenham, UK and Northampton, MA: Edward Elgar, pp. 244–65.

Rousseas, S. (1986). *Post-Keynesian Monetary Economics*, London: Macmillan.
Stiglitz, J. and A. Weiss (1981). 'Credit Rationing in Markets with Imperfect Information', *American Economic Review*, 71(3): 393–410.
Weintraub, S. (1978), *Keynes, Keynesians and Monetarists*, Philadelphia: University of Philadelphia Press.
Wolfson, M.H. (1996). 'A Post-Keynesian Theory of Credit Rationing', *Journal of Post Keynesian Economics,* 18(3): 443–70.
Wray L. R. (1992). 'Alternative Approaches to Money and Interest Rates', *Journal of Economic Issues*, XXVI (4): 1145–78.

12

New Global Players and Disharmonies in the World Orchestra: Cohesion Analysis of Business Cycles of China

Jarko Fidrmuc, Iikka Korhonen and Ivana Bátorová

12.1 Introduction

Since the early to mid-1990s the structure of the world economy has become more complex. Before 1990, economic development was clearly dominated by the US, Japan and a number of European economies. There was also significant effort to achieve some degree of policy coordination through the Organization for Economic Co-operation and Development (OECD), the International Monetary Fund (IMF) and especially the European Union (EU). In general, emerging countries were highly dependent on economic developments in the OECD countries and also followed, to some extent, their policies.

Globalization, one of the major events in the world economy in the last few decades, has expanded significantly as a result of the growth of the Chinese economy (see Brakman and van Marrewijk, 2007). While China was a predominantly agrarian economy before 1980, it is now a global player, with a modern industrial economy and the rise of a group of private entrepreneurs (see Djankov et al., 2006; Hovey and Naughton, 2007) and booming urban regions. High trade growth was supported by large foreign direct investment (FDI) flows (see Eichengreen and Tong, 2005). Not surprisingly, growth in China has changed the distribution of economic activities across the world. Between 1980 and 2006, the share of Chinese GDP in the world economy increased from 1.7 per cent to 5.5 per cent (valued at market exchange rates; the share would be higher if purchasing power adjusted prices were used). China is now one of the world's most important exporting and importing nations. However, the degree of policy coordination remains low as China has only recently become a member of the World Trade Organization (WTO).

The shifts in weights of the world economy have important implications for business cycles worldwide. The increasing weight of the emerging countries, and China in particular, have led to higher global growth. Moreover, global economic prospects are less influenced by a few large economies (especially the US and Germany) than before. This may make countries less vulnerable to the demand shocks in a particular region.

In turn, business cycles have also become more globalized. The literature on business cycle synchronization stresses the importance of foreign trade and capital flows. Thus, the emergence of China as a large trading nation and a target for international investments is likely to have a significant impact on the business cycles of its partner countries. Inasmuch as the intensity of trade and financial relations with China are different in different countries, the opening up of China might explain some recent variations in business cycle developments.

This could be especially important for European countries. We observed a joint EU cycle until the 1980s (see Artis and Zhang, 1997; Fatás, 1997), which disappeared in the 1990s despite previous expectations (see Artis, 2003). The intensity of trading (see Bussière and Mehl, 2008) and financial (see Lane and Schmukler, 2007) links with China is very different in different EU countries. The UK, Germany, Finland and the Netherlands are linked intensively to China, while other countries have more moderate economic relationships with China.

Foreign trade and foreign direct investment (FDI) are generally seen as important factors in business cycles. However, their effects on international business cycles are ambiguous. On the one hand, Frankel and Rose (1998) find a robust positive relationship between trade intensity and the correlation of business cycles between OECD countries. This also reflects high shares of intra-industry trade between these countries. On the other hand, China's position in the international division of labour results in increased patterns of specialization. Krugman (1993) argues that this is likely to cause divergence in business cycles between countries. Moreover, FDI can be either a substitute for or a complement to exports between a pair of countries.

There is already a rich literature on trade between China and the developed countries (see Bussière and Mehl, 2008). Other authors look at the determinants of the business cycles in South East Asia; indeed, a special issue of *World Economy* was devoted to this issue (see de Grauwe and Zhang, 2006). However, there are few papers looking at the synchronization of business cycles in developed countries and in China. This chapter aims to fill this gap in the literature. Our results show that the business cycle in China is very different from that of OECD countries – with the exception of Korea. Given the increasing weight of China in the world economy, the differences between the Chinese business cycle and that of the OECD countries mean that the degree of worldwide cohesion of business cycles is much lower than that for the OECD countries.

The chapter is structured as follows. Section 12.2 discusses the determinants of international business cycles. Section 12.3 introduces the dynamic correlation analysis. Section 12.4 offers stylized facts and analyses the pattern of dynamic correlation of business cycles in China and in developed countries. Section 12.5 introduces a multivariate measure of co-movement, which is called cohesion. This section further defines the cohesion and presents the results for selected regions of the world economy. Section 12.6 concludes.

12.2 Determinants of business cycle synchronization

Economic development is determined both by domestic (for example, aggregate demand shocks and budgetary policy) and international (external demand and international prices for traded goods) factors. In open economies, the latter are playing an increasingly important role and often determine domestic policies, which try to insulate the economy from adverse external economic shocks. Frankel and Rose (1998) showed that trade and, more generally, economic integration between countries can result in increased synchronization of individual business cycles since trade links serve as a channel for the transmission of shocks across countries. In line with these considerations, Kenen (2000) shows in a Keynesian model that the correlation between changes in two countries' output increases with the intensity of trade links. In turn, Kose and Yi (2006) analyse this issue in an international real business cycle model and conclude that, although the model suggests a positive relation between trade and output co-movement, quantitatively only small effects are obtained.

However, this hypothesis of a positive relationship between trade and business cycles was not generally accepted. For example, Krugman (1993) points out that, as countries become more integrated, they increasingly specialize. That is, the importance of asymmetric or sector-specific shocks increases in the process of economic integration. This pattern may be more appropriate for the explanation of business cycles in China.

In the empirical literature, the role of trade links has been studied extensively in this context. Despite theoretical ambiguities, several authors have demonstrated that countries trading more intensively also exhibit a higher degree of output co-movement (see, for example, Frankel and Rose, 1998; Baxter and Kouparitsas, 2005). However, it is not trade relations per se which may induce business cycle synchronization. Indeed, Frankel and Rose's hypothesis emphasizes that bilateral trade is mainly intra-industry trade, although this indicator does not directly enter their analysis. Basically, the idea is that specialization increases the exposure to sector-specific shocks and these shocks are transmitted via intra-industry trade. Fontagné (1999) discusses the relation between intra-industry trade and the symmetry of shocks in a monetary union. Fidrmuc (2004) shows that intra-industry trade is a better indicator for business cycle asymmetries than simple trade intensities.

Inasmuch as China seems to specialize more vertically, this channel may be less relevant for the Chinese business cycle. Actually, the specialization forces discussed by Krugman (1993) can dominate, which can cause divergence of business cycles between China and its trading partners.

Trade relations are not the only source of synchronization of business cycles (see Artis et al., 2008). Financial integration between countries may also play an important role. However, the theory of the impact of financial integration on business cycles is also ambiguous. On the one hand tightly interlinked financial markets can be thought of as a transmission channel similar to trade links. Hence, saving and investment decisions in one country are likely to affect asset prices and the real economy in other countries via financial flows. On the other hand, access to international financial markets also allows countries to specialize (see Kalemli-Ozcan et al., 2001; Imbs, 2004; Krugman, 1993) and should therefore reduce the extent of co-fluctuations. Also, more developed and integrated financial markets may allow better risk-sharing.

So far, the literature on business cycle correlation has concentrated mainly on developed economies. However, a number of studies have looked at business cycle correlation in East Asia. For example, Sato and Zhang (2006) find common business cycles for the East Asian region. Moreover, Shin and Sohn (2006) find that trade integration (financial integration much less so) enhances the co-movements of output in East Asia. Kumakura (2005) finds that the share of electronic products in foreign trade increases business cycle correlation for the countries around the Pacific. Also Shin and Wang (2004) find that trade is a significant determinant of business cycle correlation for East Asian countries. So far, very few papers have looked at the correlation of business cycles between China and other emerging Asian economies and those of the OECD countries.

12.3 Correlation and dynamic correlation analysis

Correlation analysis is the most basic approach to studying the degrees of synchronization between economic variables. The most common measure of co-movement between time series is *classical correlation*, which is also commonly used in the literature on business cycle correlation. Unfortunately classical correlation has two main drawbacks: first, it does not allow for a separation of idiosyncratic components and common co-movements. Second, it is basically a static analysis that fails to capture any dynamics in the co-movement. An alternative measure of synchronization in the case of business cycles is the *dynamic correlation*, which was proposed by Croux et al. (2001).

Let x and y be zero-mean real stochastic processes. Let $S_x(\lambda)$ and $S_y(\lambda)$ be the spectral density functions of x and y and $C_{xy}(\lambda)$ be the co-spectrum, $-\pi \leq \lambda \leq \pi$. So the dynamic correlation, $\rho(\lambda)$, equals

$$\rho_{xy}(\lambda) = \frac{C_{xy}(\lambda)}{\sqrt{S_x(\lambda)S_y(\lambda)}} \tag{12.1}$$

Similarly to standard correlation coefficient, the dynamic correlation is defined between -1 and 1.

If two stochastic processes x and y are obtained by summing the waves of x_t and y_t within a given frequency interval, the dynamic correlation can be defined on frequency band. Set $\Lambda = [\lambda_1, \lambda_2)$, where $0 \leq \lambda_1 \leq \lambda_2 \leq \pi$. So the dynamic correlation within the frequency band Λ is defined as

$$\rho_{xy}(\Lambda) = \frac{\int_\Lambda C_{xy}(\lambda)d\lambda}{\sqrt{\int_\Lambda S_x(\lambda)d\lambda \int_\Lambda S_y(\lambda)d\lambda}} \tag{12.2}$$

The dynamic correlation within the frequency band, which is defined in (12.2), can be used to measure the co-movement of seasonal components of two economic time series, because we can select the frequency band of our interest and evaluate the dynamic correlation within this frequency band.

12.4 Stylized facts of the business cycle in China and selected countries

We use quarterly GDP data according to the International Financial Statistics of the IMF. For developed countries, the time series start in the 1970s or 1980s. If seasonal adjustment is required, we use the US Census Bureau's X12 ARIMA procedure, which was performed for the whole available period.

For China, we use national quarterly data in current prices, which was deflated by the CPI. However, we have to keep in mind that these time series have been subject to a major revision recently. So far, only annual data are available according to the new methodology. As before, we adjusted this time series by the same procedure as for other countries. Furthermore, the time series start in 1992. This restricts our analysis to the period between 1992 and 2006.

Figure 12.1 presents the dynamic correlations of business cycles in China and in selected developed economies between 1992 and 2006. As is usual in the literature, we differentiate between three components of the aggregate correlation. First, the long-run movements (over 8 years) correspond to the low frequency band below $\pi/16$. Second, the traditional business cycles (that is, cycles with a period between 1.5 and 8 years) belong to the medium part of the figure (marked as a shadow area) between $\pi/16$ and $\pi/3$. Finally, the short-run movements are defined by frequencies over $\pi/3$. Although it is usual to neglect these developments, we will look at them here because the short-run dependencies of economic development may be more important in the case of China.

We can see that business cycles in China and selected economies vary significantly over the frequencies. Few countries show a comparatively high positive correlation of long-run cycles with China. Many of these are non-European OECD countries (the US, Korea, Australia and Japan). To a lesser degree, we can also see small positive correlations of long-run development in Denmark, Italy, Norway, and perhaps the UK. In general, the non-European OECD countries trade more intensively with China than the remaining countries of our sample, which may go towards explaining the extent of business cycle correlation. For the European countries this explanation is less credible.

We can see a more homogeneous picture for the traditional business cycle frequencies (between $\pi/16 \approx 0.2$ and $\pi/3 \approx 1$). In general, negative correlations of business cycles in China and in OECD countries dominate. Generally, only Korea, Denmark and Spain show positive correlation over the whole interval of business cycle frequencies. This

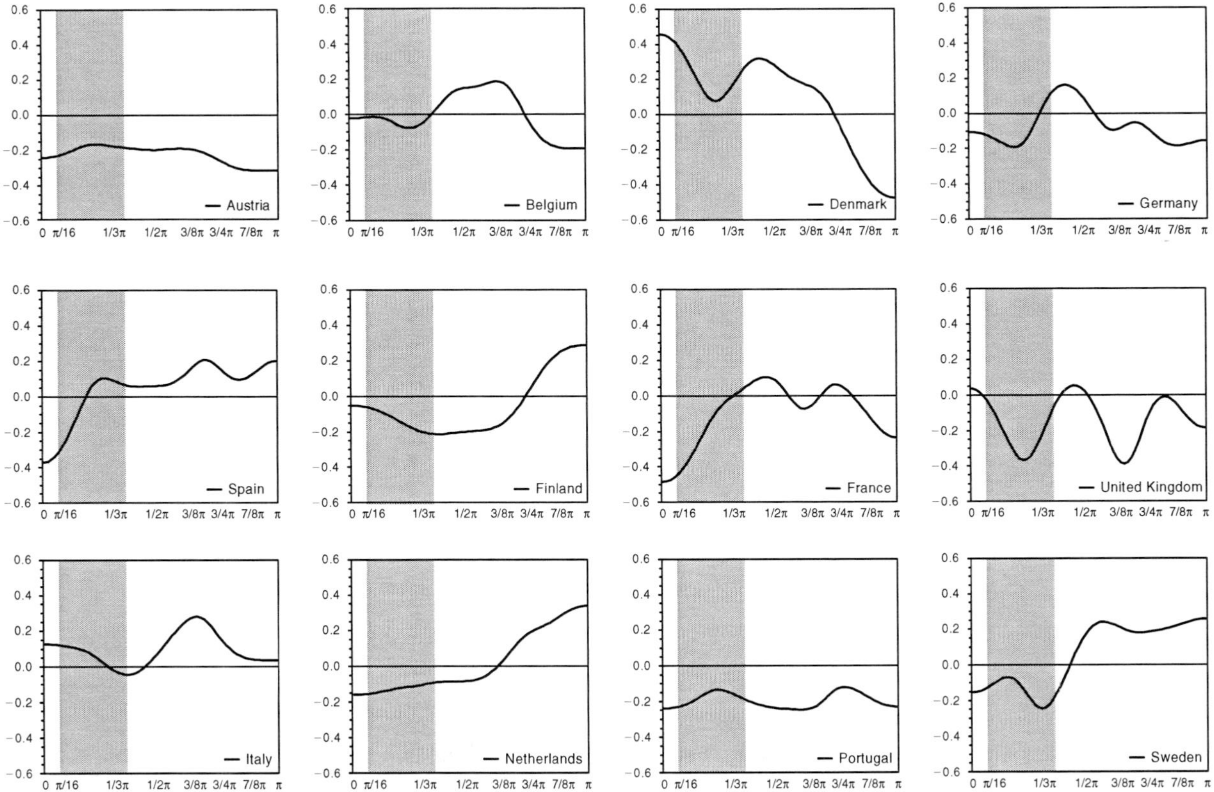

Figure 12.1 Dynamic correlations between China and selected countries, 1992–2006
Note: Business cycle frequencies are marked by the shaded area.

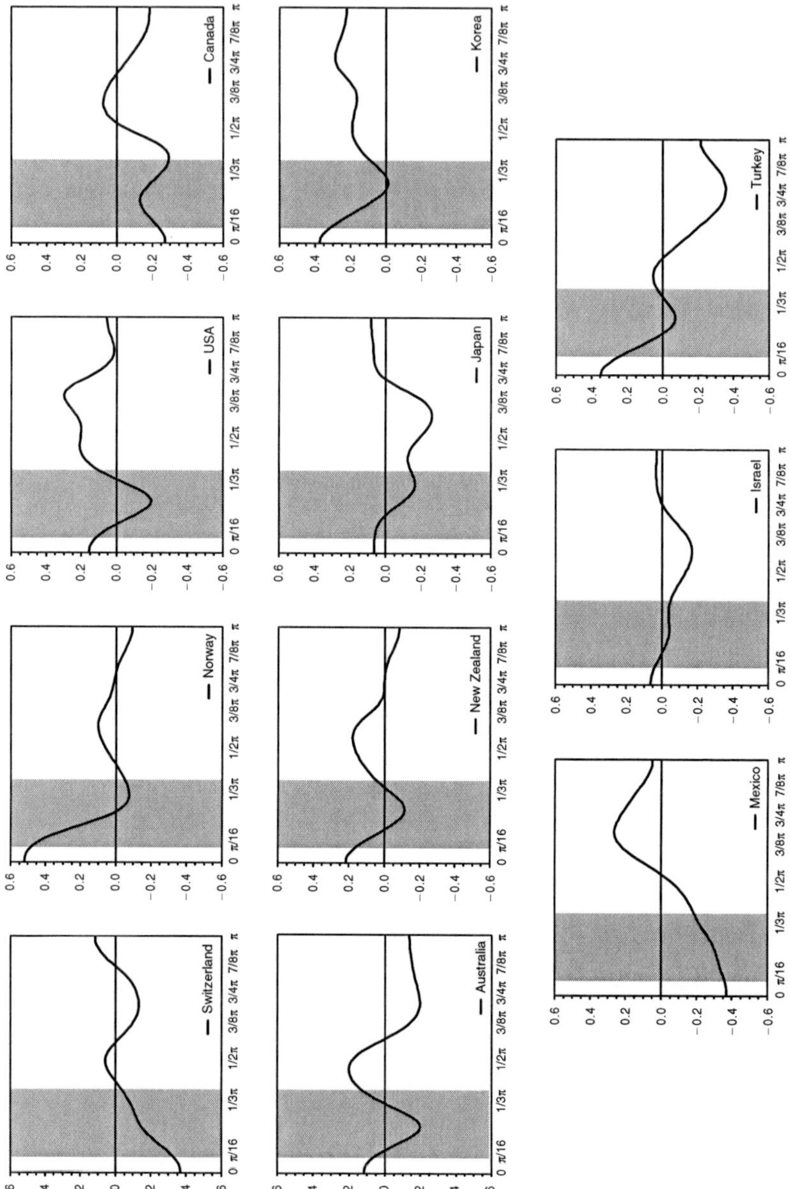

Figure 12.1 (*Continued*)

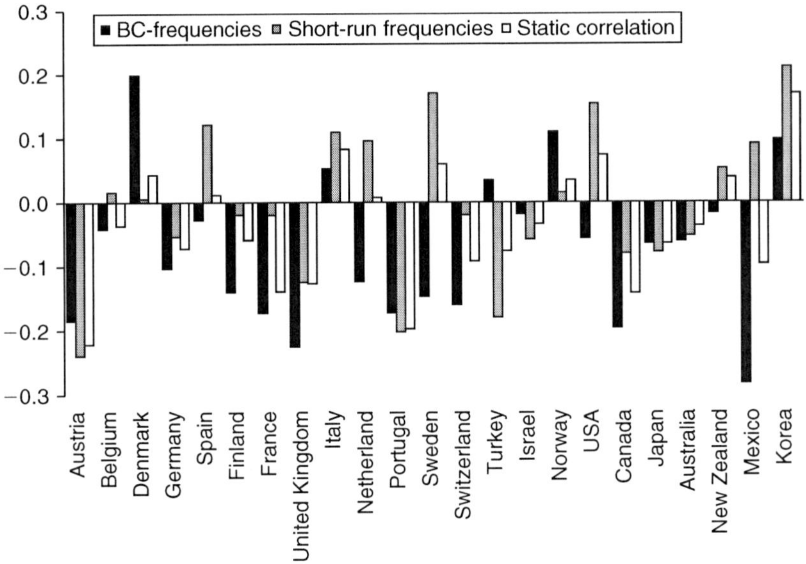

Figure 12.2 Aggregate correlations of business cycles in China and selected countries, 1992–2006

confirms the earlier findings by Shin and Sohn (2006) and Sato and Zhang (2006). As before, the non-European OECD countries show a positive correlation at the lower range of the interval (close to eight years). Only Italy and Spain show positive correlation at frequencies close to 1.5 years.

Finally, we can see also large differences between various short-run frequencies. In general, the dynamic correlations tend to increase at the right end of the spectrum (see Figure 12.1). This would correspond to strong business linkages between suppliers from China and final producers in the developed countries. Among the European countries short-term correlation appears to be high for Finland, Netherlands and Sweden. Short-run correlation is high also for the US and Korea, but only marginally positive for Japan. All these countries can be characterized as having highly intensive relationships with China over a longer period.

Figure 12.2 compares average dynamic correlations of the business cycle and the short-run frequencies with the static correlations for the sample. We can see that the negative correlations dominate for nearly all countries especially for the business cycle frequencies. Only Korea, Denmark, Spain and Italy show a positive correlation of business cycles with China. At the same time, several countries show low negative or even positive dynamic correlations for the short-run frequencies. This is especially strong for Korea, Finland, the Netherlands, Sweden and the US. Thus, there could be also some signs of increasing similarities of business cycles. Cui and Syed (2007) find that China is moving away from traditional assembly operations in its processing activities and its exports have started to rely more on domestically sourced components.

12.5 Cohesion analysis and the Chinese effect on world business cycles

Cohesion, defined in frequency domain, is a measure of dynamic co-movement between time series. In the bivariate case, the measure is reduced to the dynamic correlation. Cohesion is useful in studying problems of business cycle synchronization and in investigating the short-run and long-run dynamic properties of multiple time series. It is an appropriate technique for obtaining the facts on co-movements of macroeconomic variables at a specified frequency band.

Let $x_t = (x_{1t}, \ldots, x_{2t})$ be a vector of $N \geq 2$ variables and $w = (w_1, \ldots, w_N)$ be a vector of the non-normalized positive weights to the variables in x_t. We use the shares of countries in global output. The cohesion of the variables in x_t is defined as the weighted average of dynamic correlation between all possible pairs of series. Thus, the cohesion is defined as

$$coh_x(\lambda) = \frac{\sum_{i \neq j} w_i w_j \rho_{x_i x_j}(\lambda)}{\sum_{i \neq j} w_i w_j} \tag{12.3}$$

As with dynamic correlation, cohesion is also defined between −1 and 1.

In order to illustrate synchronization across the countries, it is possible to compute the cohesion, which provides a better measure of the dynamic co-movements between time series than do alternative methods.

Figure 12.3 presents a graphical representation of cohesion in selected regions of the world economy at all frequencies. The figure provides a comparison of the cohesion of the OECD countries (except Japan and Korea, which are included in the Asia group), Asian countries and members of the European Union.

We can see that OECD countries show a high level of cohesion for all frequencies. In general, we confirm a high degree of synchronization of business cycles in OECD countries. Not surprisingly, the highest values of cohesion are found for the European Union (defined as 15 member states

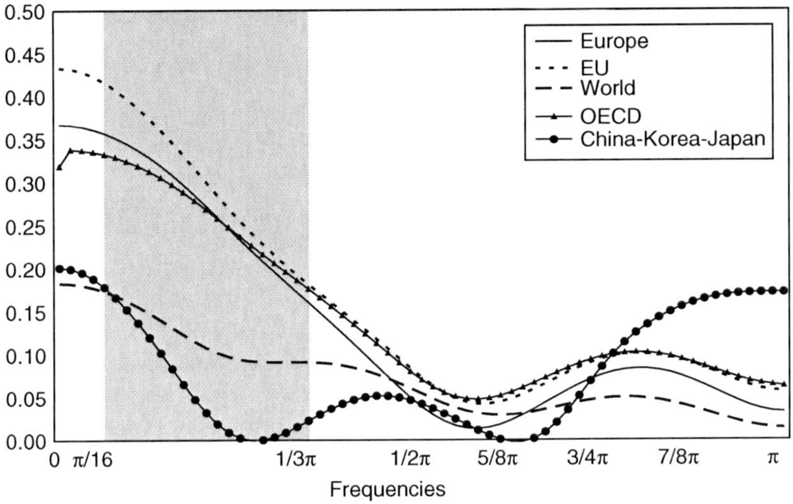

Figure 12.3 Cohesion of business cycles in selected regions, 1992–2006
Note: Business cycle frequencies are marked by the shaded area.

before 2004). Nevertheless, the addition of the non-European OECD countries does not change the picture significantly.

By contrast, the level of cohesion between China, Korea and Japan is close to zero in the business cycle frequencies. In turn, Asian cohesion is higher for the very short-term frequencies than in other regions. The inclusion of the Asian countries to the worldwide level of cohesion makes a difference, although we reflect the different size of the countries by using the GDP weights. For business cycle frequencies, we can see that the degree of cohesion drops approximately by one half and it stays at relatively low levels also for the short-run movements. Future developments could result in even further declines of the worldwide level of cohesion as the weights of emerging countries increase. The evidence on business cycle decoupling indicates that this process can be counteracted only slowly with the convergence of business cycles in emerging countries with those in OECD countries (see Kose et al., 2008).

12.6 Conclusions

Globalization and the rise of China as a global player in the world trade system has been one of the major events in the world economy in recent decades. During this unprecedented process, China has gained in economic strength and influenced economic developments around the world. Thus, China has become a global player affecting the growth of the global economy. Increasingly, trade with China is also influencing the business cycles of its partners. Furthermore, it has motivated developing countries to attract foreign investors (see Dollar, 2008).

We show that the interdependencies between economic development in China and in developed economies are varied. In particular, many countries show highly correlated short-run movements. Many transnational companies use China as a part of their production process. Actually, this observation is especially true for the other Asian countries (Japan and Korea). It seems that countries that have more intensive economic and financial relationships with China also have higher dynamic correlations with the Chinese economy. In turn, most countries show a negative correlation with China for the traditional business cycles (cycles with periods between 1.5 and 8 years).

In sum, our initial results confirm a specific position of China in the business cycles of the global economy. Despite the increased trade links between the countries, the Chinese business cycle behaves differently from the rest of the world economy. This may correspond to the replacement of production from the OECD countries to China. The low dynamic correlation means that the world economy shows a low degree of cohesion especially at the business cycles frequencies.

References

Artis, M. J. (2003). 'Is there a European Business Cycle?', Working Paper 1053, CESifo, Munich, http://www.cesifo.de/DocCIDL/1053.pdf

Artis, M. J. and W. Zhang (1997). 'International Business Cycles and the ERM: is there a European Business Cycle?', *International Journal of Finance and Economics*, 2: 1099–158.

Artis, M. J., J. Fidrmuc and J. Scharler (2008). 'The Transmission of Business Cycles: Implications for EMU Enlargement', *Economics of Transition*, 16(3): 559–82.

Baxter, M. and M.A. Kouparitsas (2005). 'Determinants of Business Cycle Comovement: a Robust Analysis', *Journal of Monetary Economics*, 52: 113–57.

Brakman, S. and C. van Marrewijk (2007). 'It's a Big World After All', Working Paper No. 1964, CESifo, Munich.

Bussière, M. and A. Mehl (2008). 'China's and India's Roles in Global Trade and Finance: Twin Titans for the New Millennium', Occasional Paper Series NO 80/2008, ECB.

Croux, C., M. Forni and L. Reichlin (2001). 'A measure of Co-movement for Economic Variables: Theory and Empirics', *Review of Economics and Statistics*, 83: 232–41.

Cui, L. and M.H. Syed (2007). 'The Shifting Structure of China's Trade and Production', Working Paper No. 07/214, IMF, Washington.

De Grauwe, P. and Z. Zhang (2006). 'Introduction: Monetary and Economic Integration in the East Asian Region', *World Economy*, 29(12): 1643–7.

Djankov, S., Y. Qian, G. Roland and E. Zhuravskaya (2006). 'Who are China's Entrepreneurs?' *American Economic Review*, 96(2): 348–52.

Dollar, D. (2008). 'Lessons from China for Africa', Policy Research Working Paper No. 4531, World Bank, Washington.

Eichengreen, B. and H. Tong (2005). 'Is China's FDI Coming at the Expense of Other Countries', Working Paper No. 11335, National Bureau of Economic Research, Cambridge, MA, http://www.nber.org/papers/w11335.

Fatás, A. (1997). 'EMU: Countries or Regions?', *European Economic Review*, 41: 753–60.

Fidrmuc, J. (2004). 'The Endogeneity of the Optimum Currency Area Criteria, Intra-Industry Trade, and EMU Enlargement', *Contemporary Economic Policy*, 22: 1–12.

Fontagné, L. (1999). 'Endogenous Symmetry of Shocks in a Monetary Union', *Open Economies Review*, 10: 263–87.

Frankel, J.A. and A.K. Rose (1998). 'The Endogeneity of the Optimum Currency Area Criteria', *Economic Journal*, 108: 1009–25.

Hovey, M. and T. Naughton (2007). 'A Survey of Enterprise Reforms in China', *Economic Systems*, 31(2): 138–56.

Imbs, J. (2004). 'Trade, Finance, Specialization, and Synchronization', *Review of Economics and Statistics*, 86: 723–34.

Kalemli-Ozcan, S., B. Sorensen and O. Yosha (2001). 'Economic Integration, Industrial Specialization, and the Asymmetry of Macroeconomic Fluctuations', *Journal of International Economics*, 55(1): 107–37.

Kenen, P.B. (2000). 'Currency Areas, Policy Domains, and the Institutionalization of Fixed Exchange Rates', Discussion Paper No. 467, London School of Economics, Centre for Economic Performance, London, http://cep.lse.ac.uk/pubs/download/dp0467.pdf

Kose, M.A. and K.-M. Yi (2006). 'Can the Standard International Business Cycle Model Explain the Relation between Trade and Comovement?', *Journal of International Economics*, 68(2): 267–95.

Kose, M.A., C. Otrok and E. Prasad (2008). 'Global Business Cycles: Convergence or Decoupling?' mimeo, IMF, Washington.

Krugman, P.R. (1993). 'Lessons of Massachusetts for EMU', in F. Torres and F. Giavazzi (eds), *Adjustment and Growth in the European Monetary Union*, Cambridge: Cambridge University Press and CEPR, pp. 241–61.

Kumakura, M. (2005). 'Trade and Business Cycle Correlations in Asia-Pacific', Institute of Developing Economies Discussion Paper No. 44.

Lane, P. and L. S. Schmukler (2007). 'International Financial Integration of China and India', in L.A. Winter and S. Yusuf (eds), *Dancing with Giants*, Washington: World Bank, pp. 101–32.

Sato, K. and Z. Zhang (2006). 'Real Output Co-movements in East Asia: Any Evidence for a Monetary Union?', *World Economy*, 29(12): 1671–89.

Shin, K. and C.-H. Sohn (2006). 'Trade and Financial Integration in East Asia: Effects on Co-movements', *World Economy*, 29(12): 1649–69.

Shin, K. and Y. Wang (2004). 'Trade Integration and Business Cycle Co-movements: the Case of Korea with Other Asian Countries', *Japan and the World Economy*, 16: 213–30.

Index